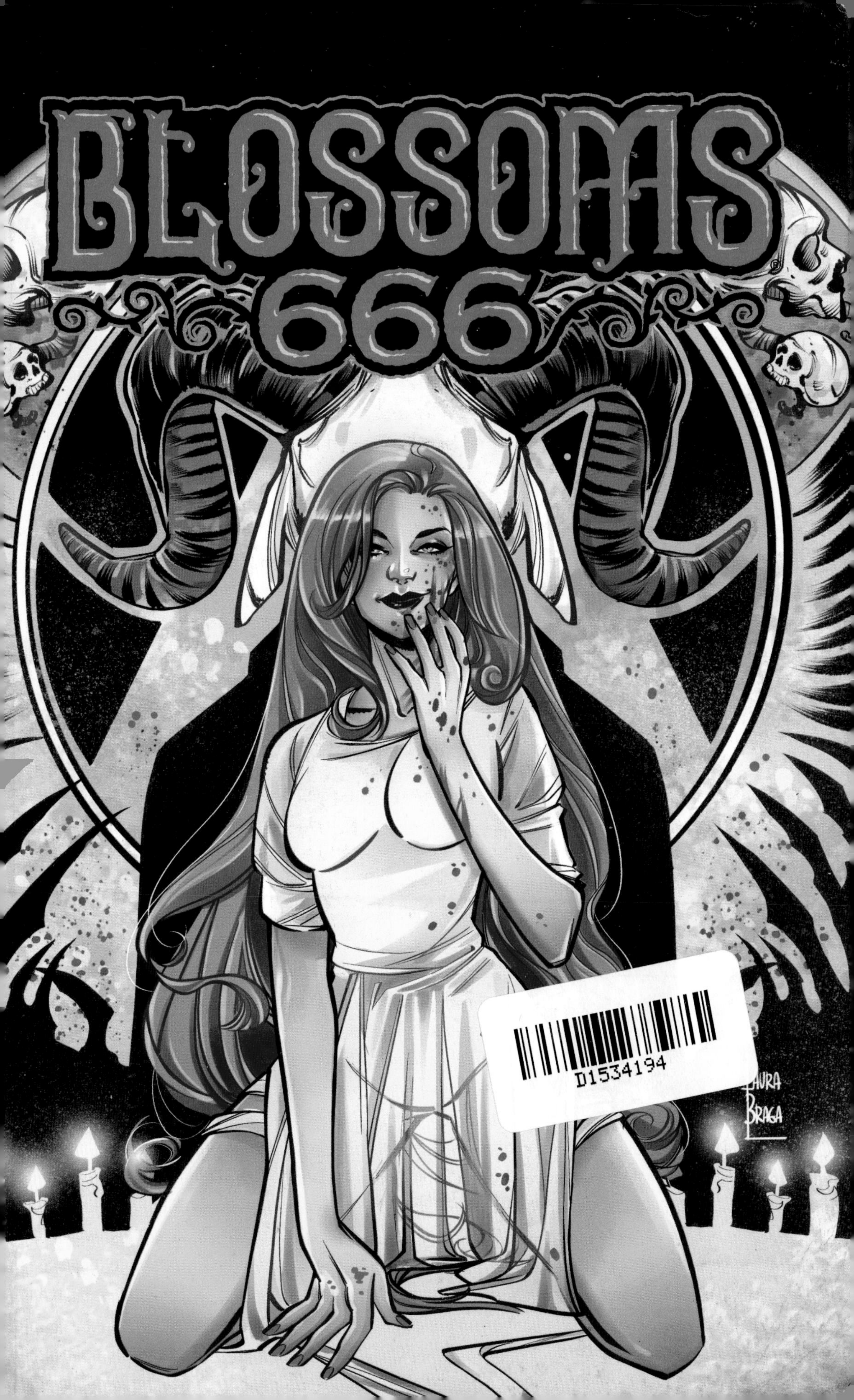
BLOSSOMS
666
LAURA
BRAGA

BLOSSOMS 666

STORY BY
CULLEN BUNN

ART BY
LAURA BRAGA

LETTERING BY
JACK MORELLI

COLORING BY
MATT HERMS

EDITOR-IN-CHIEF
VICTOR GORELICK

GRAPHIC DESIGN BY
KARI MCLACHLAN

CREATIVE CONSULTANT
SHANNON GOLDWATER

EDITORS
ALEX SEGURA AND
JAMIE LEE ROTANTE

ASSOCIATE EDITOR
STEPHEN OSWALD

PUBLISHER
JON GOLDWATER

ASSISTANT EDITOR
VINCENT LOVALLO

Archie and the Anti-Christ were big parts of my formative years.

As a kid, I read more than my fair share of superhero comics. My dad would buy them for me by the grocery sack-full at garage sales and flea markets—big mixed up collections of tales of daring spandex-clad adventure. There were often other books to be found in the dog-eared stacks. Horror comics, sure, and I gobbled those up. But also Archie comics. And I loved them. I loved the Riverdale Gang and the beautiful reprieve they gave me from the masked vigilantes and villains.

Now, around this same time—and I was just five or six years old here—I became aware of a couple of movies. *The Omen*, the story of a cherub-faced Anti-Christ, hit theaters. And that got people talking about another devil-infused movie that had come out a few years earlier—*The Exorcist*. Somehow, I caught little glimpses of these stories. It might have been my older siblings talking about them. It might have been the trailers. Maybe *The Exorcist* aired in a greatly-edited version as a movie of the week. Either way, the bits and pieces I put together formed into something wholly terrifying.

Archie and the Anti-Christ... Though at the time I never dreamed of smashing the two together.

Until now.

I've been talking to the good folks at Archie for a while. I knew we'd someday do a book together. I knew it would be one of the horror titles. But I wanted to wait until the perfect opportunity. I wanted my first foray into Archie Horror to be special. Luckily for me, along came *Blossoms 666*, and the opportunity to throw the wholesome world of Archie and the world of infernal horror together was just too amazing to pass up.

If you're revisiting this story, I hope you find some new twists and turns among these pages. If you're reading it for the first time, I hope you have as much fun with this tale of demonic destinies as I did. It's a twisted little story, if I do say so myself, but I'll bet you already knew that. I'll bet that's why you're here in the first place, you creepy little freaks.

Don't take it the wrong way.

Creepy little freaks are
my kind of people.

—Cullen Bunn

CHAPTER ONE

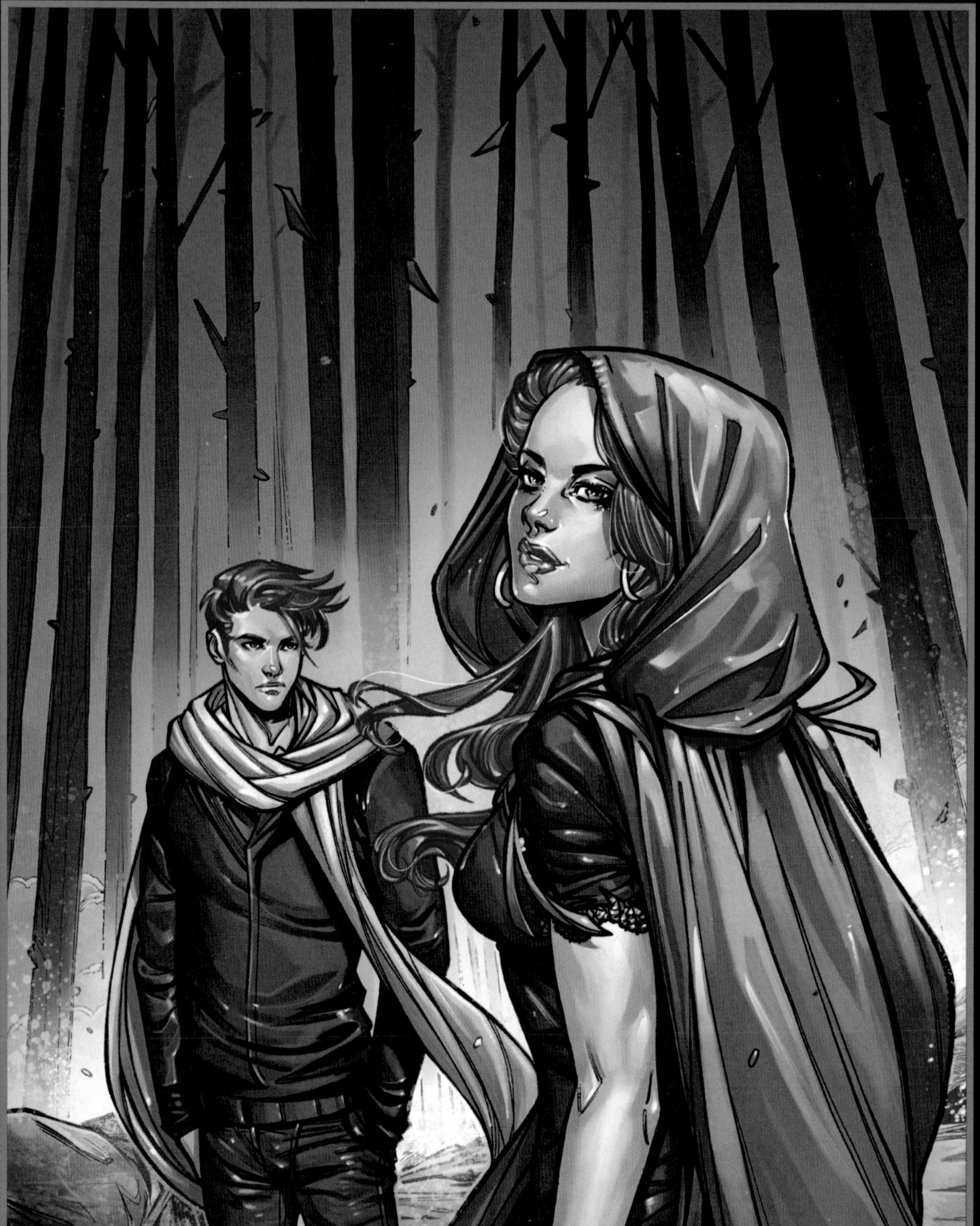
LAURA
BRAGA
2018

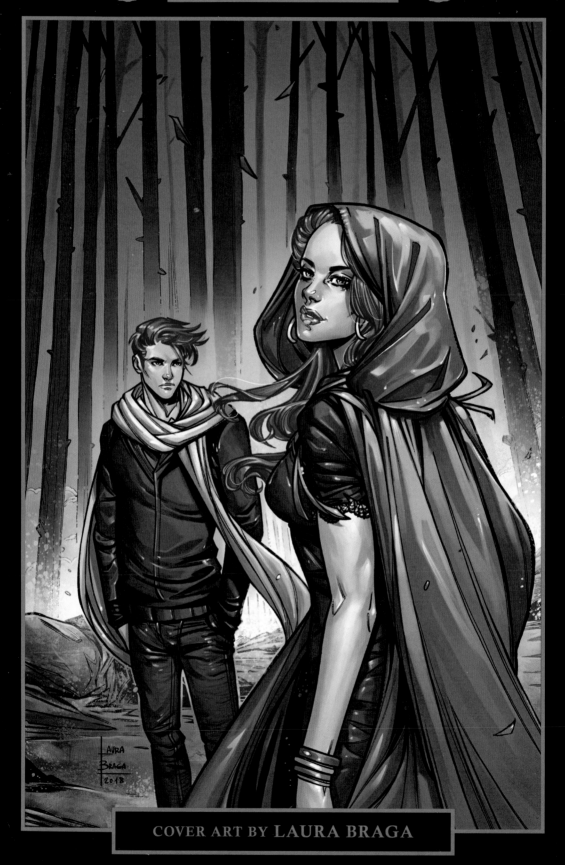

COVER ART BY LAURA BRAGA

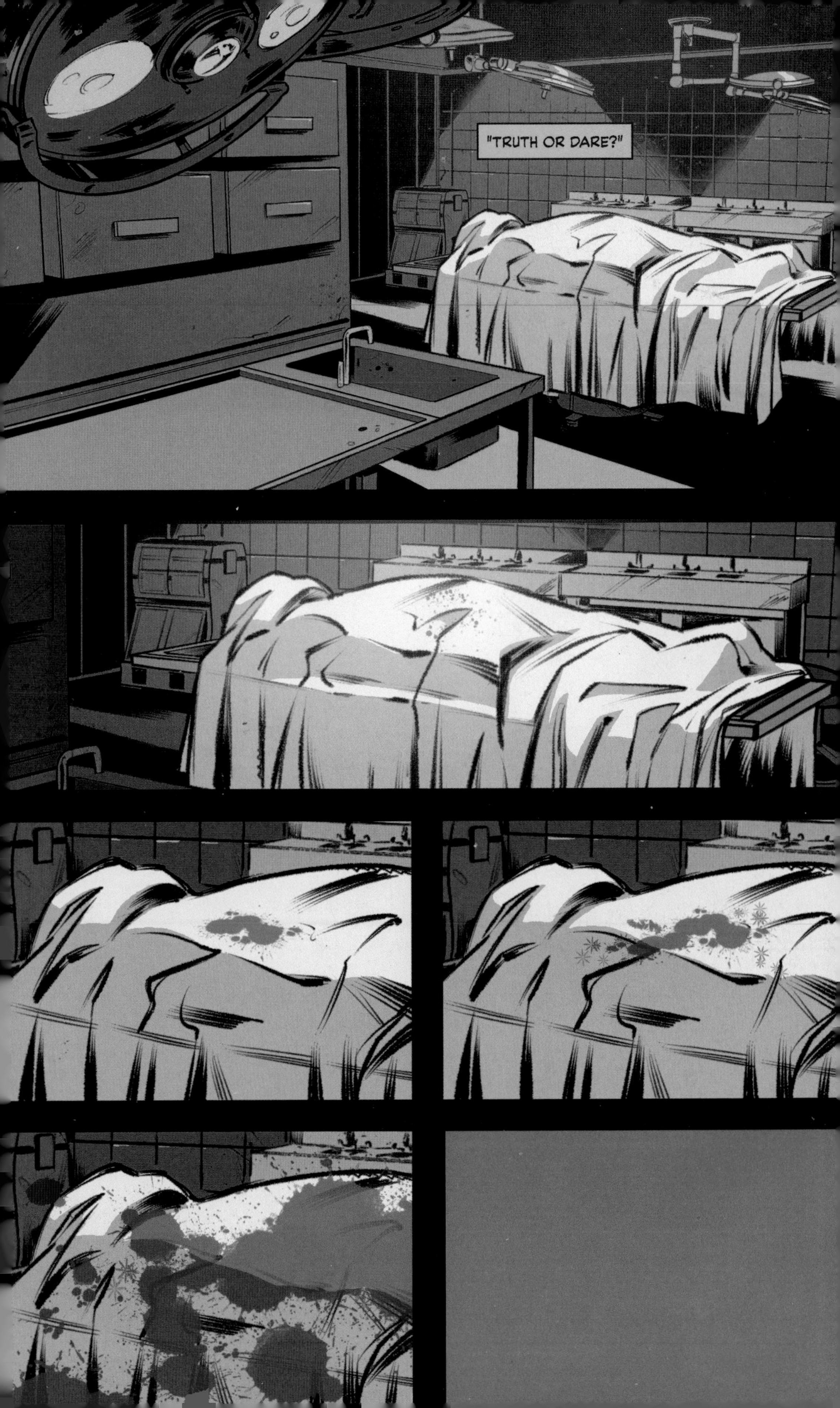
"TRUTH OR DARE?"

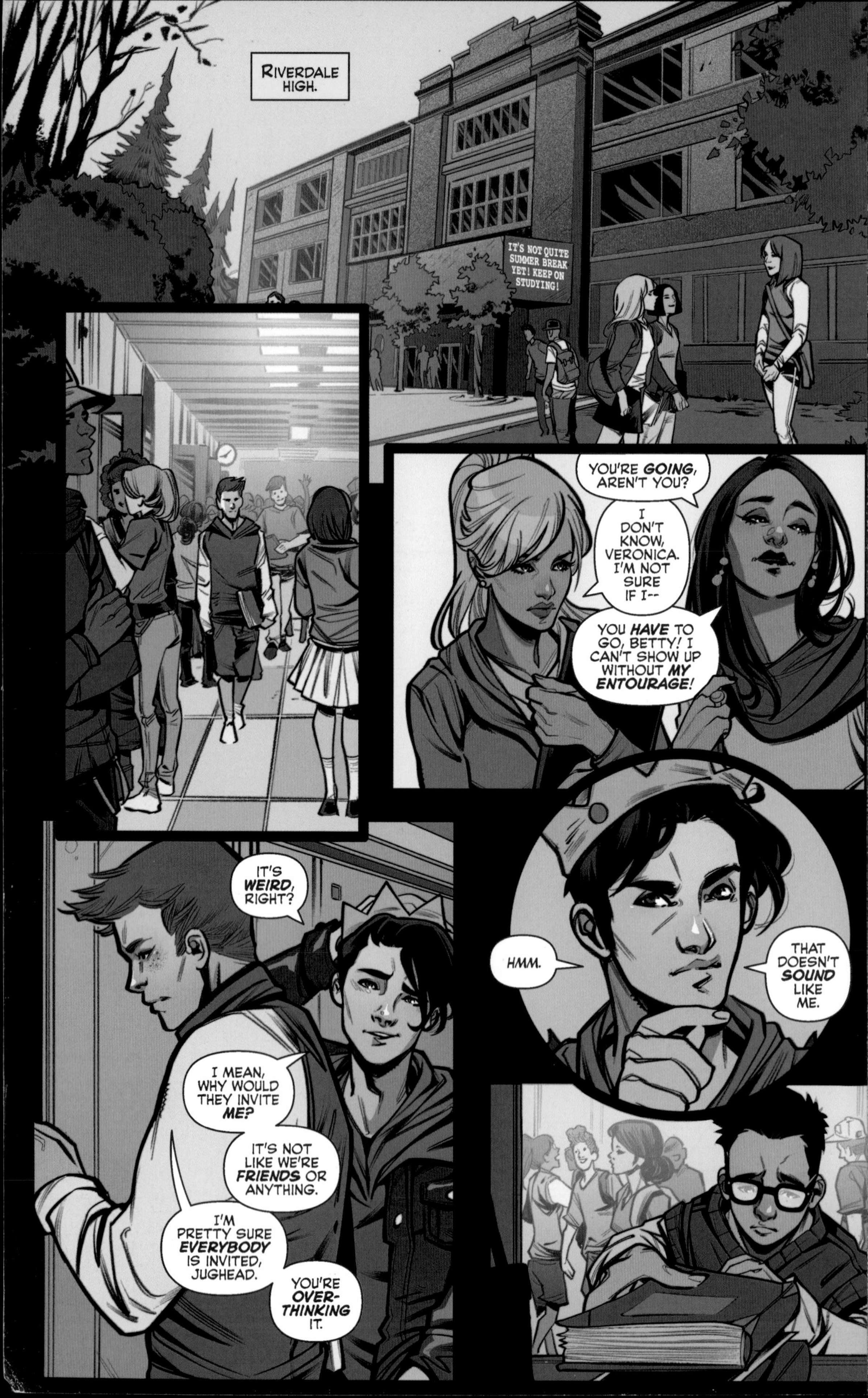
RIVERDALE HIGH.
IT'S NOT QUITE SUMMER BREAK YET! KEEP ON STUDYING!
YOU'RE **GOING**, AREN'T YOU?
I DON'T KNOW, VERONICA. I'M NOT SURE IF I--
YOU **HAVE** TO GO, BETTY! I CAN'T SHOW UP WITHOUT **MY ENTOURAGE**!
IT'S **WEIRD**, RIGHT?
I MEAN, WHY WOULD THEY INVITE **ME?**
IT'S NOT LIKE WE'RE **FRIENDS** OR ANYTHING.
I'M PRETTY SURE **EVERYBODY** IS INVITED, JUGHEAD.
YOU'RE **OVER-THINKING** IT.
HMM.
THAT DOESN'T **SOUND** LIKE ME.

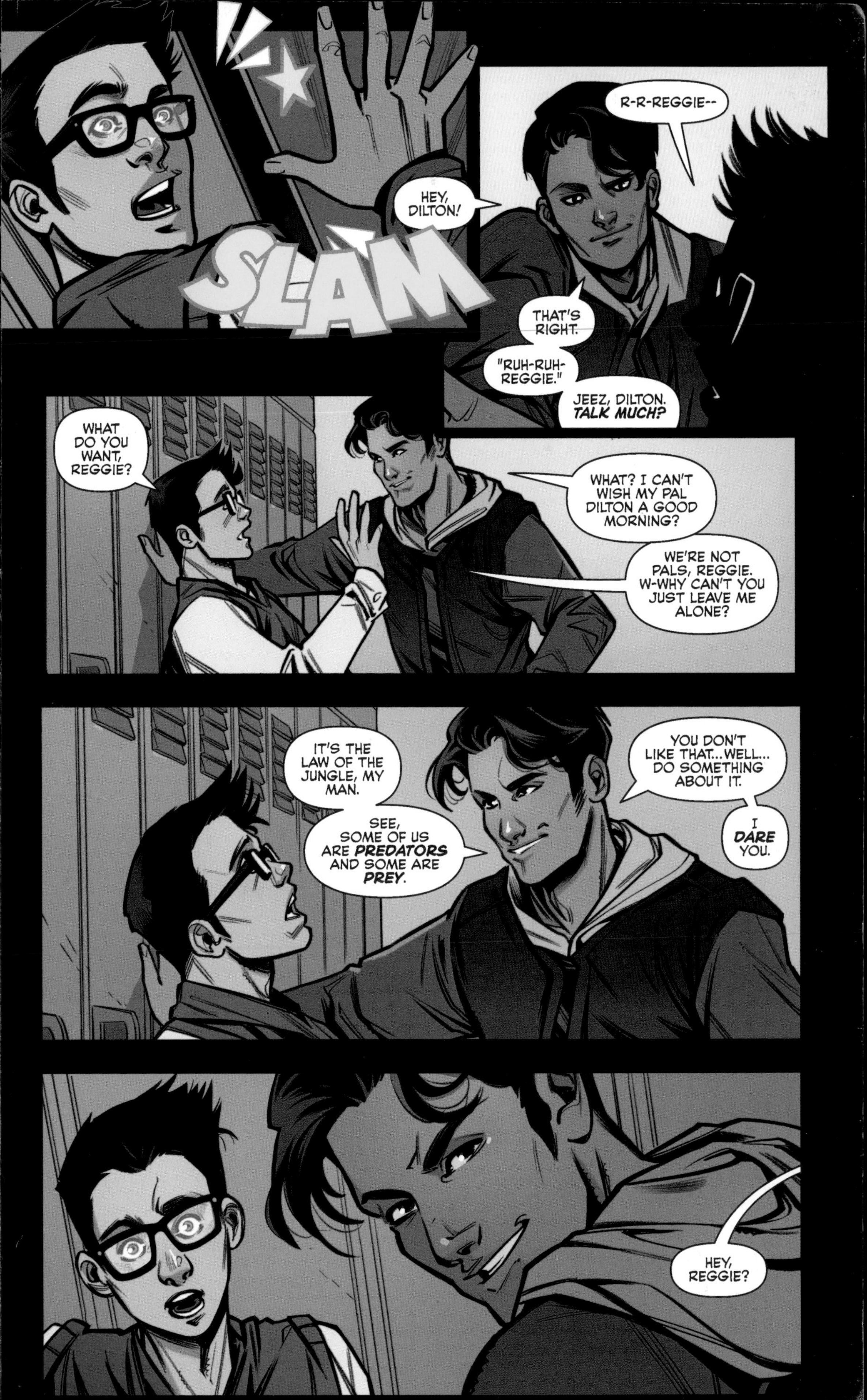
SLAM
HEY, DILTON!
R-R-REGGIE--
THAT'S RIGHT.
"RUH-RUH-REGGIE."
JEEZ, DILTON. TALK MUCH?
WHAT DO YOU WANT, REGGIE?
WHAT? I CAN'T WISH MY PAL DILTON A GOOD MORNING?
WE'RE NOT PALS, REGGIE. W-WHY CAN'T YOU JUST LEAVE ME ALONE?
IT'S THE LAW OF THE JUNGLE, MY MAN.
SEE, SOME OF US ARE PREDATORS AND SOME ARE PREY.
YOU DON'T LIKE THAT...WELL... DO SOMETHING ABOUT IT.
I DARE YOU.
HEY, REGGIE?

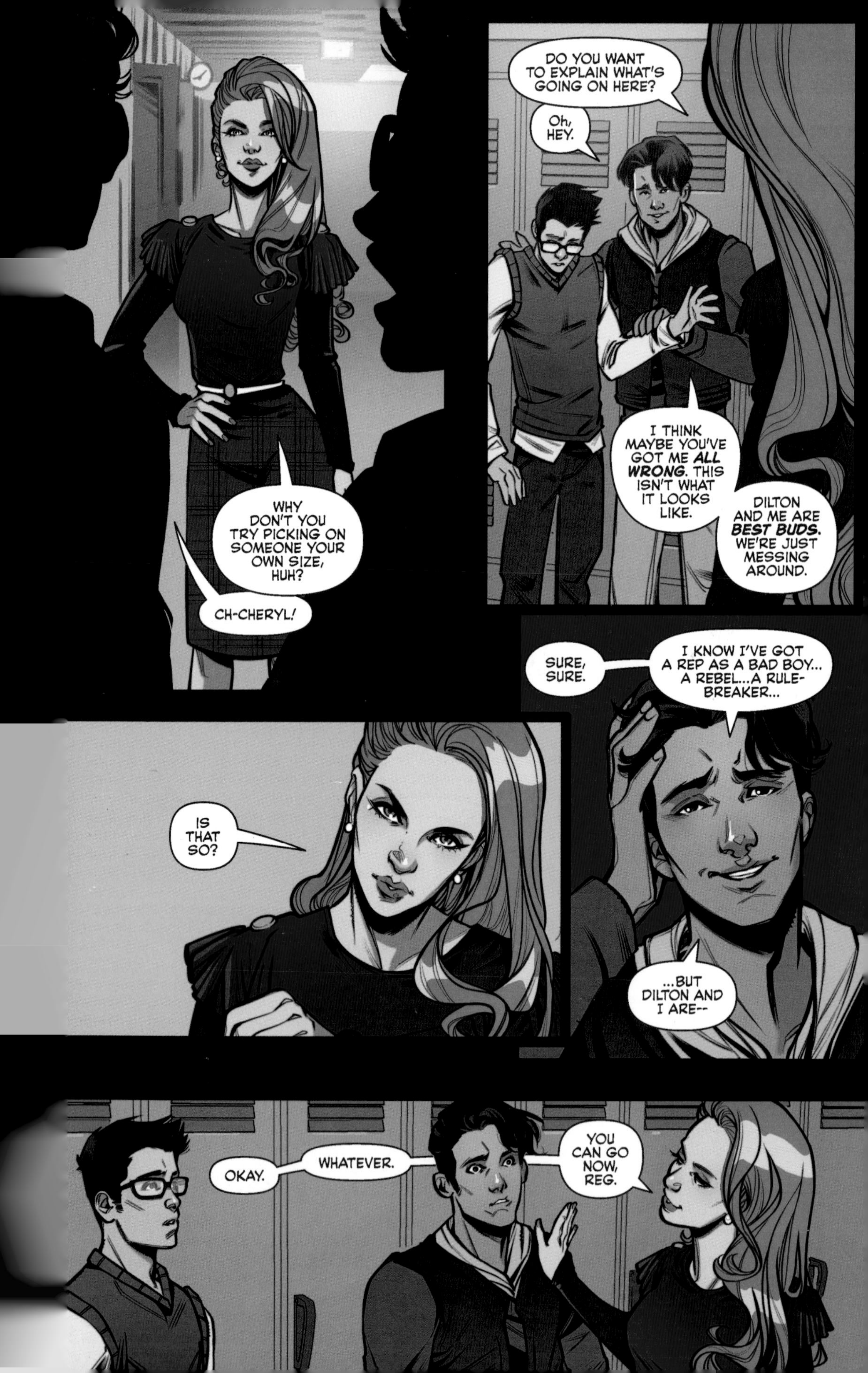
WHY DON'T YOU TRY PICKING ON SOMEONE YOUR OWN SIZE, HUH?
CH-CHERYL!
DO YOU WANT TO EXPLAIN WHAT'S GOING ON HERE?
Oh, HEY.
I THINK MAYBE YOU'VE GOT ME ALL WRONG. THIS ISN'T WHAT IT LOOKS LIKE.
DILTON AND ME ARE BEST BUDS. WE'RE JUST MESSING AROUND.
I KNOW I'VE GOT A REP AS A BAD BOY... A REBEL...A RULE-BREAKER...
SURE, SURE.
IS THAT SO?
...BUT DILTON AND I ARE--
YOU CAN GO NOW, REG.
WHATEVER.
OKAY.

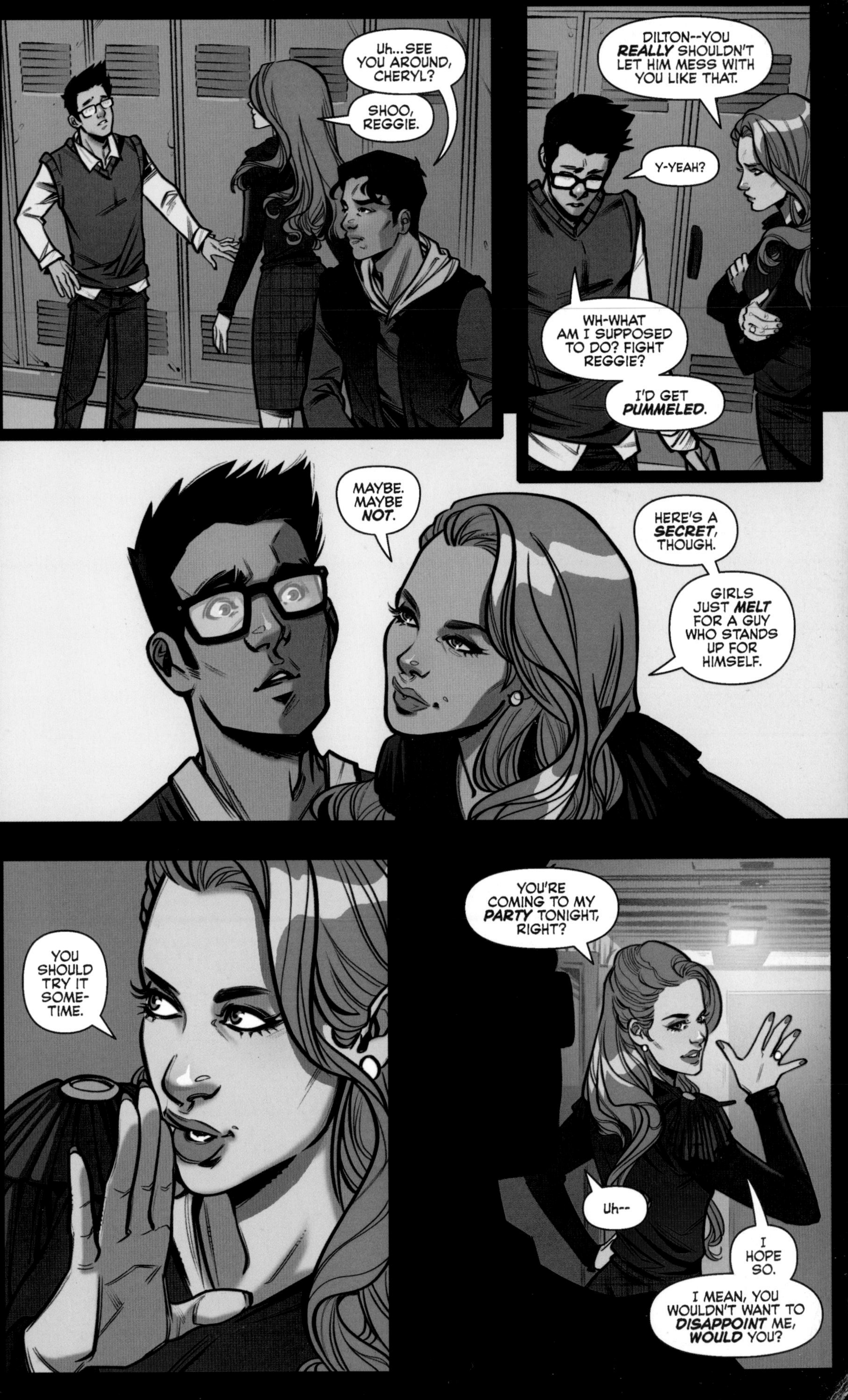
UH...SEE YOU AROUND, CHERYL?
SHOO, REGGIE.
DILTON--YOU *REALLY* SHOULDN'T LET HIM MESS WITH YOU LIKE THAT.
Y-YEAH?
WH-WHAT AM I SUPPOSED TO DO? FIGHT REGGIE?
I'D GET *PUMMELED*.
MAYBE. MAYBE *NOT*.
HERE'S A *SECRET*, THOUGH.
GIRLS JUST *MELT* FOR A GUY WHO STANDS UP FOR HIMSELF.
YOU SHOULD TRY IT SOME-TIME.
YOU'RE COMING TO MY *PARTY* TONIGHT, RIGHT?
UH--
I HOPE SO.
I MEAN, YOU WOULDN'T WANT TO *DISAPPOINT* ME, *WOULD* YOU?

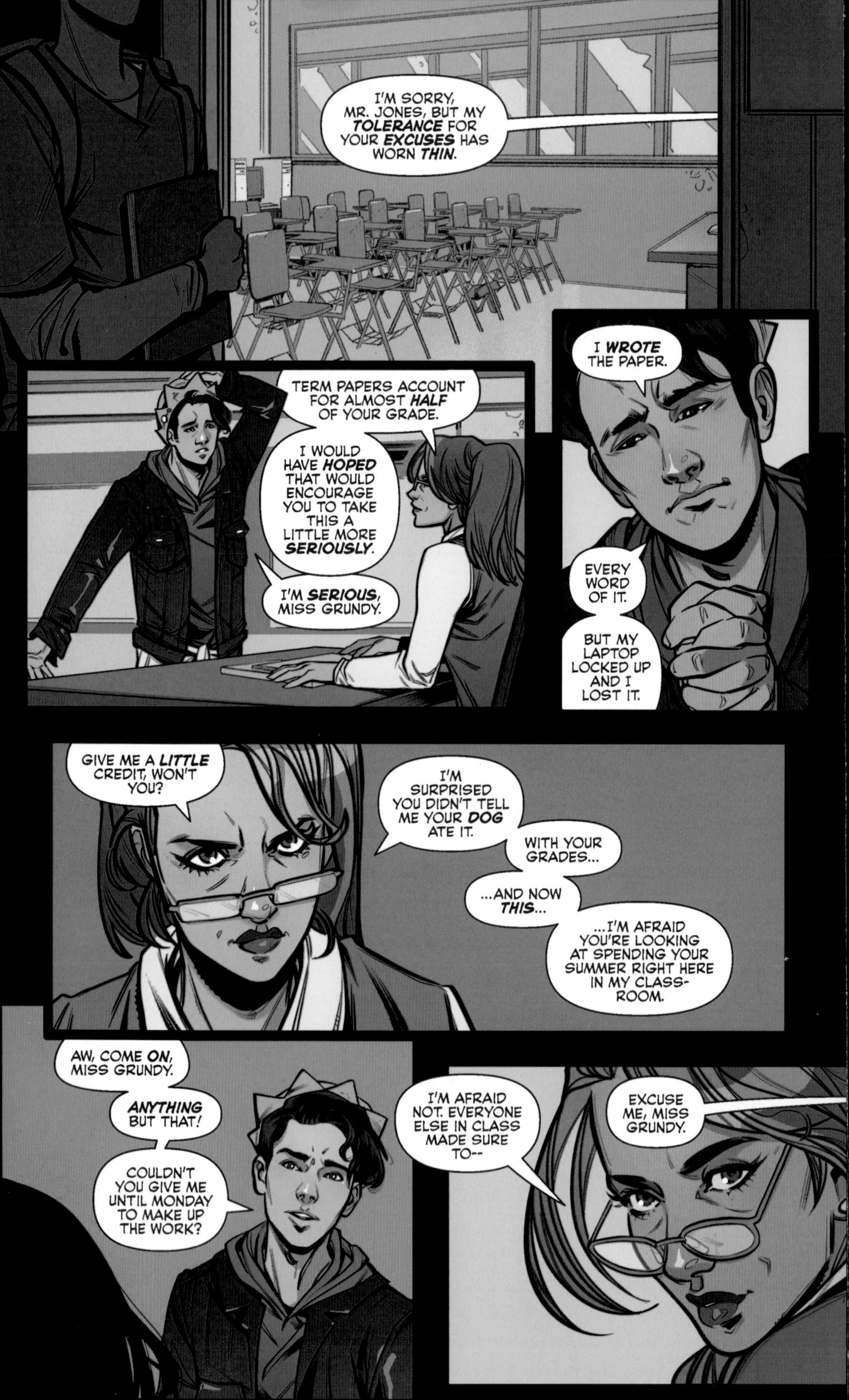
I'M SORRY, MR. JONES, BUT MY TOLERANCE FOR YOUR EXCUSES HAS WORN THIN.
TERM PAPERS ACCOUNT FOR ALMOST HALF OF YOUR GRADE.
I WOULD HAVE HOPED THAT WOULD ENCOURAGE YOU TO TAKE THIS A LITTLE MORE SERIOUSLY.
I'M SERIOUS, MISS GRUNDY.
I WROTE THE PAPER.
EVERY WORD OF IT.
BUT MY LAPTOP LOCKED UP AND I LOST IT.
GIVE ME A LITTLE CREDIT, WON'T YOU?
I'M SURPRISED YOU DIDN'T TELL ME YOUR DOG ATE IT.
WITH YOUR GRADES...
...AND NOW THIS...
...I'M AFRAID YOU'RE LOOKING AT SPENDING YOUR SUMMER RIGHT HERE IN MY CLASS-ROOM.
AW, COME ON, MISS GRUNDY.
ANYTHING BUT THAT!
COULDN'T YOU GIVE ME UNTIL MONDAY TO MAKE UP THE WORK?
I'M AFRAID NOT. EVERYONE ELSE IN CLASS MADE SURE TO--
EXCUSE ME, MISS GRUNDY.

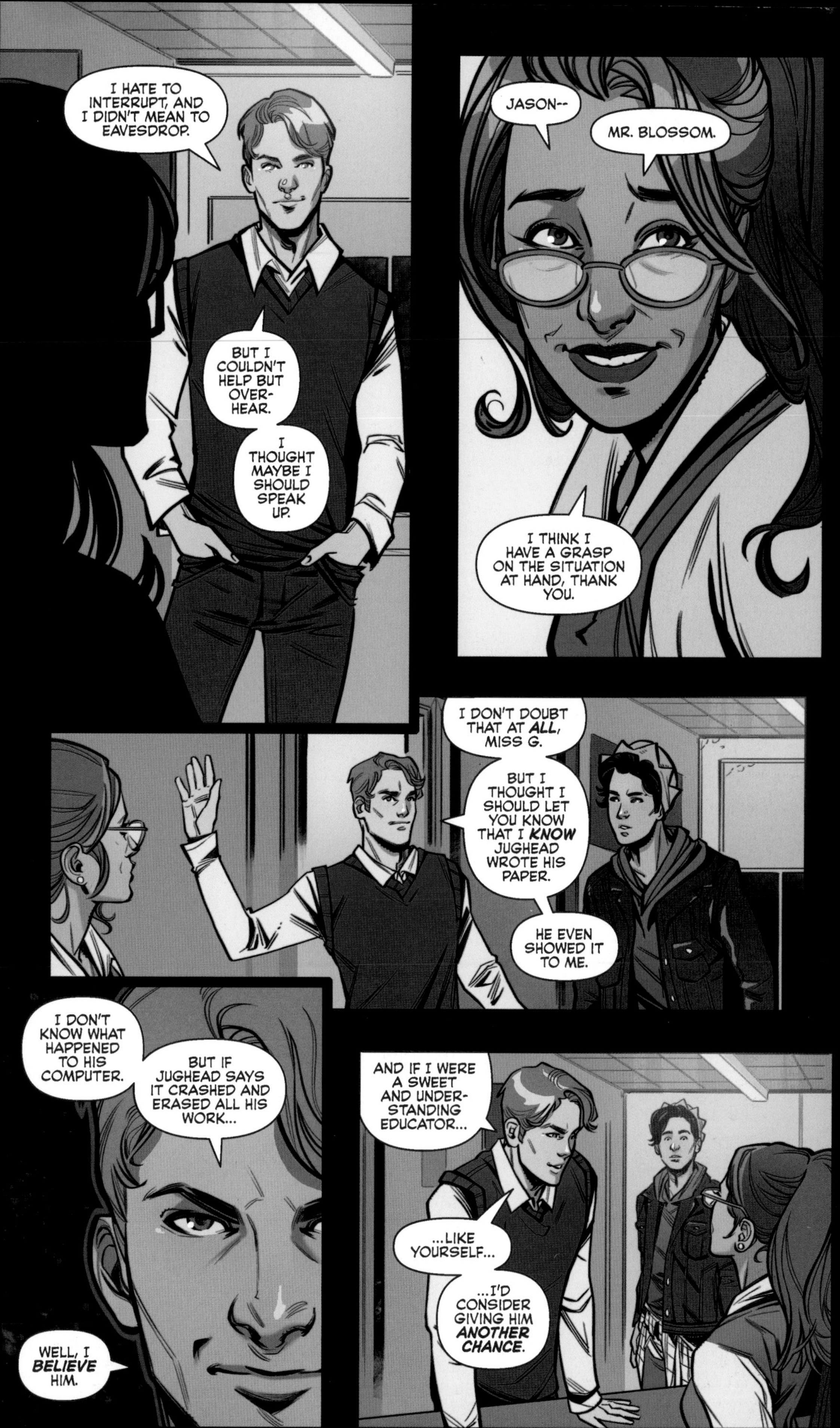
I HATE TO INTERRUPT, AND I DIDN'T MEAN TO EAVESDROP.
BUT I COULDN'T HELP BUT OVER-HEAR.
I THOUGHT MAYBE I SHOULD SPEAK UP.
JASON--
MR. BLOSSOM.
I THINK I HAVE A GRASP ON THE SITUATION AT HAND, THANK YOU.
I DON'T DOUBT THAT AT *ALL*, MISS G.
BUT I THOUGHT I SHOULD LET YOU KNOW THAT I *KNOW* JUGHEAD WROTE HIS PAPER.
HE EVEN SHOWED IT TO ME.
I DON'T KNOW WHAT HAPPENED TO HIS COMPUTER.
BUT IF JUGHEAD SAYS IT CRASHED AND ERASED ALL HIS WORK...
WELL, I *BELIEVE* HIM.
AND IF I WERE A SWEET AND UNDER-STANDING EDUCATOR...
...LIKE YOURSELF...
...I'D CONSIDER GIVING HIM *ANOTHER CHANCE*.

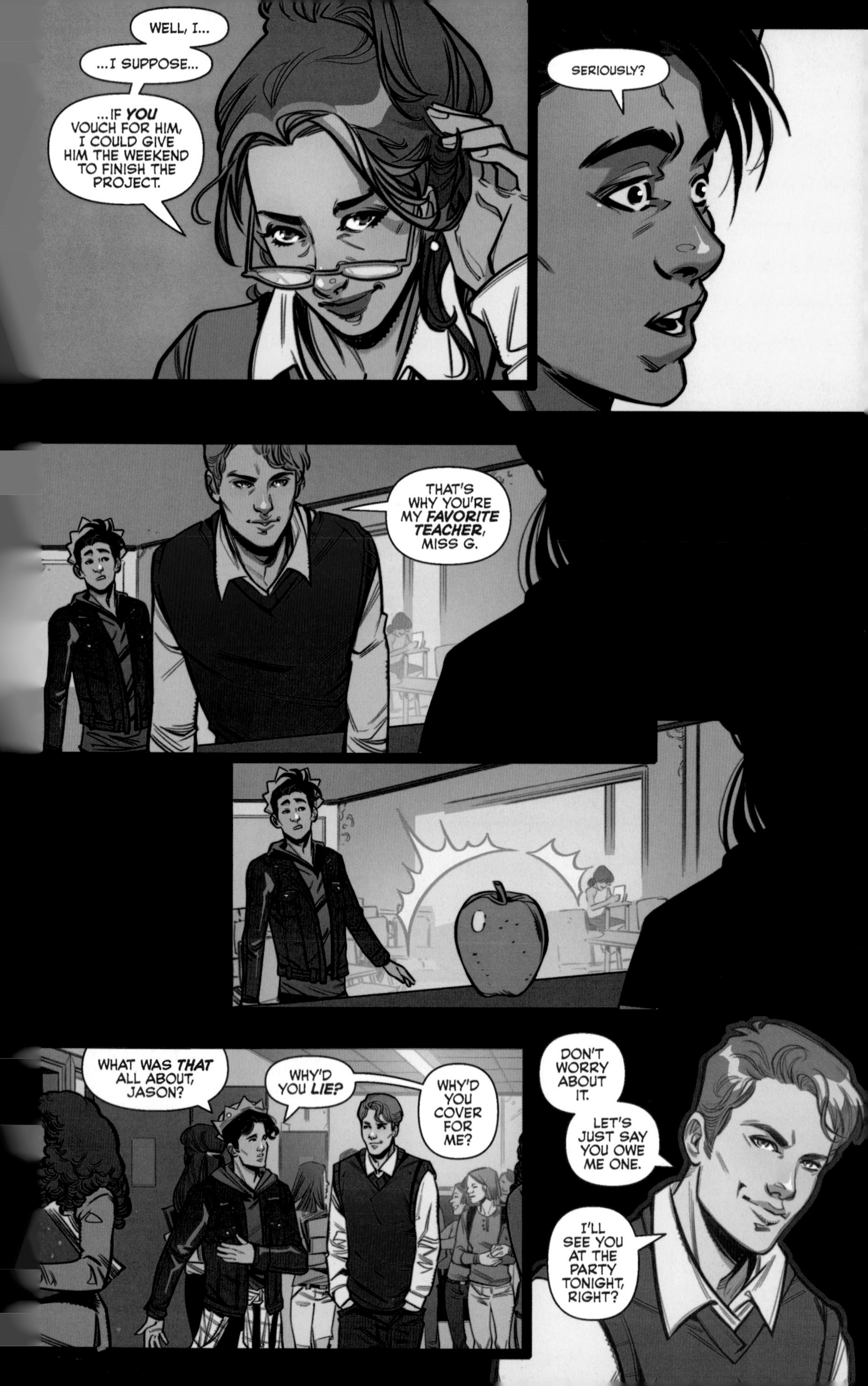
WELL, I...
...I SUPPOSE...
...IF **YOU** VOUCH FOR HIM, I COULD GIVE HIM THE WEEKEND TO FINISH THE PROJECT.
SERIOUSLY?
THAT'S WHY YOU'RE MY **FAVORITE TEACHER**, MISS G.
WHAT WAS **THAT** ALL ABOUT, JASON?
WHY'D YOU **LIE**?
WHY'D YOU COVER FOR ME?
DON'T WORRY ABOUT IT.
LET'S JUST SAY YOU OWE ME ONE.
I'LL SEE YOU AT THE PARTY TONIGHT, RIGHT?

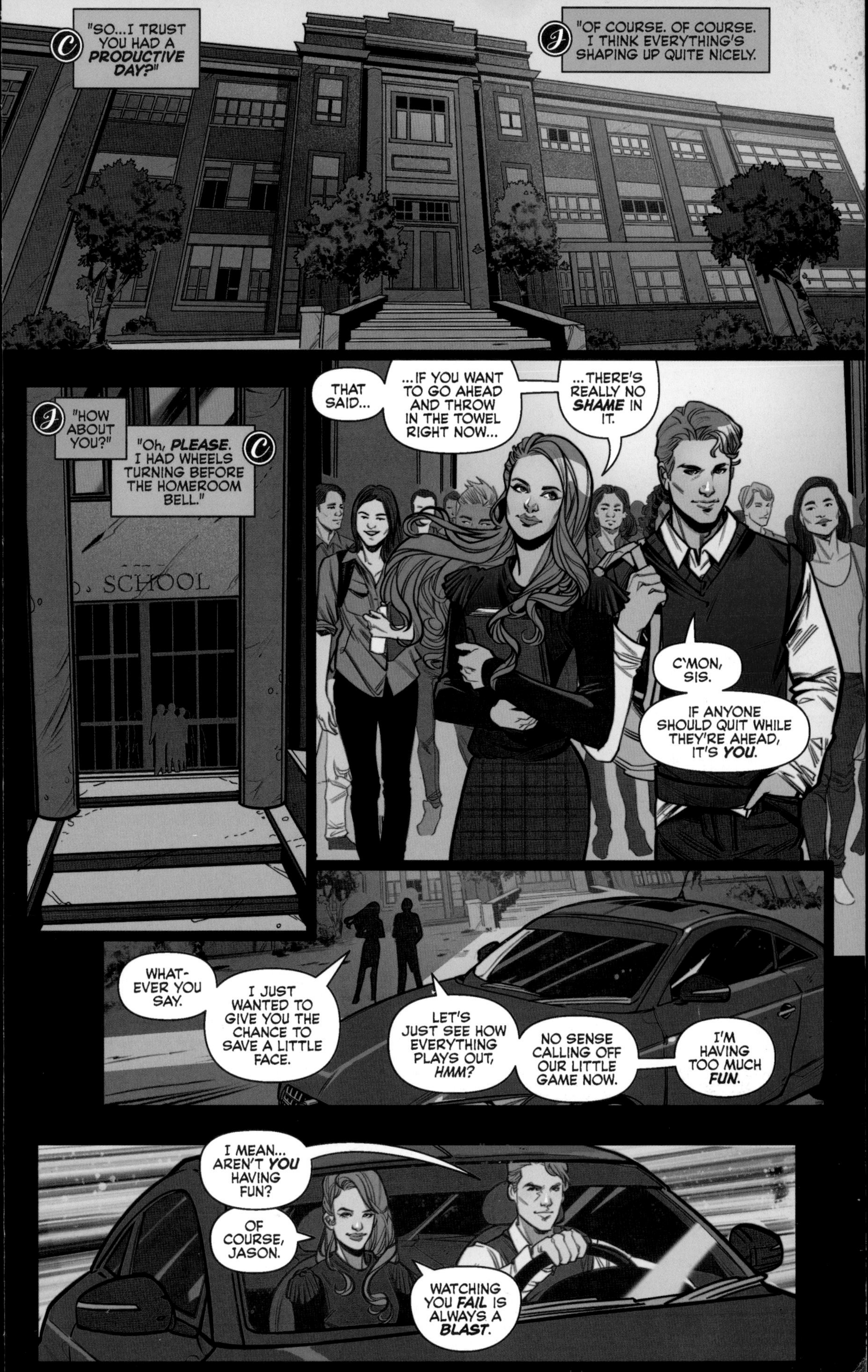
"SO...I TRUST YOU HAD A PRODUCTIVE DAY?"
"OF COURSE. OF COURSE. I THINK EVERYTHING'S SHAPING UP QUITE NICELY.
"HOW ABOUT YOU?"
"Oh, PLEASE. I HAD WHEELS TURNING BEFORE THE HOMEROOM BELL."
SCHOOL
THAT SAID...
...IF YOU WANT TO GO AHEAD AND THROW IN THE TOWEL RIGHT NOW...
...THERE'S REALLY NO SHAME IN IT.
C'MON, SIS.
IF ANYONE SHOULD QUIT WHILE THEY'RE AHEAD, IT'S YOU.
WHAT-EVER YOU SAY.
I JUST WANTED TO GIVE YOU THE CHANCE TO SAVE A LITTLE FACE.
LET'S JUST SEE HOW EVERYTHING PLAYS OUT, HMM?
NO SENSE CALLING OFF OUR LITTLE GAME NOW.
I'M HAVING TOO MUCH FUN.
I MEAN... AREN'T YOU HAVING FUN?
OF COURSE, JASON.
WATCHING YOU FAIL IS ALWAYS A BLAST.

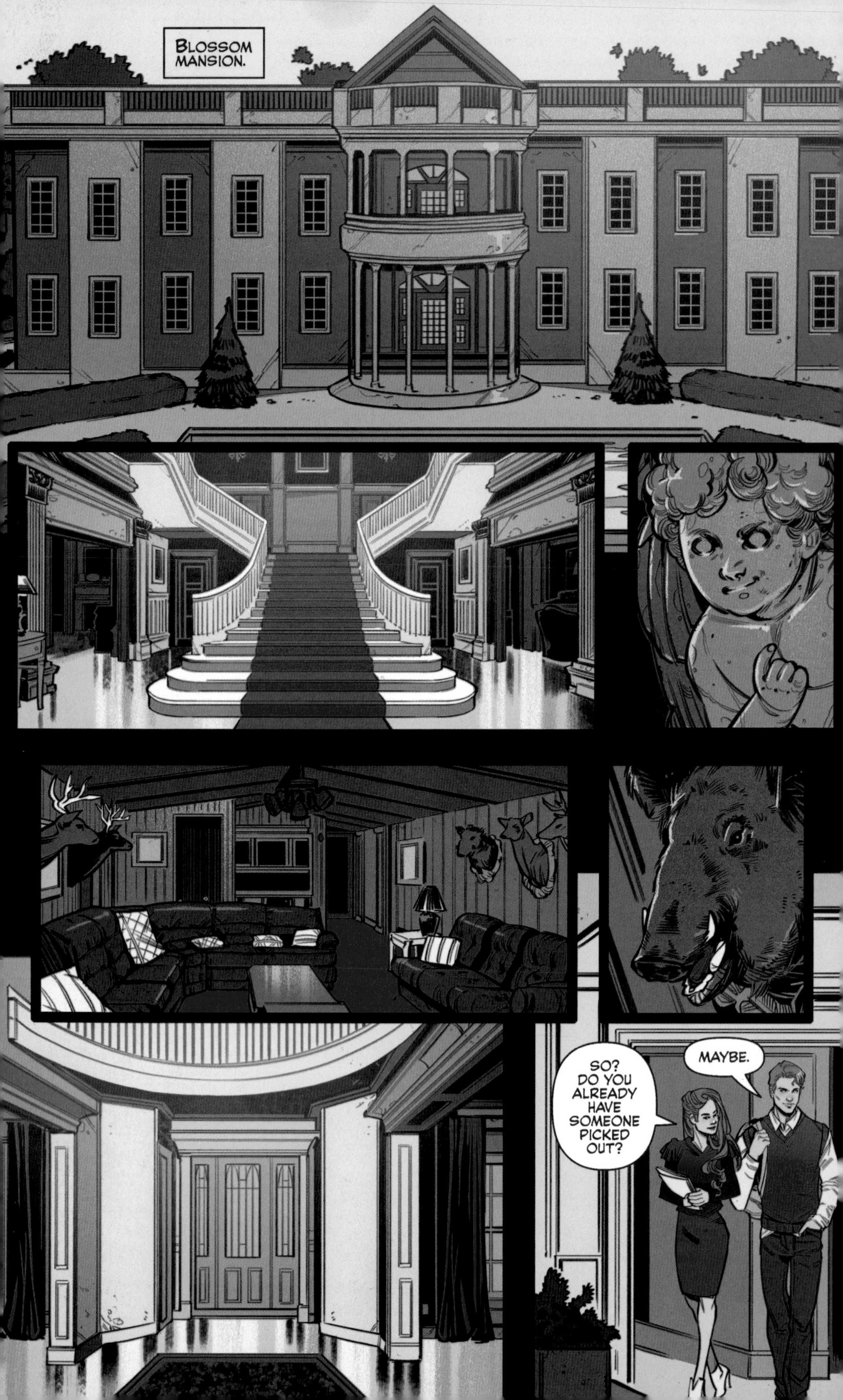
BLOSSOM MANSION.
SO? DO YOU ALREADY HAVE SOMEONE PICKED OUT?
MAYBE.

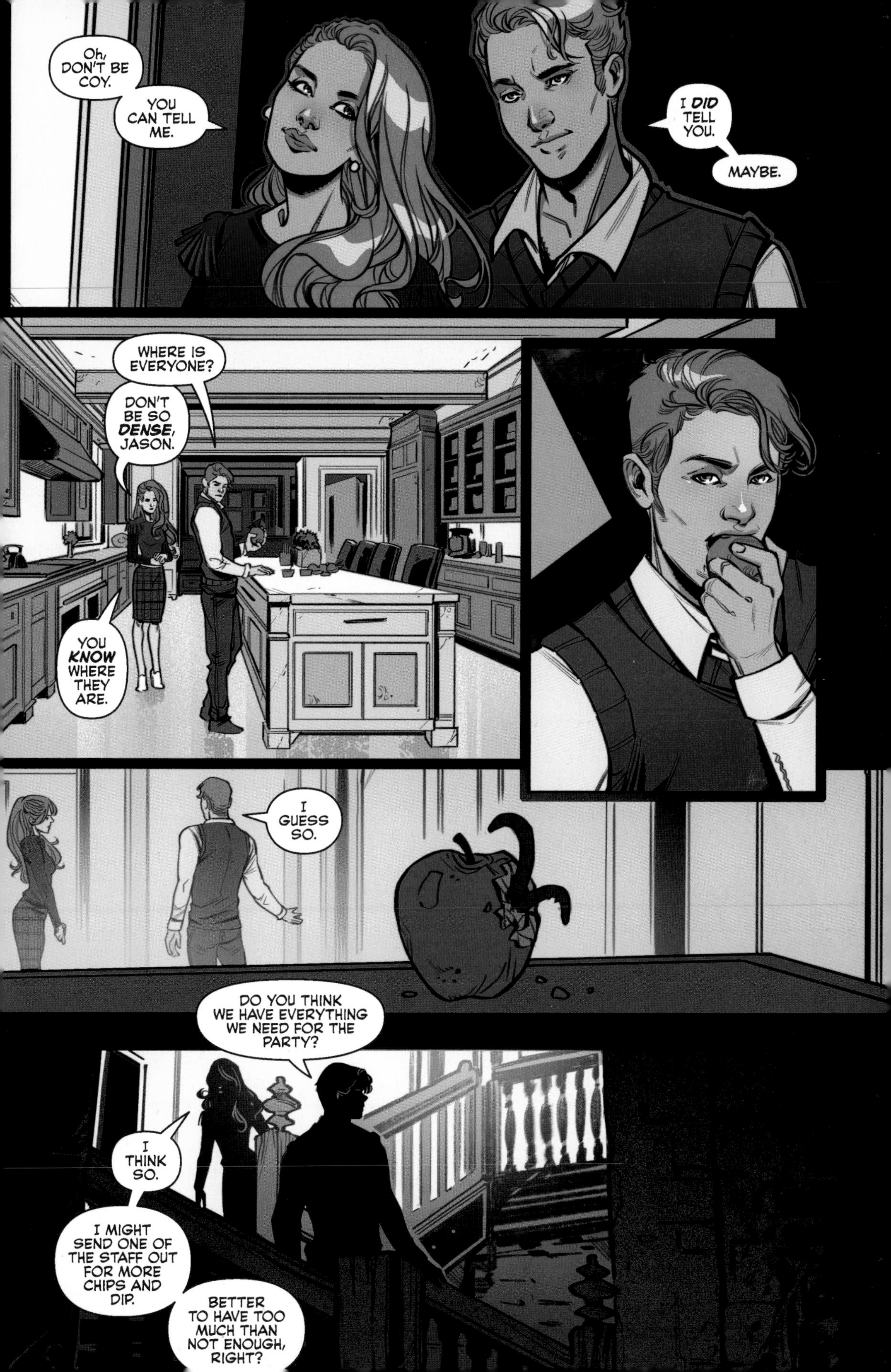

Oh, DON'T BE COY.
YOU CAN TELL ME.
I DID TELL YOU.
MAYBE.
WHERE IS EVERYONE?
DON'T BE SO DENSE, JASON.
YOU KNOW WHERE THEY ARE.
I GUESS SO.
DO YOU THINK WE HAVE EVERYTHING WE NEED FOR THE PARTY?
I THINK SO.
I MIGHT SEND ONE OF THE STAFF OUT FOR MORE CHIPS AND DIP.
BETTER TO HAVE TOO MUCH THAN NOT ENOUGH, RIGHT?

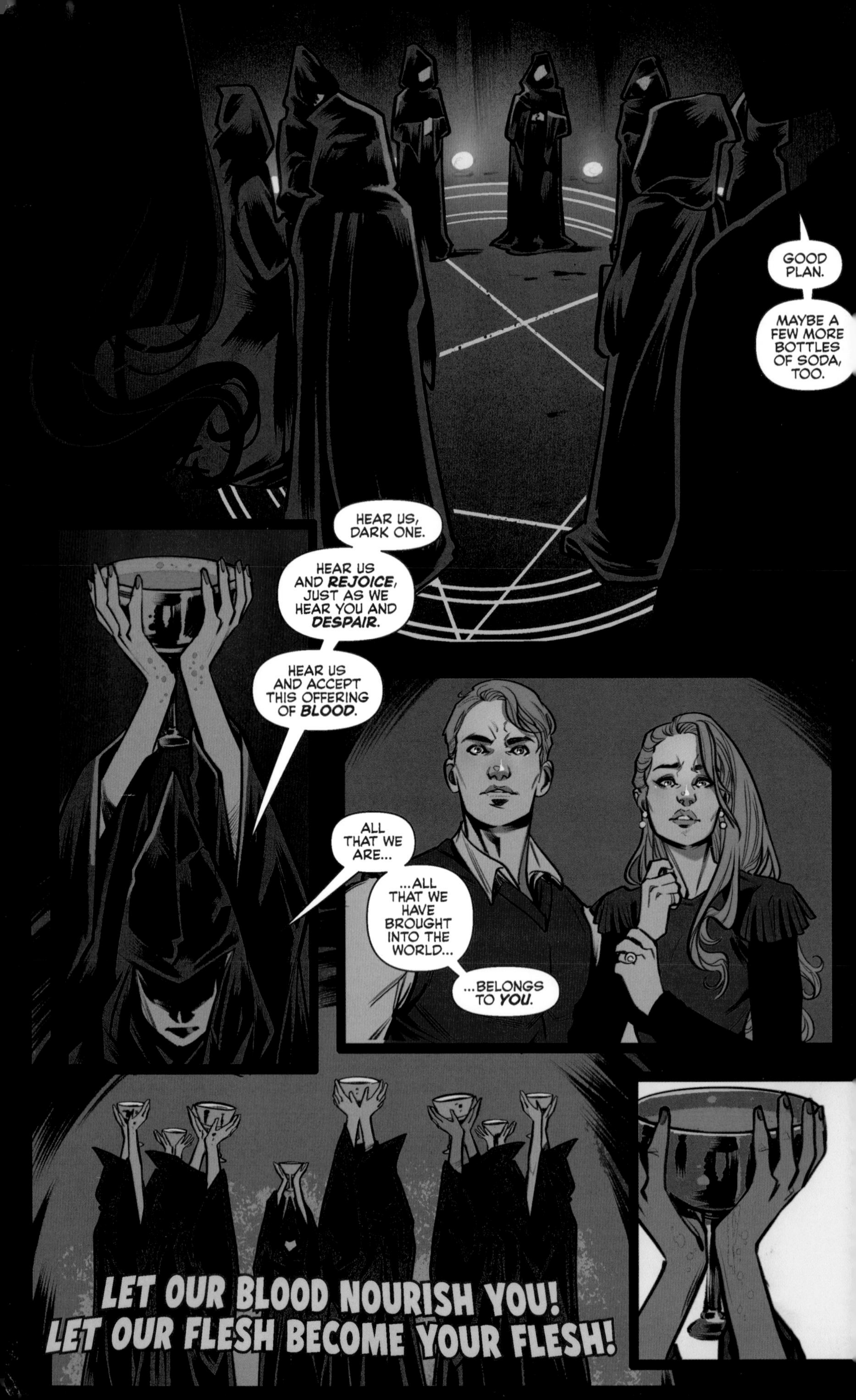
GOOD PLAN.
MAYBE A FEW MORE BOTTLES OF SODA, TOO.
HEAR US, DARK ONE.
HEAR US AND REJOICE, JUST AS WE HEAR YOU AND DESPAIR.
HEAR US AND ACCEPT THIS OFFERING OF BLOOD.
ALL THAT WE ARE...
...ALL THAT WE HAVE BROUGHT INTO THE WORLD...
...BELONGS TO YOU.
LET OUR BLOOD NOURISH YOU! LET OUR FLESH BECOME YOUR FLESH!

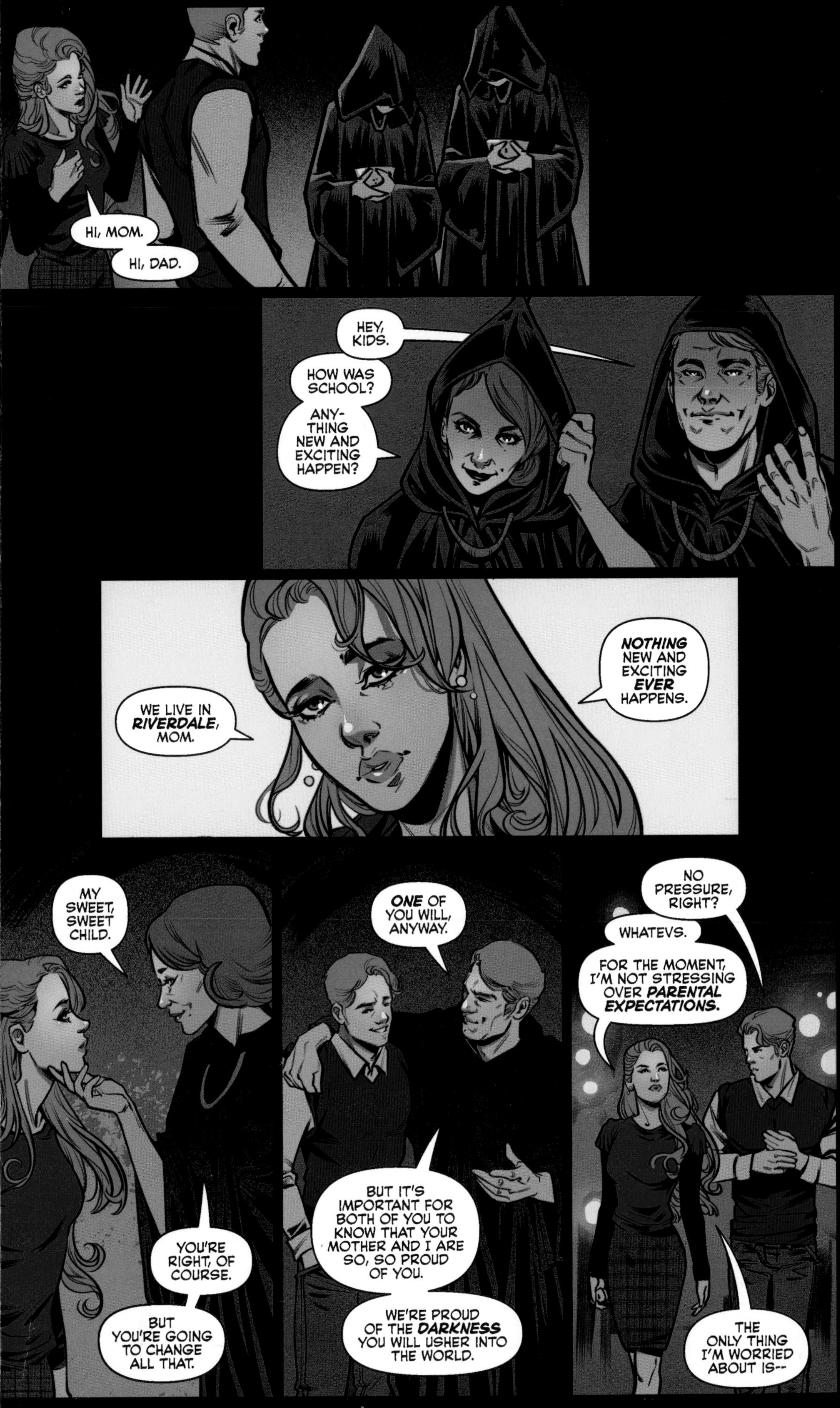
HI, MOM.
HI, DAD.
HEY, KIDS.
HOW WAS SCHOOL?
ANY-THING NEW AND EXCITING HAPPEN?
WE LIVE IN *RIVERDALE*, MOM.
NOTHING NEW AND EXCITING *EVER* HAPPENS.
MY SWEET, SWEET CHILD.
YOU'RE RIGHT, OF COURSE.
BUT YOU'RE GOING TO CHANGE ALL THAT.
ONE OF YOU WILL, ANYWAY.
BUT IT'S IMPORTANT FOR BOTH OF YOU TO KNOW THAT YOUR MOTHER AND I ARE SO, SO PROUD OF YOU.
WE'RE PROUD OF THE *DARKNESS* YOU WILL USHER INTO THE WORLD.
NO PRESSURE, RIGHT?
WHATEVS.
FOR THE MOMENT, I'M NOT STRESSING OVER *PARENTAL EXPECTATIONS.*
THE ONLY THING I'M WORRIED ABOUT IS--

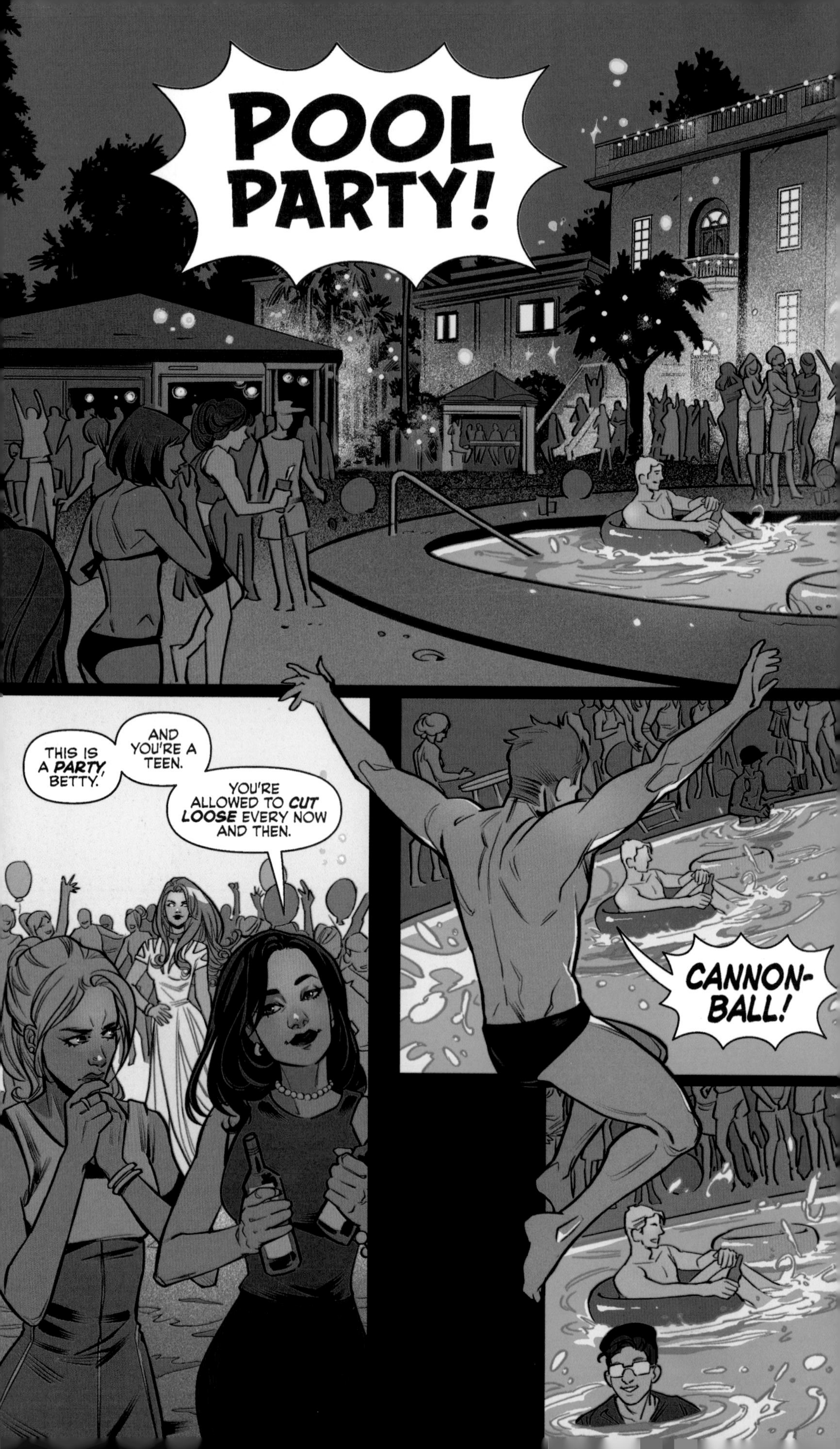
POOL PARTY!
THIS IS A PARTY, BETTY.
AND YOU'RE A TEEN.
YOU'RE ALLOWED TO CUT LOOSE EVERY NOW AND THEN.
CANNON-BALL!

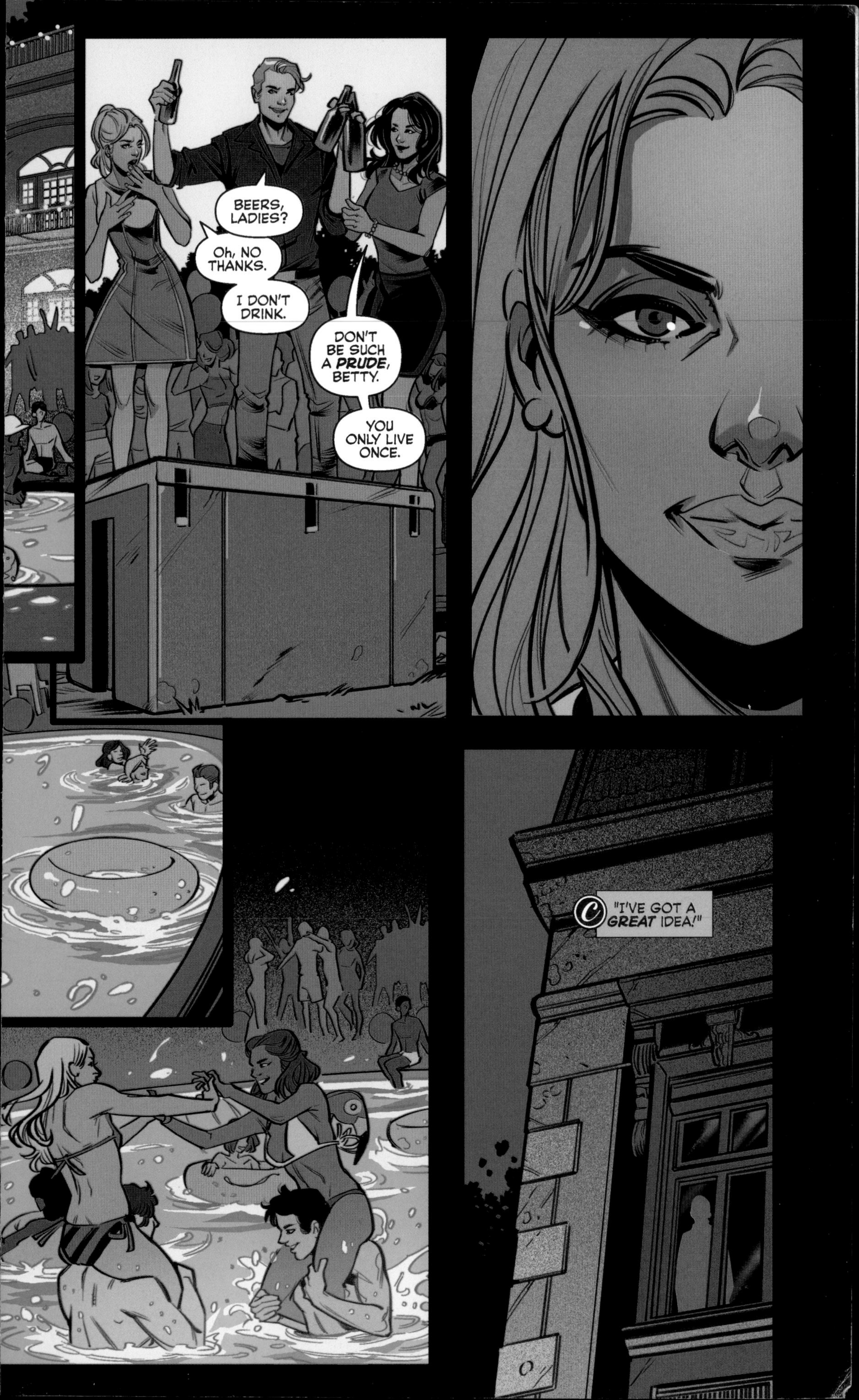
BEERS, LADIES?
Oh, NO THANKS.
I DON'T DRINK.
DON'T BE SUCH A **PRUDE**, BETTY.
YOU ONLY LIVE ONCE.
"I'VE GOT A **GREAT** IDEA!"

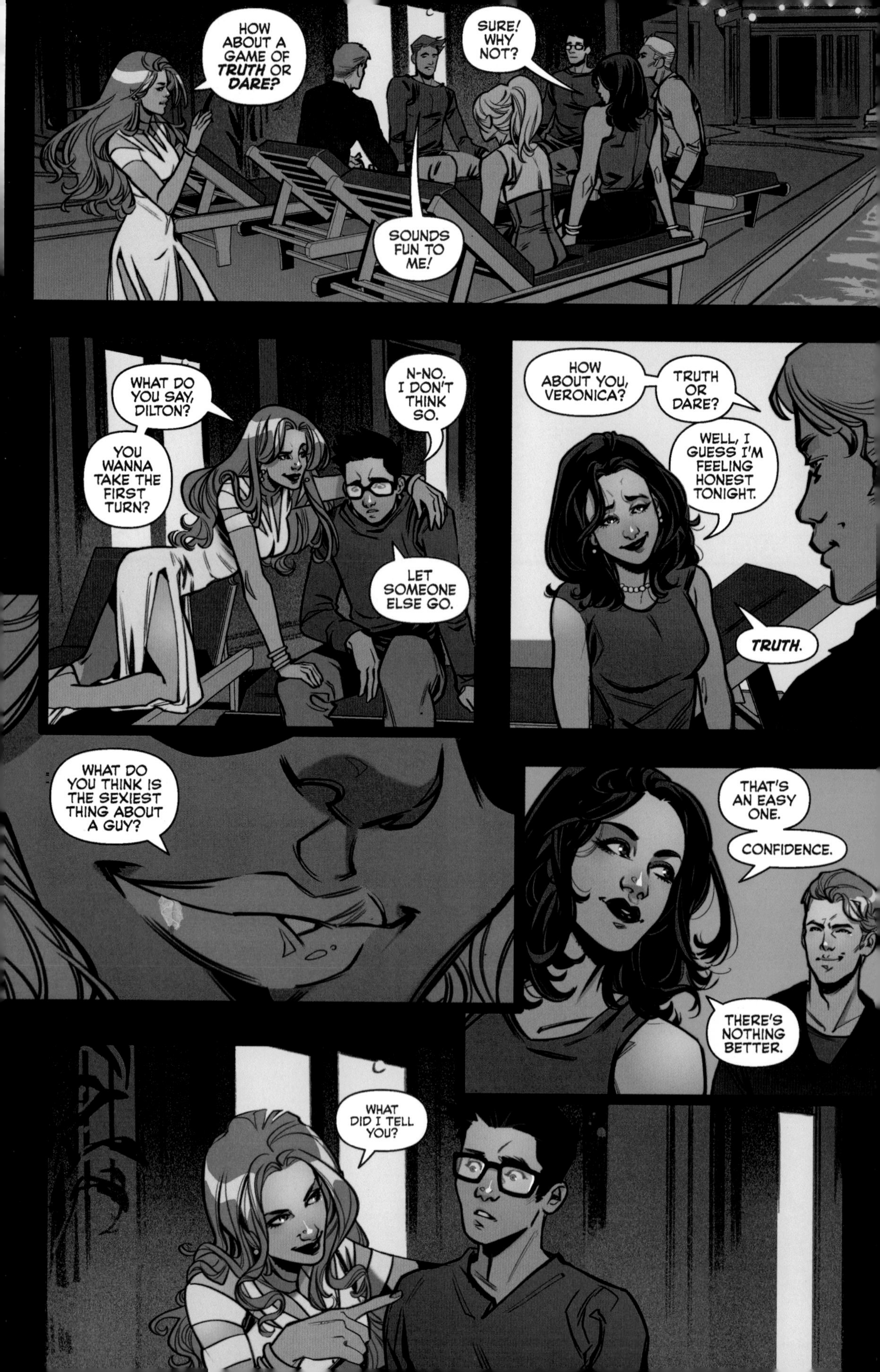
HOW ABOUT A GAME OF *TRUTH* OR *DARE?*
SURE! WHY NOT?
SOUNDS FUN TO ME!
WHAT DO YOU SAY, DILTON?
YOU WANNA TAKE THE FIRST TURN?
N-NO. I DON'T THINK SO.
LET SOMEONE ELSE GO.
HOW ABOUT YOU, VERONICA?
TRUTH OR DARE?
WELL, I GUESS I'M FEELING HONEST TONIGHT.
TRUTH.
WHAT DO YOU THINK IS THE SEXIEST THING ABOUT A GUY?
THAT'S AN EASY ONE.
CONFIDENCE.
THERE'S NOTHING BETTER.
WHAT DID I TELL YOU?

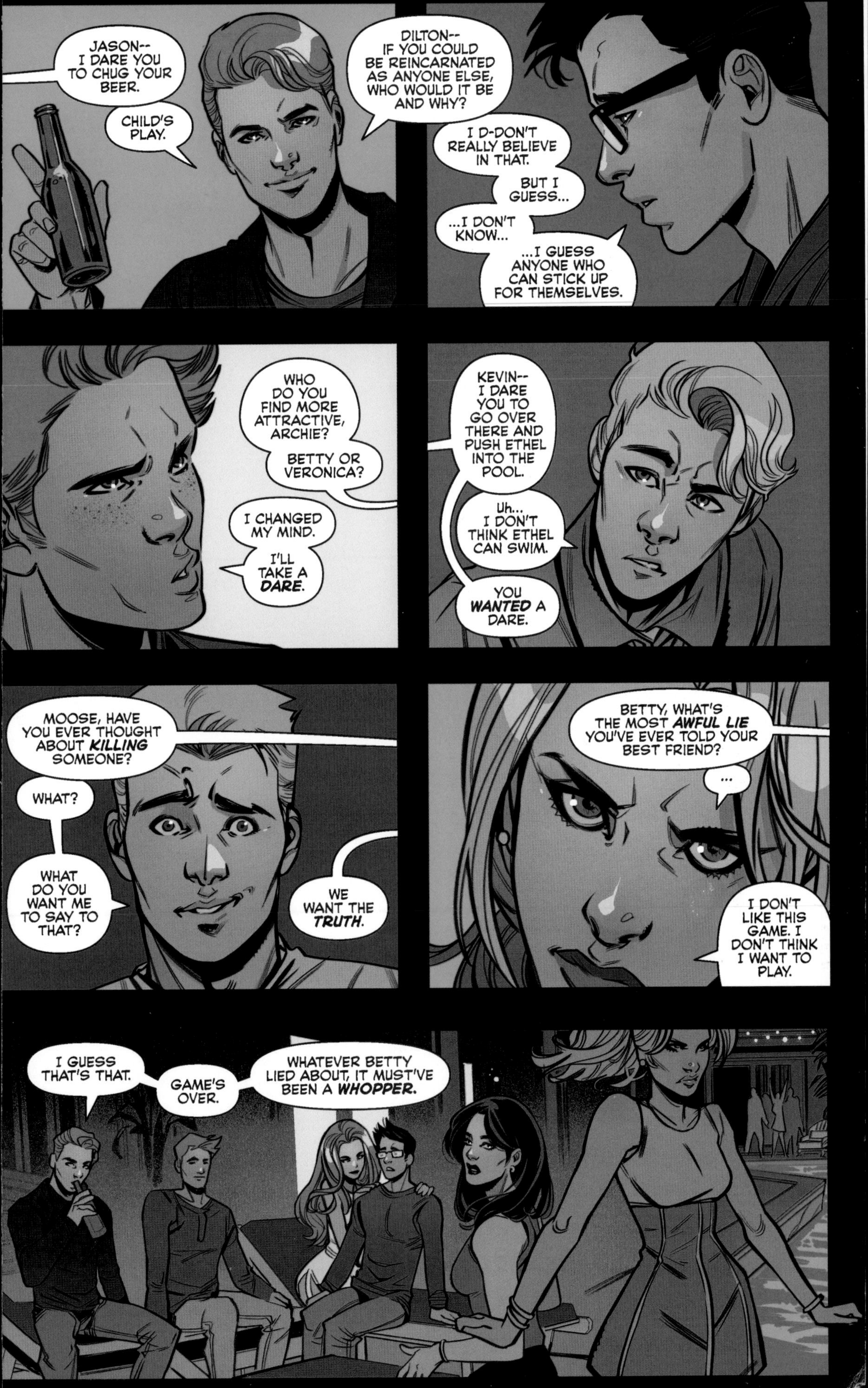
JASON-- I DARE YOU TO CHUG YOUR BEER.
CHILD'S PLAY.
DILTON-- IF YOU COULD BE REINCARNATED AS ANYONE ELSE, WHO WOULD IT BE AND WHY?
I D-DON'T REALLY BELIEVE IN THAT.
BUT I GUESS...
...I DON'T KNOW...
...I GUESS ANYONE WHO CAN STICK UP FOR THEMSELVES.
WHO DO YOU FIND MORE ATTRACTIVE, ARCHIE?
BETTY OR VERONICA?
I CHANGED MY MIND.
I'LL TAKE A *DARE*.
KEVIN-- I DARE YOU TO GO OVER THERE AND PUSH ETHEL INTO THE POOL.
UH... I DON'T THINK ETHEL CAN SWIM.
YOU *WANTED* A DARE.
MOOSE, HAVE YOU EVER THOUGHT ABOUT *KILLING* SOMEONE?
WHAT?
WHAT DO YOU WANT ME TO SAY TO THAT?
WE WANT THE *TRUTH*.
BETTY, WHAT'S THE MOST *AWFUL LIE* YOU'VE EVER TOLD YOUR BEST FRIEND?
...
I DON'T LIKE THIS GAME. I DON'T THINK I WANT TO PLAY.
I GUESS THAT'S THAT.
GAME'S OVER.
WHATEVER BETTY LIED ABOUT, IT MUST'VE BEEN A *WHOPPER*.

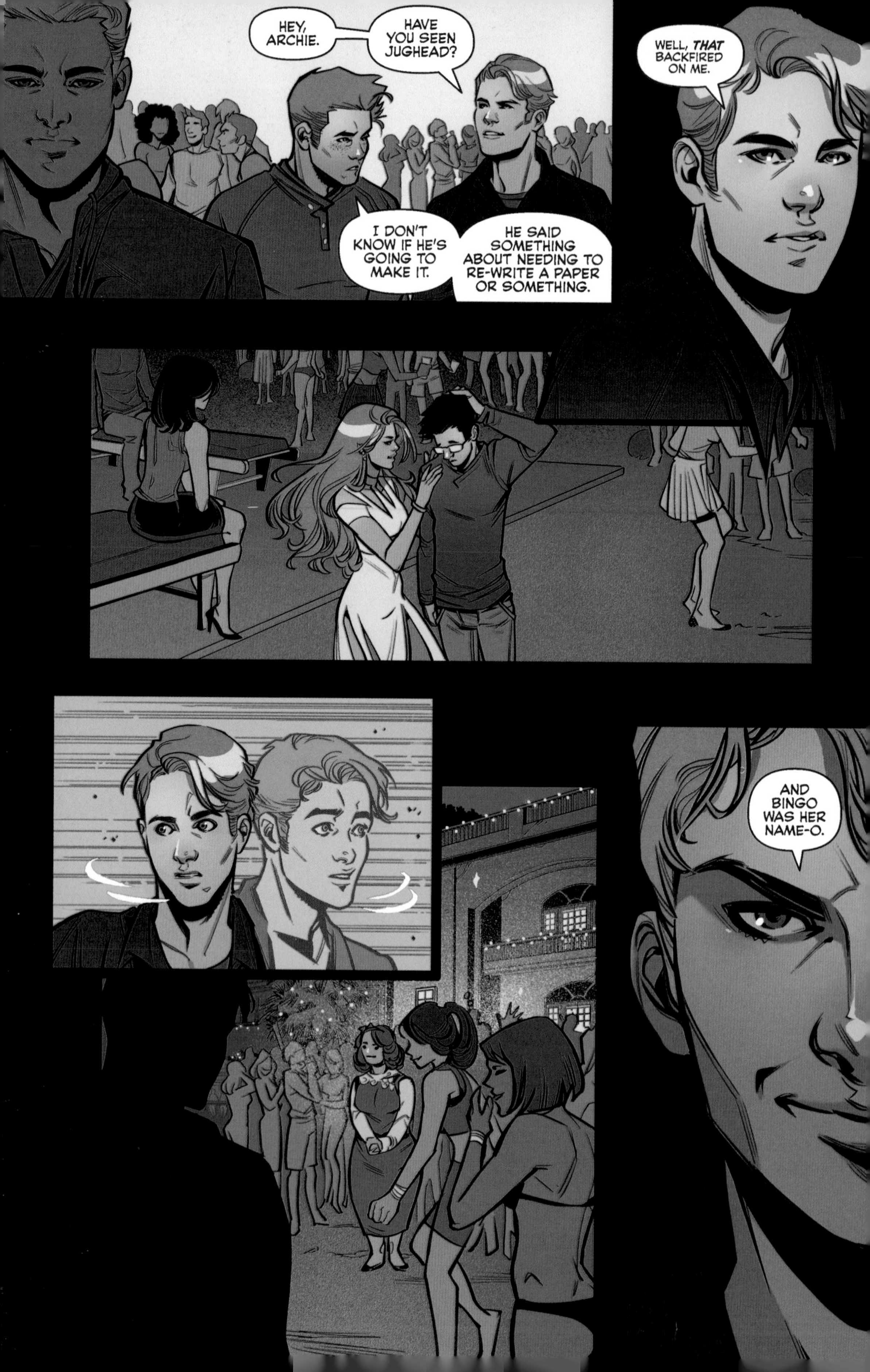
HEY, ARCHIE.
HAVE YOU SEEN JUGHEAD?
I DON'T KNOW IF HE'S GOING TO MAKE IT.
HE SAID SOMETHING ABOUT NEEDING TO RE-WRITE A PAPER OR SOMETHING.
WELL, ***THAT*** BACKFIRED ON ME.
AND BINGO WAS HER NAME-O.

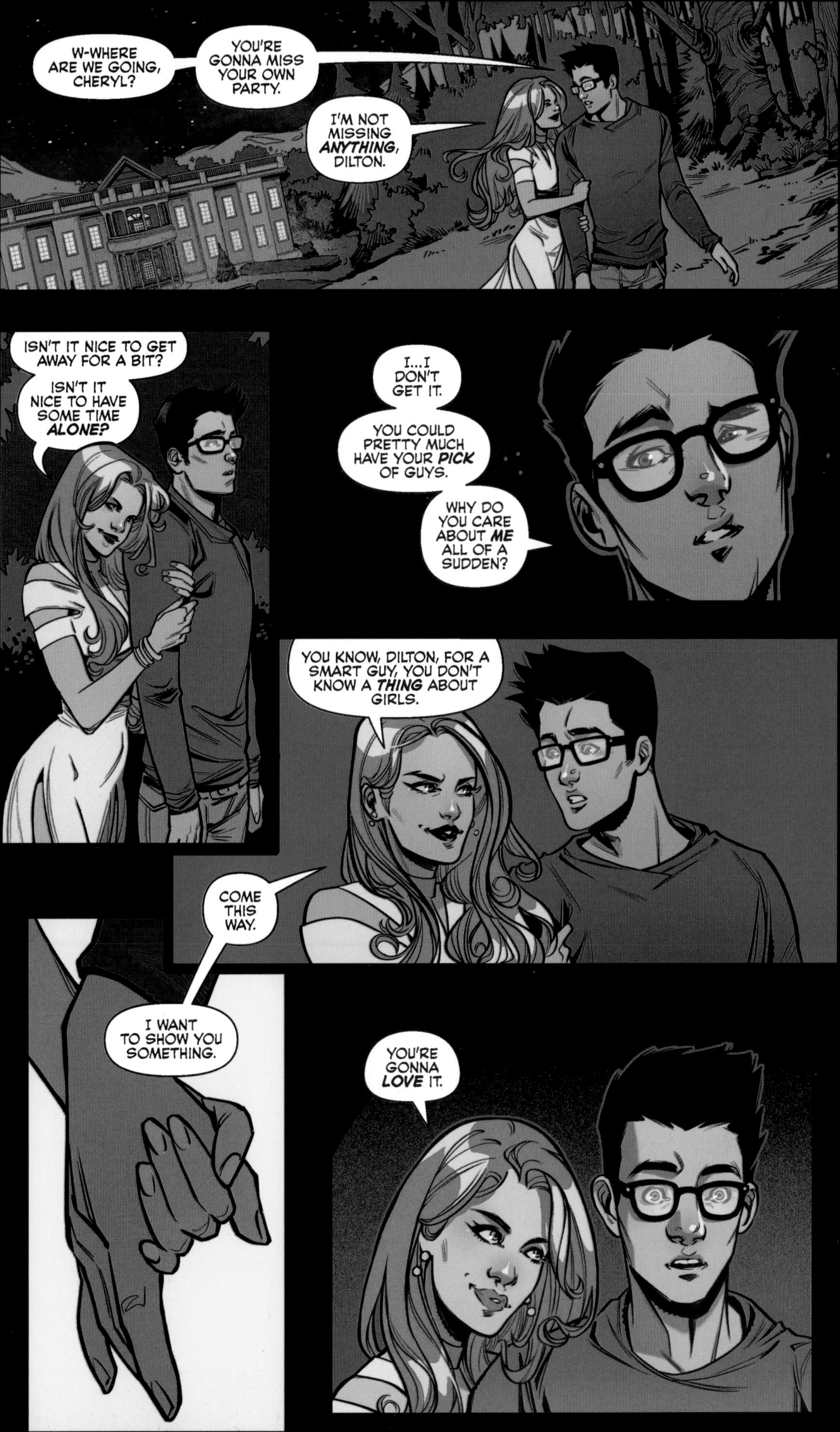
W-WHERE ARE WE GOING, CHERYL?
YOU'RE GONNA MISS YOUR OWN PARTY.
I'M NOT MISSING *ANYTHING*, DILTON.
ISN'T IT NICE TO GET AWAY FOR A BIT?
ISN'T IT NICE TO HAVE SOME TIME *ALONE?*
I...I DON'T GET IT.
YOU COULD PRETTY MUCH HAVE YOUR *PICK* OF GUYS.
WHY DO YOU CARE ABOUT *ME* ALL OF A SUDDEN?
YOU KNOW, DILTON, FOR A SMART GUY, YOU DON'T KNOW A *THING* ABOUT GIRLS.
COME THIS WAY.
I WANT TO SHOW YOU SOMETHING.
YOU'RE GONNA *LOVE* IT.

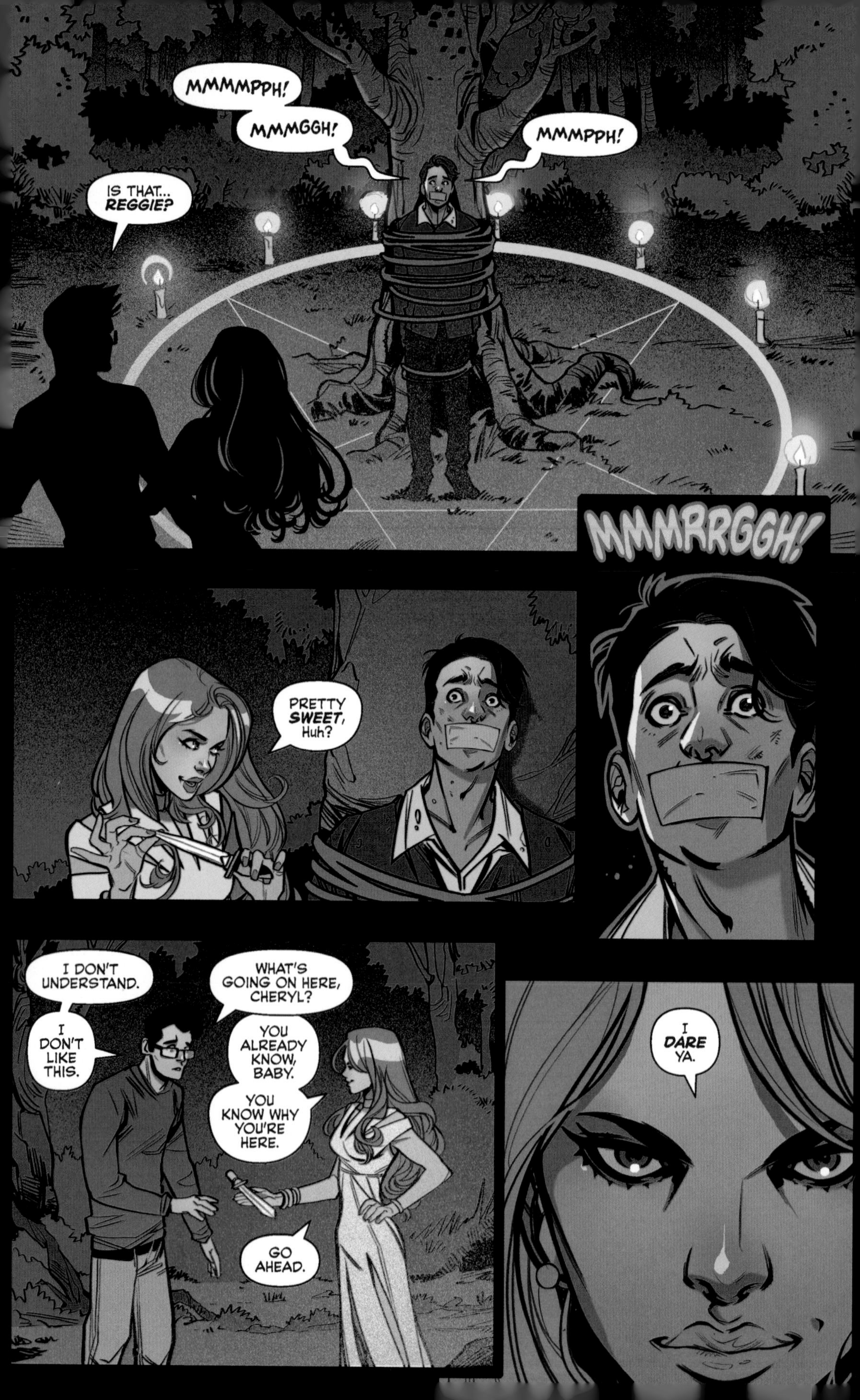
MMMMPPH!
MMMGGH!
MMMPPH!
IS THAT... REGGIE?
MMMRRGGH!
PRETTY SWEET, Huh?
I DON'T UNDERSTAND.
I DON'T LIKE THIS.
WHAT'S GOING ON HERE, CHERYL?
YOU ALREADY KNOW, BABY.
YOU KNOW WHY YOU'RE HERE.
GO AHEAD.
I DARE YA.

TO BE CONTINUED...

CHAPTER TWO

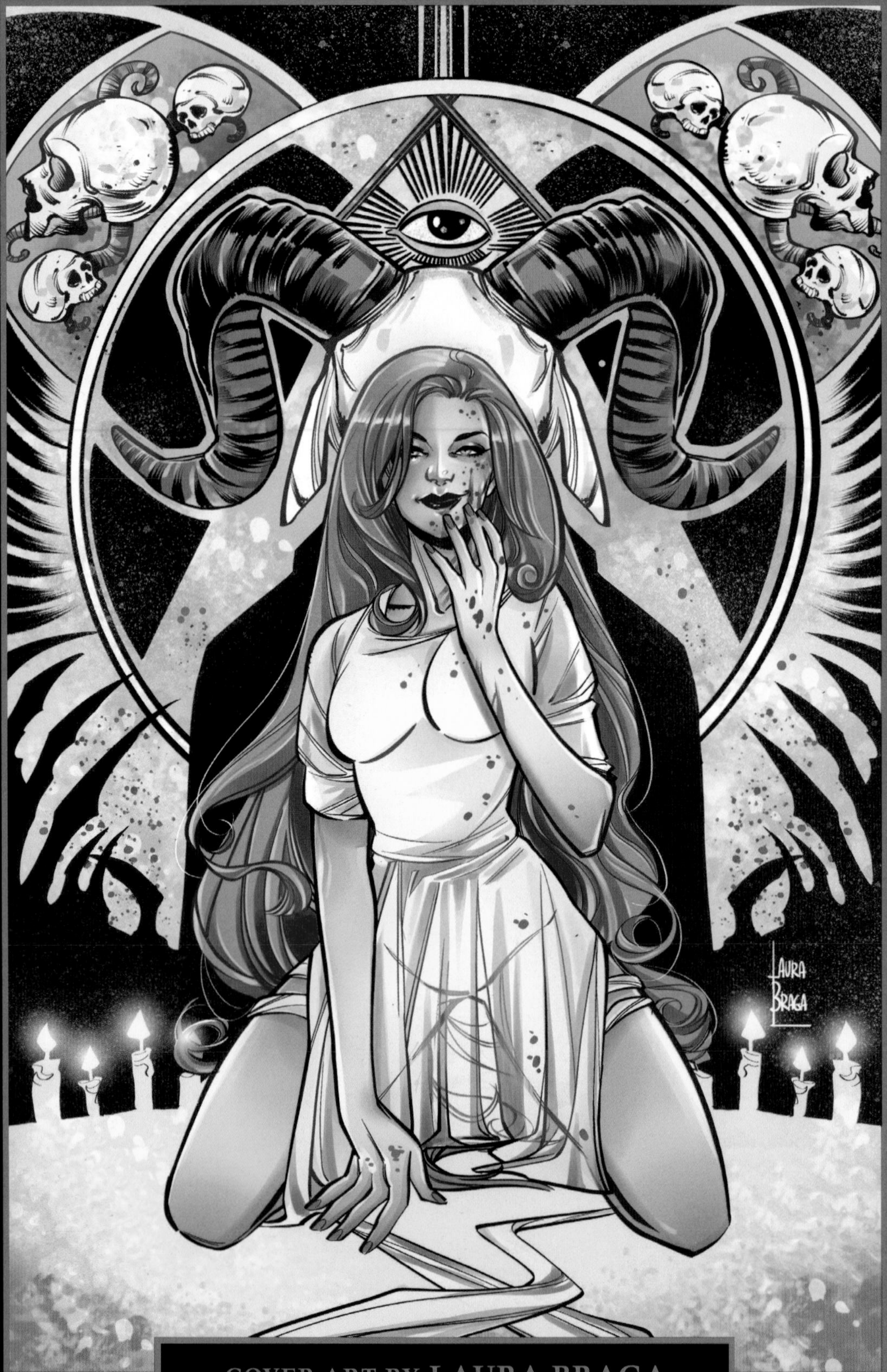
LAURA BRAGA

COVER ART BY LAURA BRAGA

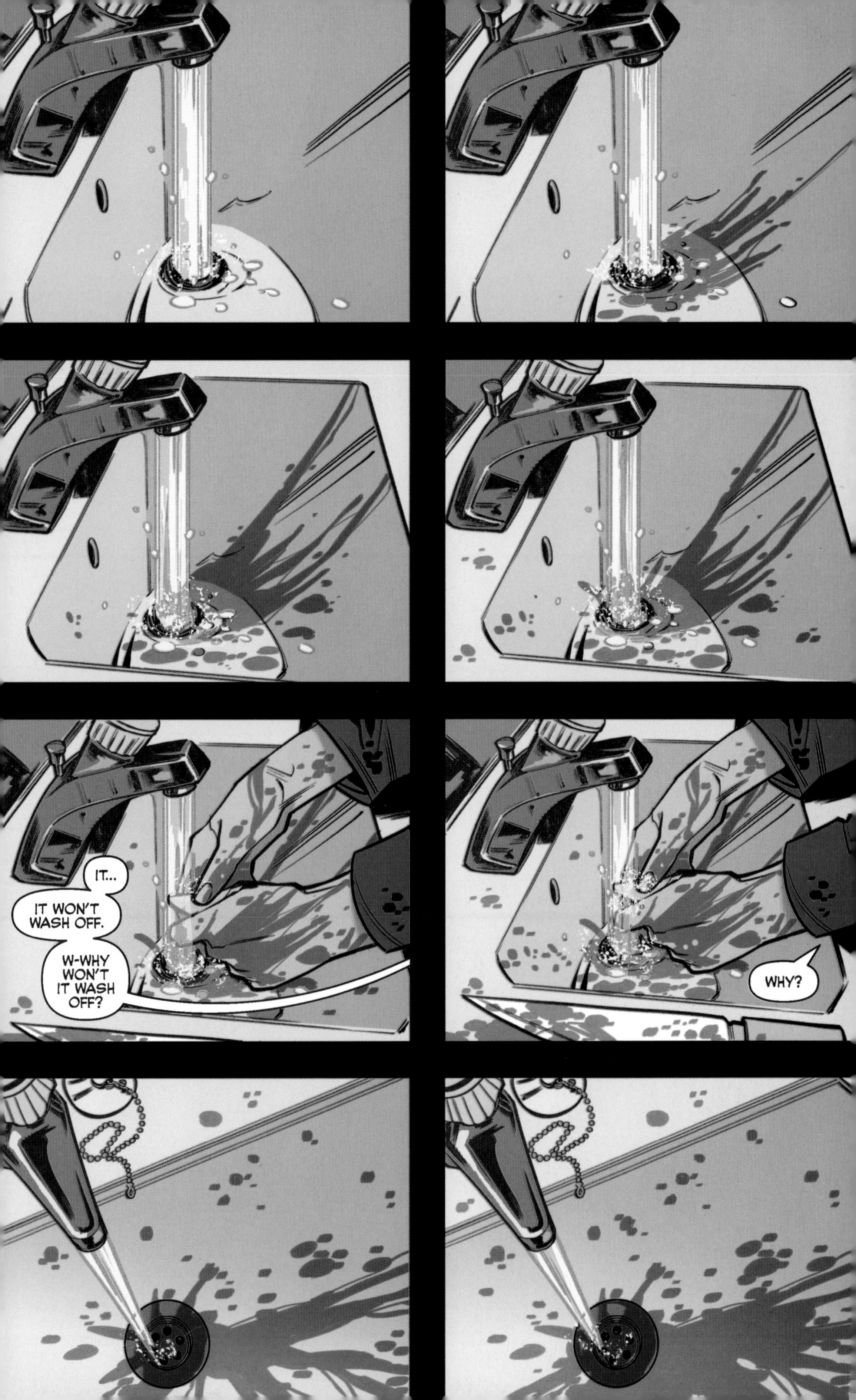
IT...
IT WON'T WASH OFF.
W-WHY WON'T IT WASH OFF?
WHY?

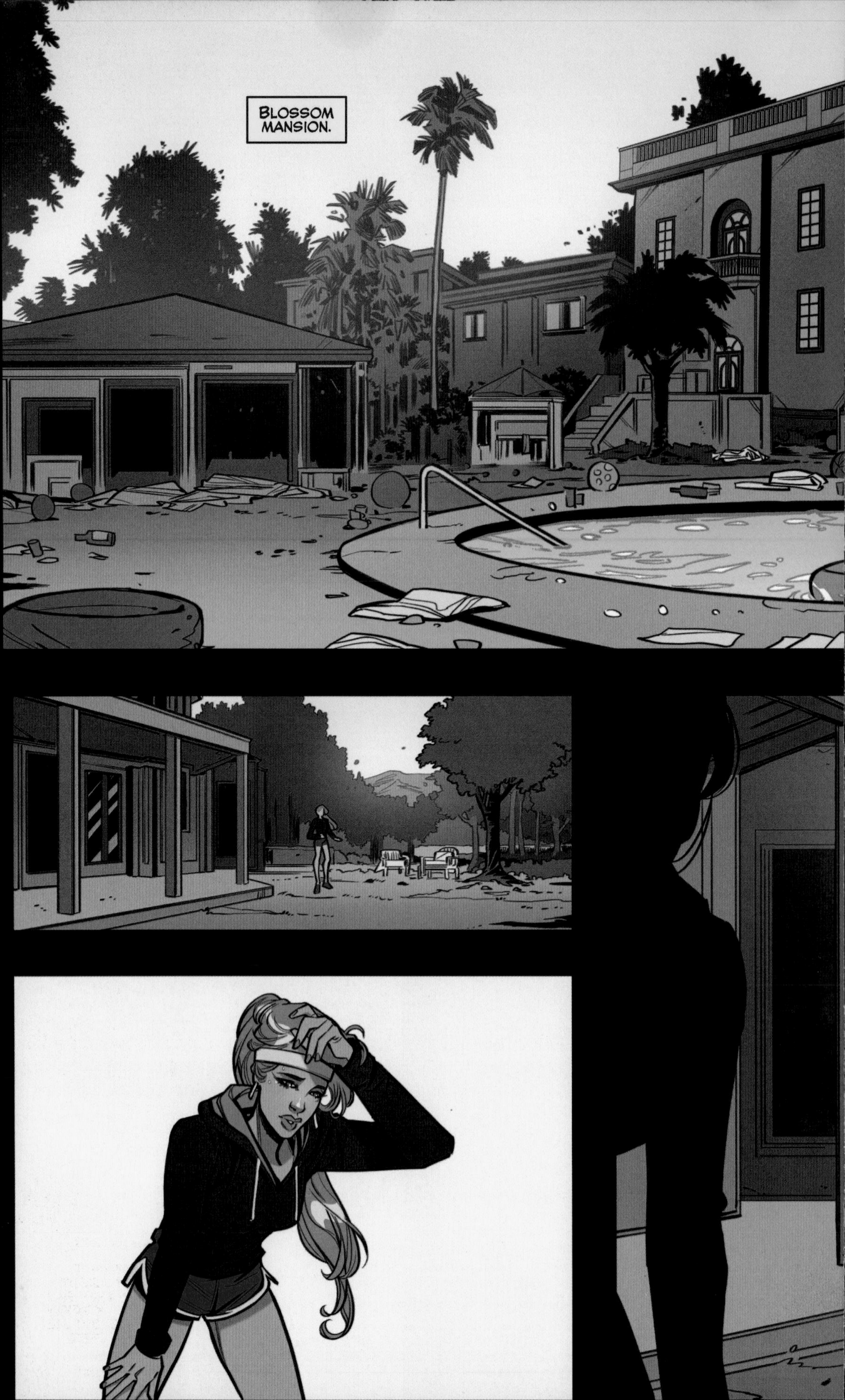
BLOSSOM MANSION.

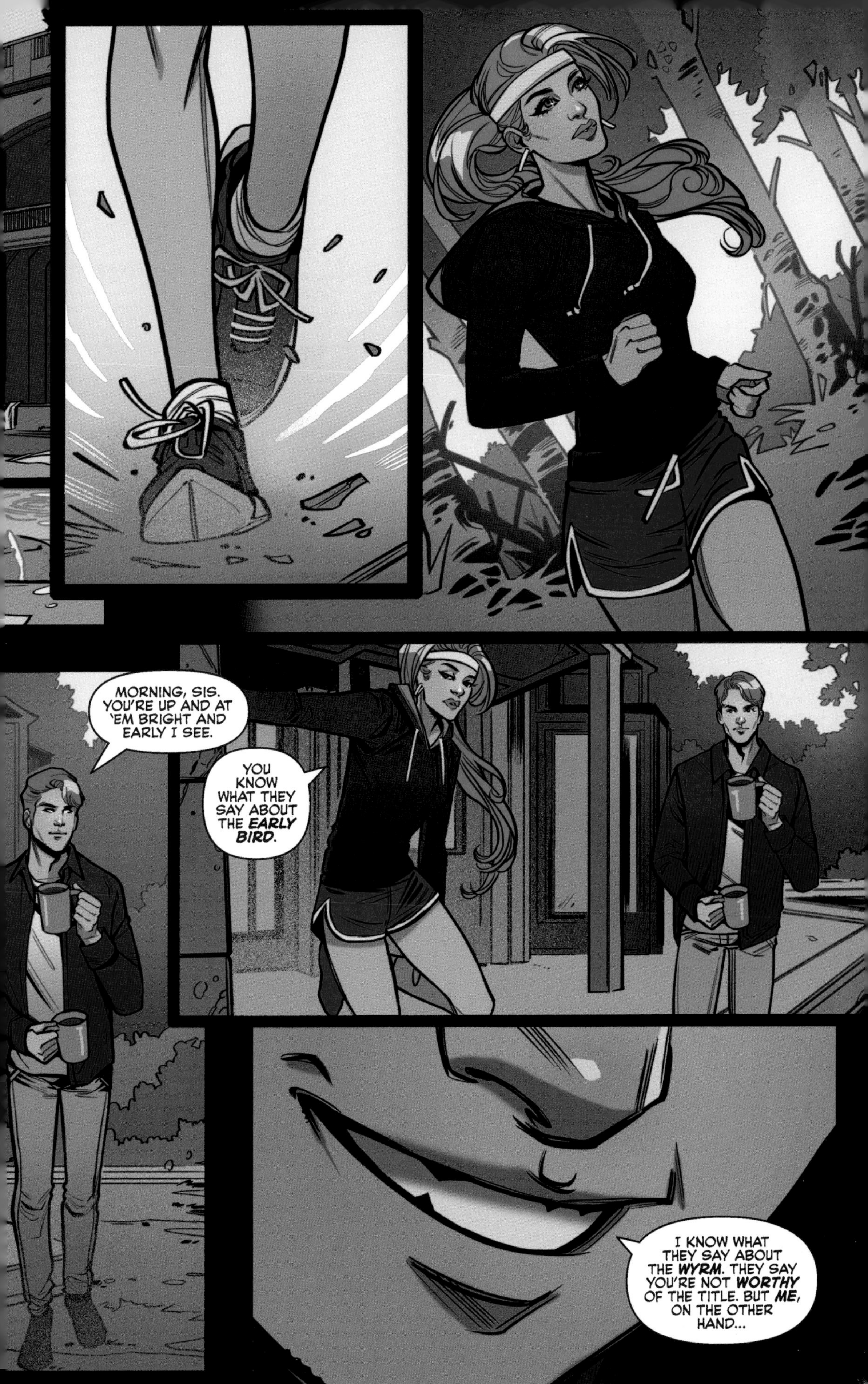
MORNING, SIS. YOU'RE UP AND AT 'EM BRIGHT AND EARLY I SEE.
YOU KNOW WHAT THEY SAY ABOUT THE EARLY BIRD.
I KNOW WHAT THEY SAY ABOUT THE WYRM. THEY SAY YOU'RE NOT WORTHY OF THE TITLE. BUT ME, ON THE OTHER HAND...

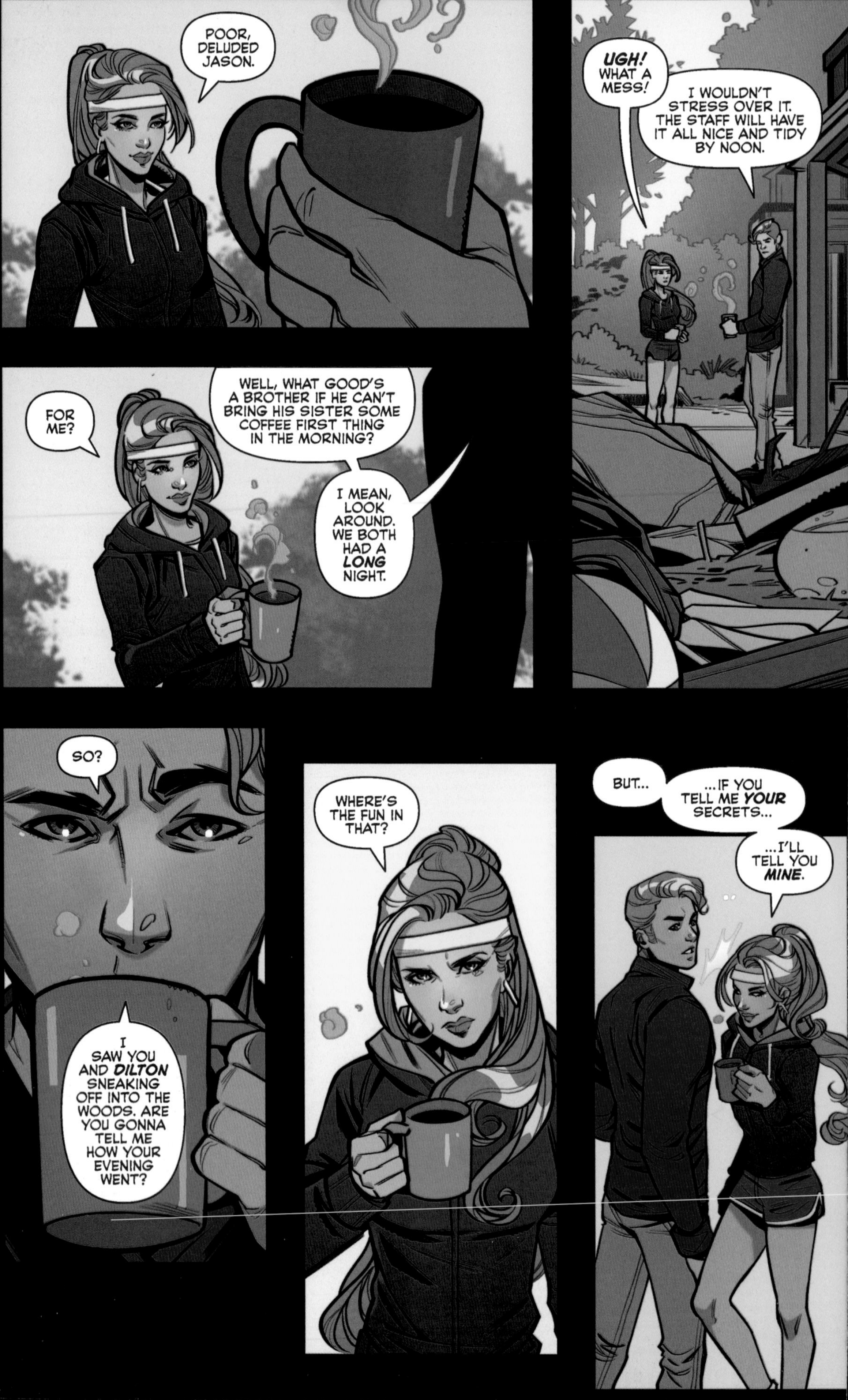
POOR, DELUDED JASON.
UGH! WHAT A MESS!
I WOULDN'T STRESS OVER IT. THE STAFF WILL HAVE IT ALL NICE AND TIDY BY NOON.
FOR ME?
WELL, WHAT GOOD'S A BROTHER IF HE CAN'T BRING HIS SISTER SOME COFFEE FIRST THING IN THE MORNING?
I MEAN, LOOK AROUND. WE BOTH HAD A LONG NIGHT.
SO?
I SAW YOU AND DILTON SNEAKING OFF INTO THE WOODS. ARE YOU GONNA TELL ME HOW YOUR EVENING WENT?
WHERE'S THE FUN IN THAT?
BUT...
...IF YOU TELL ME YOUR SECRETS...
...I'LL TELL YOU MINE.

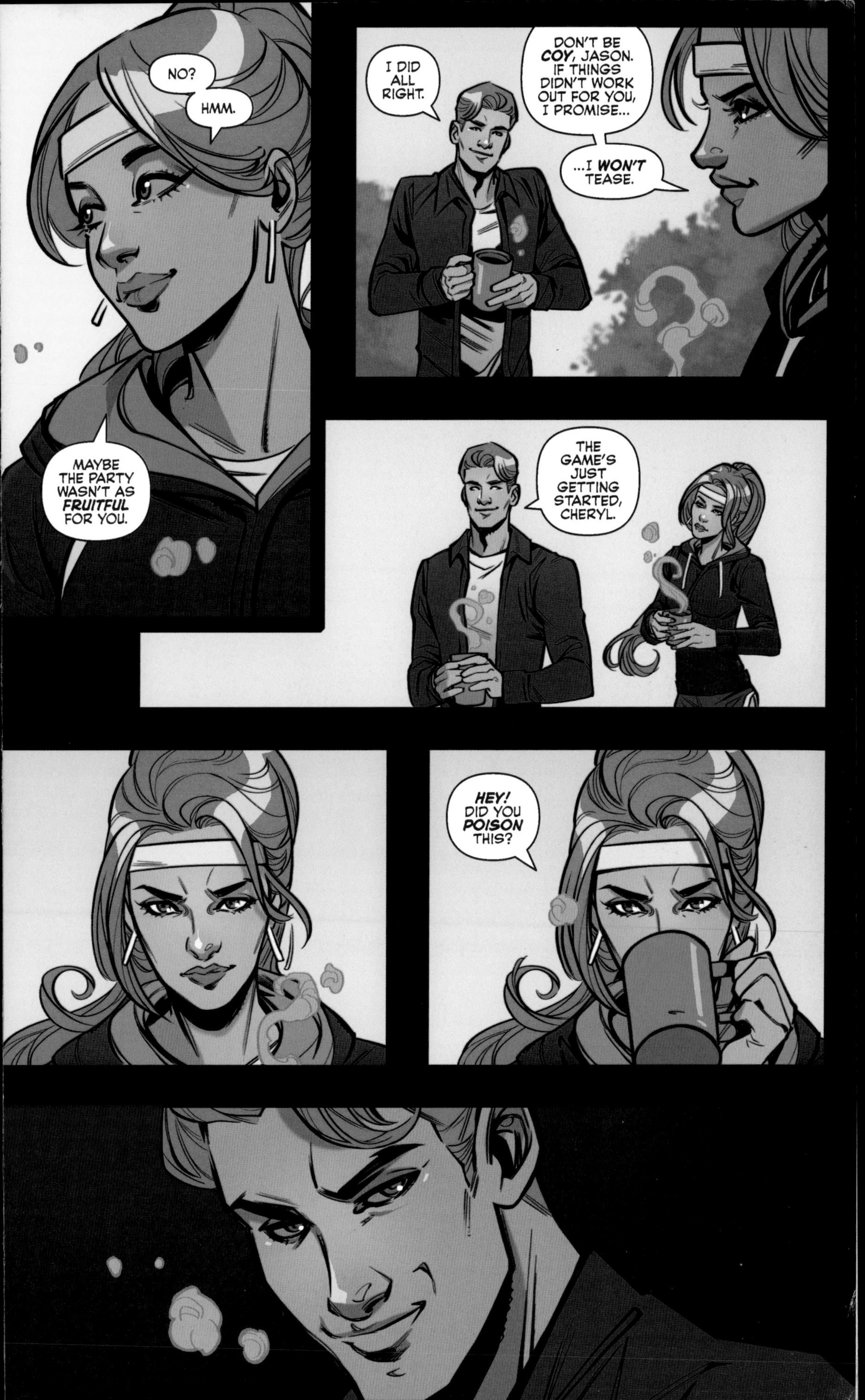
NO?
HMM.
MAYBE THE PARTY WASN'T AS FRUITFUL FOR YOU.
I DID ALL RIGHT.
DON'T BE COY, JASON. IF THINGS DIDN'T WORK OUT FOR YOU, I PROMISE...
...I WON'T TEASE.
THE GAME'S JUST GETTING STARTED, CHERYL.
HEY! DID YOU POISON THIS?

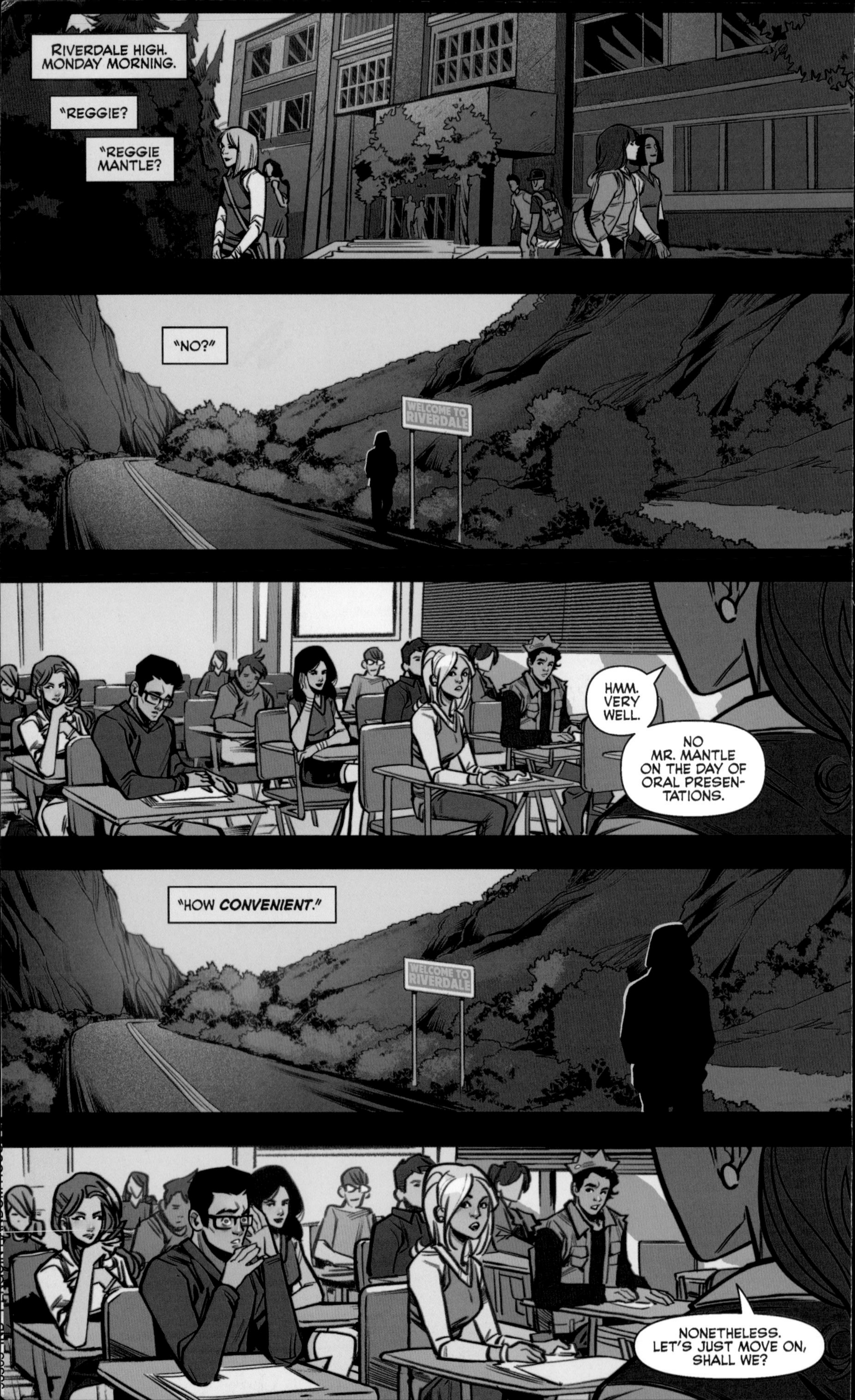

RIVERDALE HIGH. MONDAY MORNING.
"REGGIE?
"REGGIE MANTLE?
"NO?"
WELCOME TO RIVERDALE
HMM. VERY WELL.
NO MR. MANTLE ON THE DAY OF ORAL PRESEN-TATIONS.
"HOW CONVENIENT."
WELCOME TO RIVERDALE
NONETHELESS. LET'S JUST MOVE ON, SHALL WE?

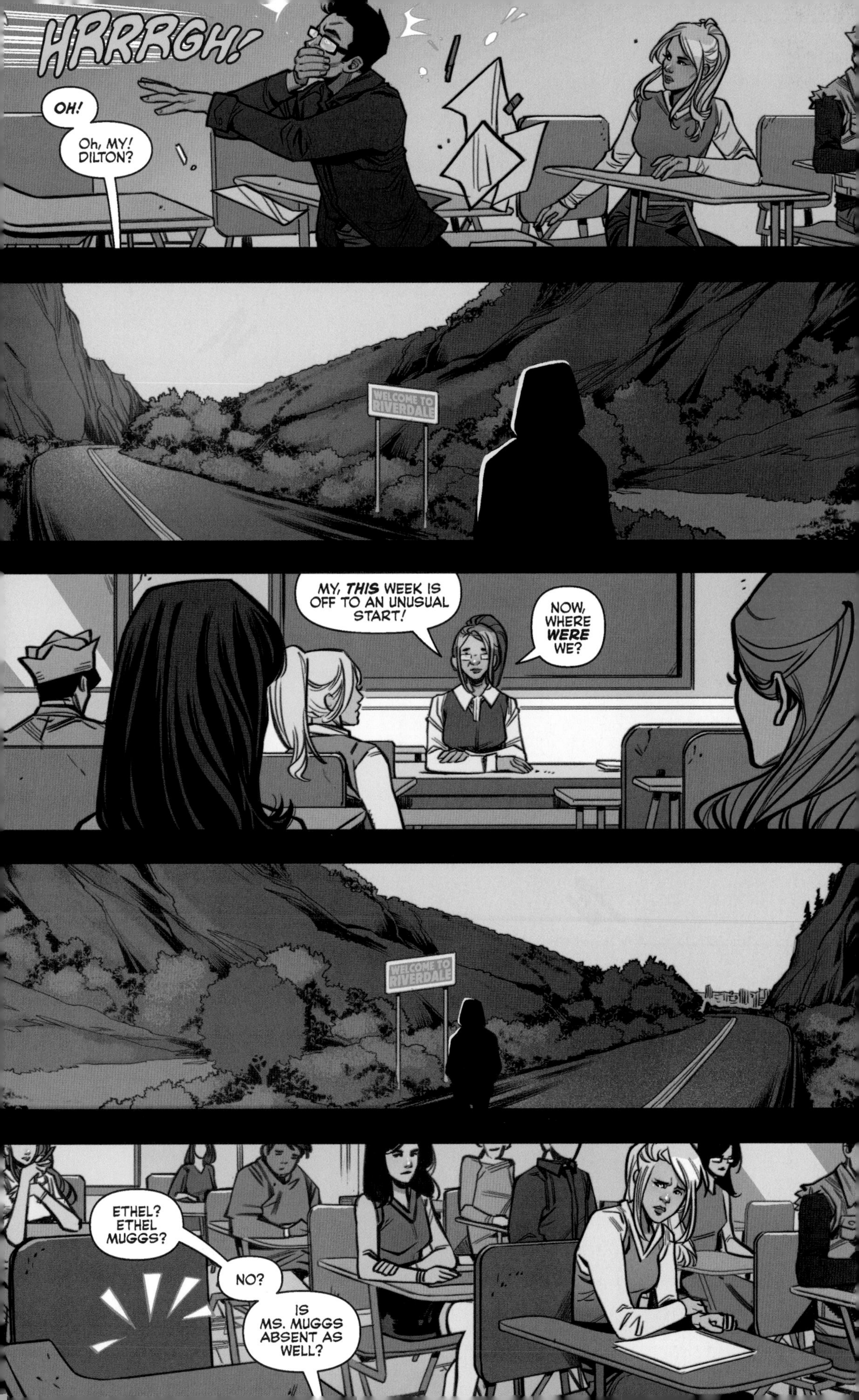
HRRRGH!
OH!
Oh, MY! DILTON?
WELCOME TO RIVERDALE
MY, THIS WEEK IS OFF TO AN UNUSUAL START!
NOW, WHERE WERE WE?
WELCOME TO RIVERDALE
ETHEL? ETHEL MUGGS?
NO?
IS MS. MUGGS ABSENT AS WELL?

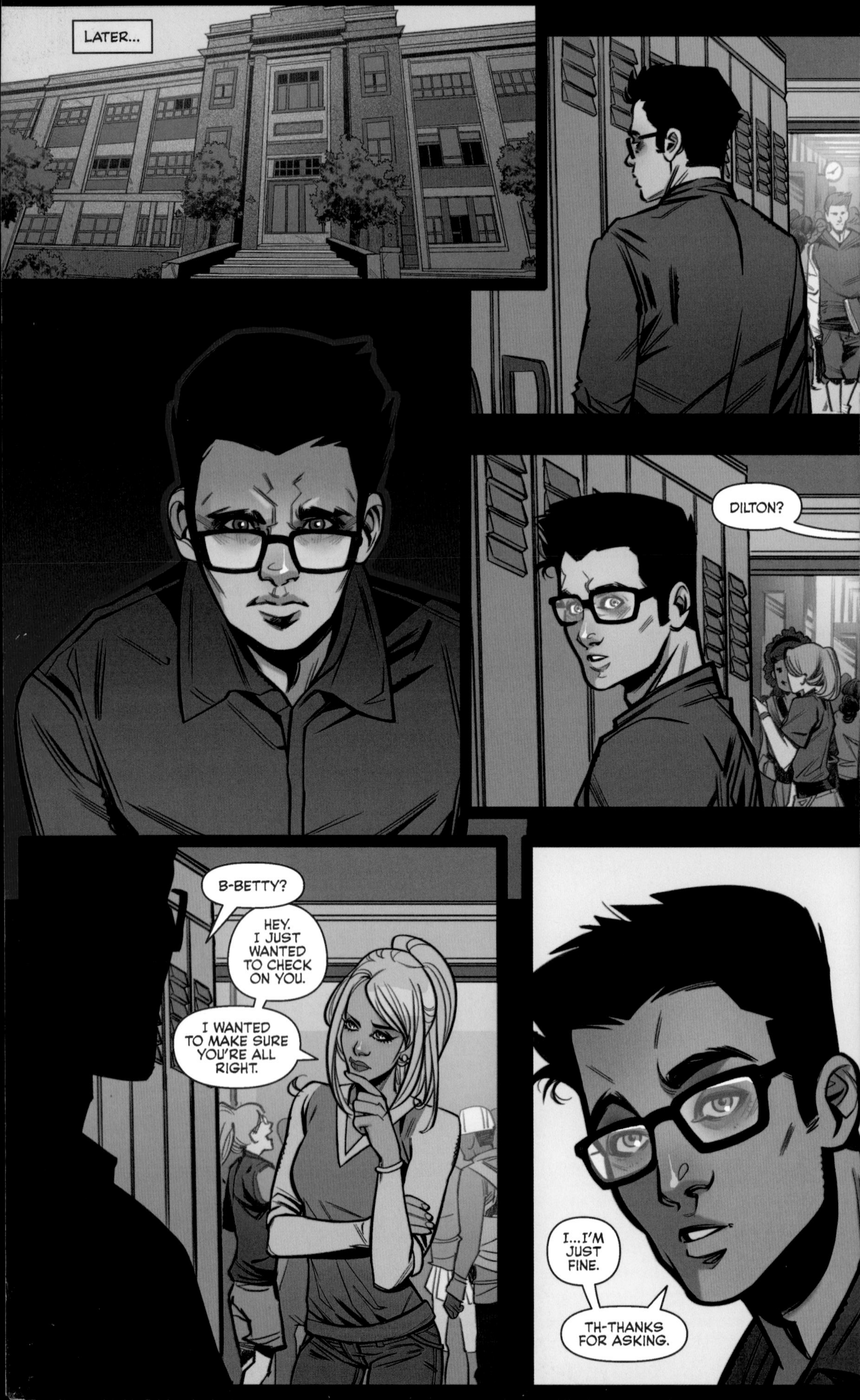
LATER...
DILTON?
B-BETTY?
HEY. I JUST WANTED TO CHECK ON YOU.
I WANTED TO MAKE SURE YOU'RE ALL RIGHT.
I...I'M JUST FINE.
TH-THANKS FOR ASKING.

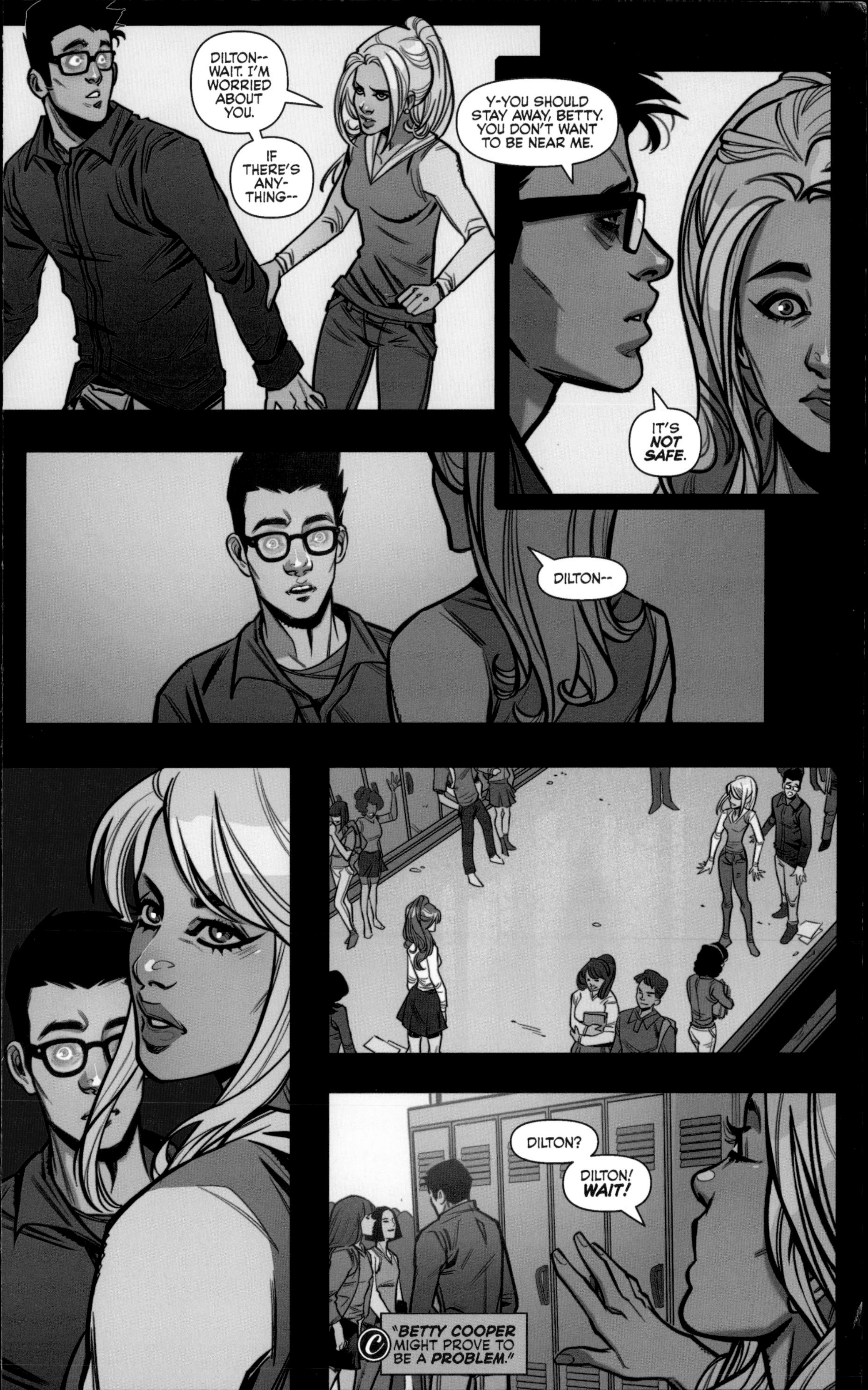
DILTON-- WAIT. I'M WORRIED ABOUT YOU.
IF THERE'S ANY-THING--
Y-YOU SHOULD STAY AWAY, BETTY. YOU DON'T WANT TO BE NEAR ME.
IT'S NOT SAFE.
DILTON--
DILTON?
DILTON! WAIT!
"BETTY COOPER MIGHT PROVE TO BE A PROBLEM."

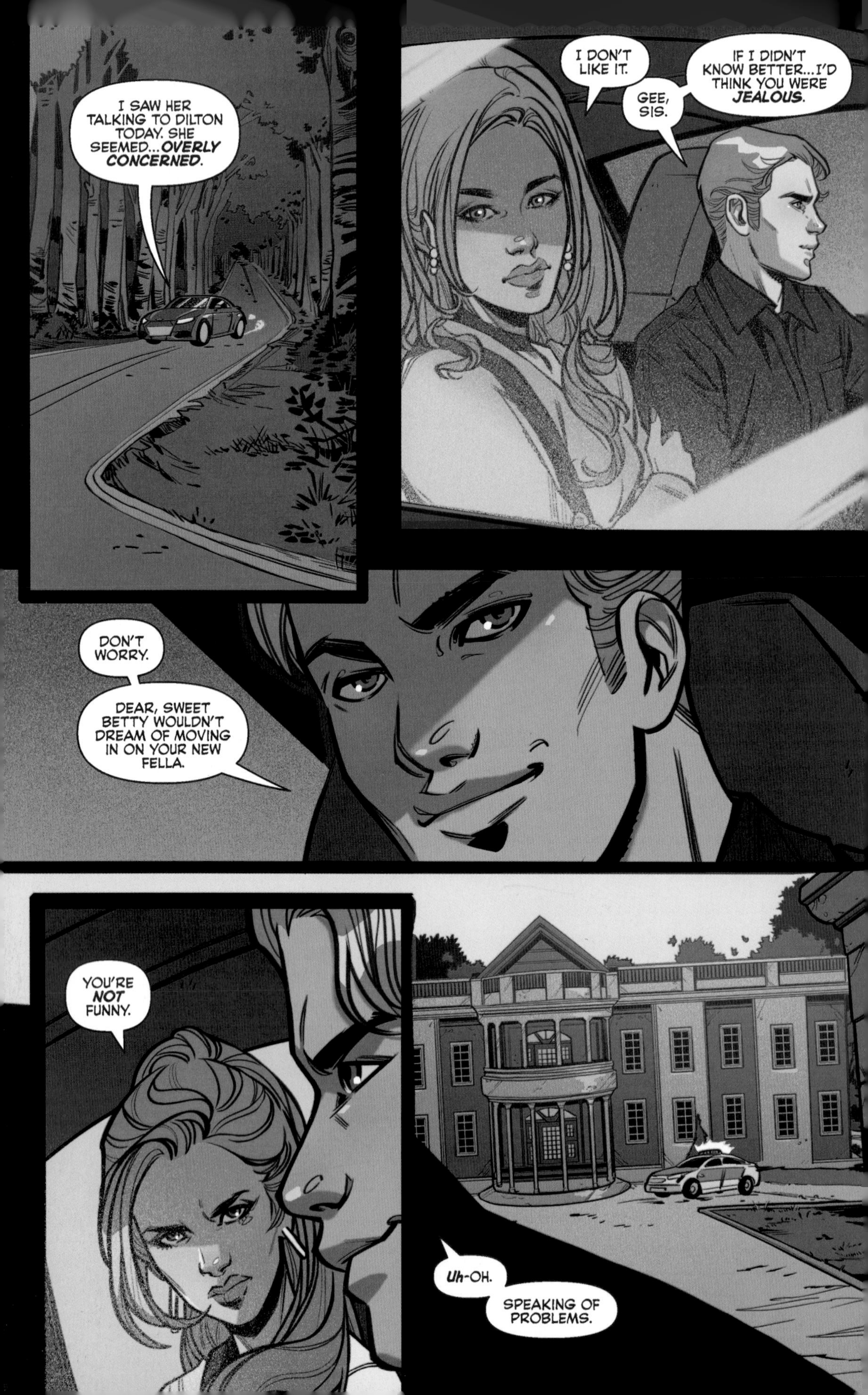
I SAW HER TALKING TO DILTON TODAY. SHE SEEMED...OVERLY CONCERNED.
I DON'T LIKE IT.
GEE, SIS.
IF I DIDN'T KNOW BETTER...I'D THINK YOU WERE JEALOUS.
DON'T WORRY.
DEAR, SWEET BETTY WOULDN'T DREAM OF MOVING IN ON YOUR NEW FELLA.
YOU'RE NOT FUNNY.
Uh-OH.
SPEAKING OF PROBLEMS.

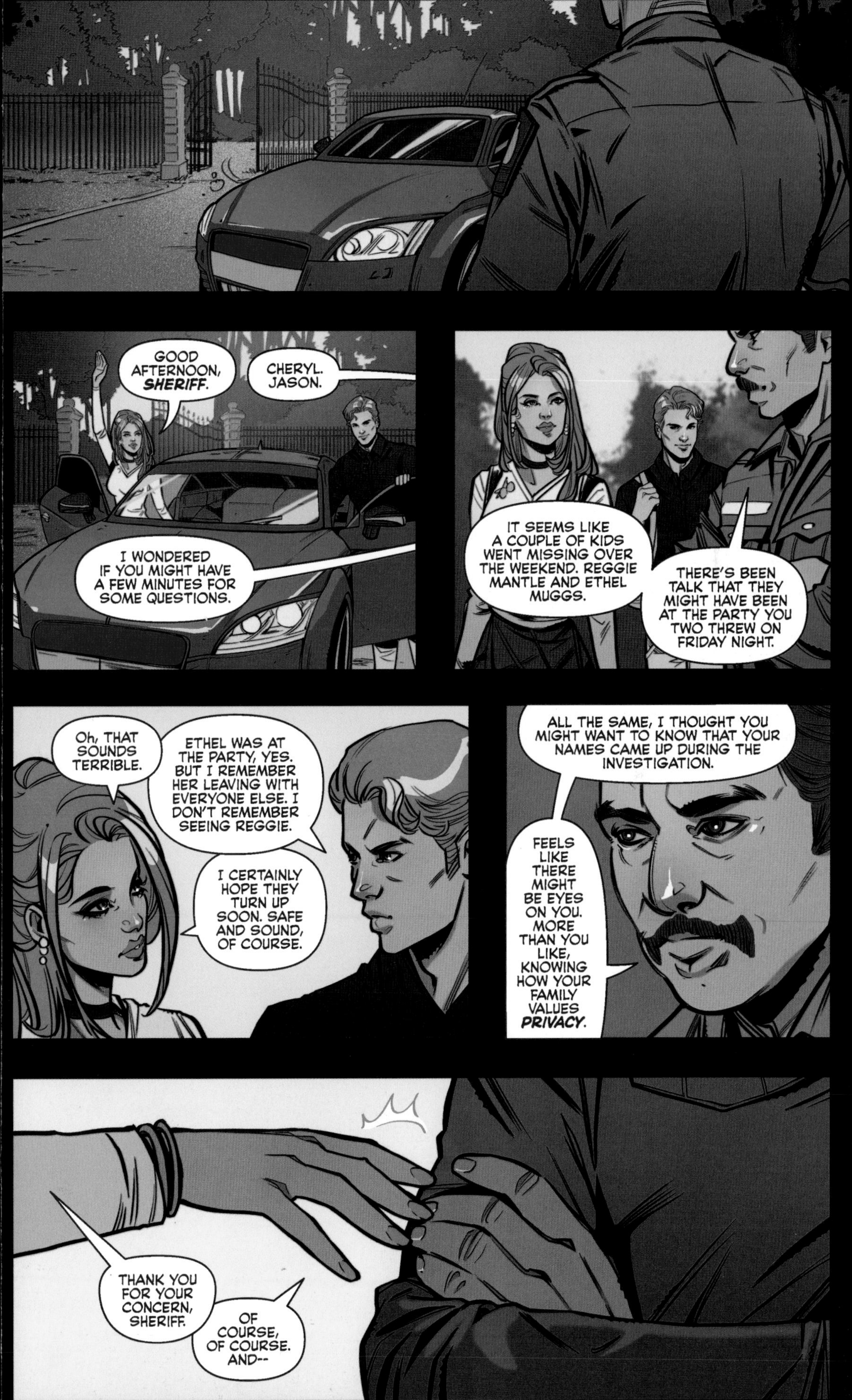
GOOD AFTERNOON, SHERIFF.
CHERYL. JASON.
I WONDERED IF YOU MIGHT HAVE A FEW MINUTES FOR SOME QUESTIONS.
IT SEEMS LIKE A COUPLE OF KIDS WENT MISSING OVER THE WEEKEND. REGGIE MANTLE AND ETHEL MUGGS.
THERE'S BEEN TALK THAT THEY MIGHT HAVE BEEN AT THE PARTY YOU TWO THREW ON FRIDAY NIGHT.
Oh, THAT SOUNDS TERRIBLE.
ETHEL WAS AT THE PARTY, YES. BUT I REMEMBER HER LEAVING WITH EVERYONE ELSE. I DON'T REMEMBER SEEING REGGIE.
I CERTAINLY HOPE THEY TURN UP SOON. SAFE AND SOUND, OF COURSE.
ALL THE SAME, I THOUGHT YOU MIGHT WANT TO KNOW THAT YOUR NAMES CAME UP DURING THE INVESTIGATION.
FEELS LIKE THERE MIGHT BE EYES ON YOU. MORE THAN YOU LIKE, KNOWING HOW YOUR FAMILY VALUES PRIVACY.
THANK YOU FOR YOUR CONCERN, SHERIFF.
OF COURSE, OF COURSE. AND--

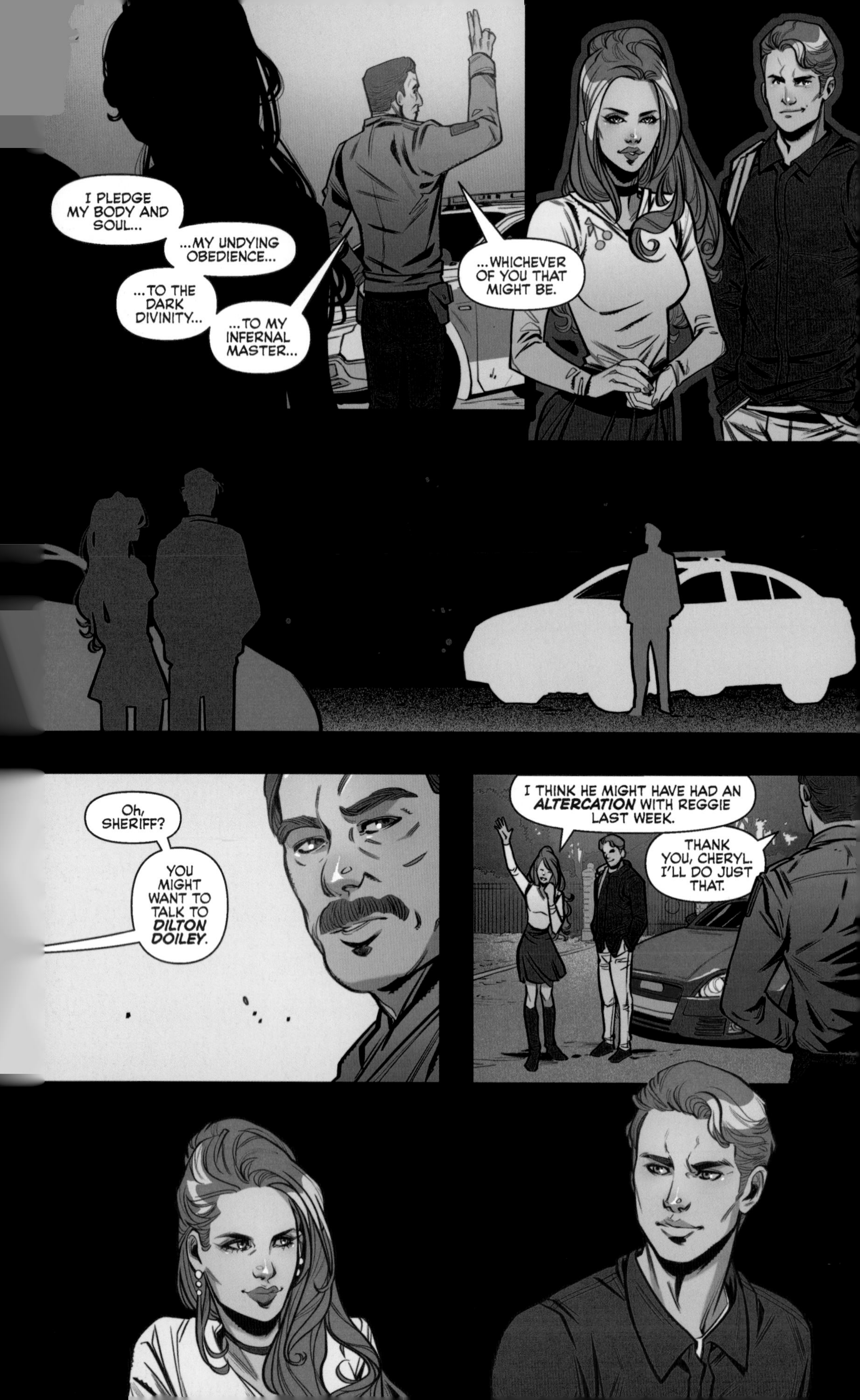

I PLEDGE MY BODY AND SOUL...
...MY UNDYING OBEDIENCE...
...TO THE DARK DIVINITY...
...TO MY INFERNAL MASTER...
...WHICHEVER OF YOU THAT MIGHT BE.
Oh, SHERIFF?
YOU MIGHT WANT TO TALK TO *DILTON DOILEY*.
I THINK HE MIGHT HAVE HAD AN *ALTERCATION* WITH REGGIE LAST WEEK.
THANK YOU, CHERYL. I'LL DO JUST THAT.

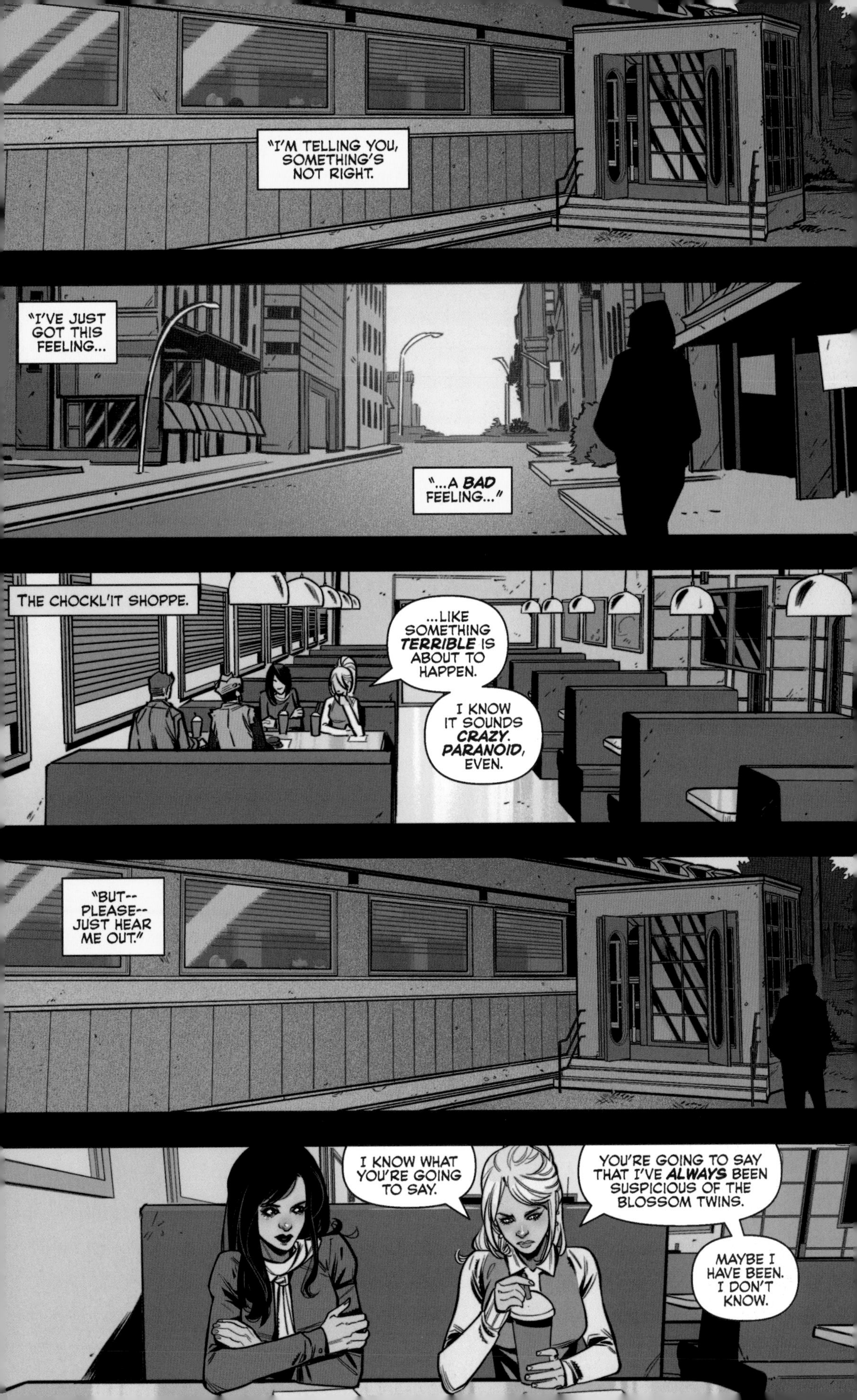

"I'M TELLING YOU, SOMETHING'S NOT RIGHT.
"I'VE JUST GOT THIS FEELING...
"...A BAD FEELING..."
THE CHOCKL'IT SHOPPE.
...LIKE SOMETHING TERRIBLE IS ABOUT TO HAPPEN.
I KNOW IT SOUNDS CRAZY. PARANOID, EVEN.
"BUT-- PLEASE-- JUST HEAR ME OUT."
I KNOW WHAT YOU'RE GOING TO SAY.
YOU'RE GOING TO SAY THAT I'VE ALWAYS BEEN SUSPICIOUS OF THE BLOSSOM TWINS.
MAYBE I HAVE BEEN. I DON'T KNOW.

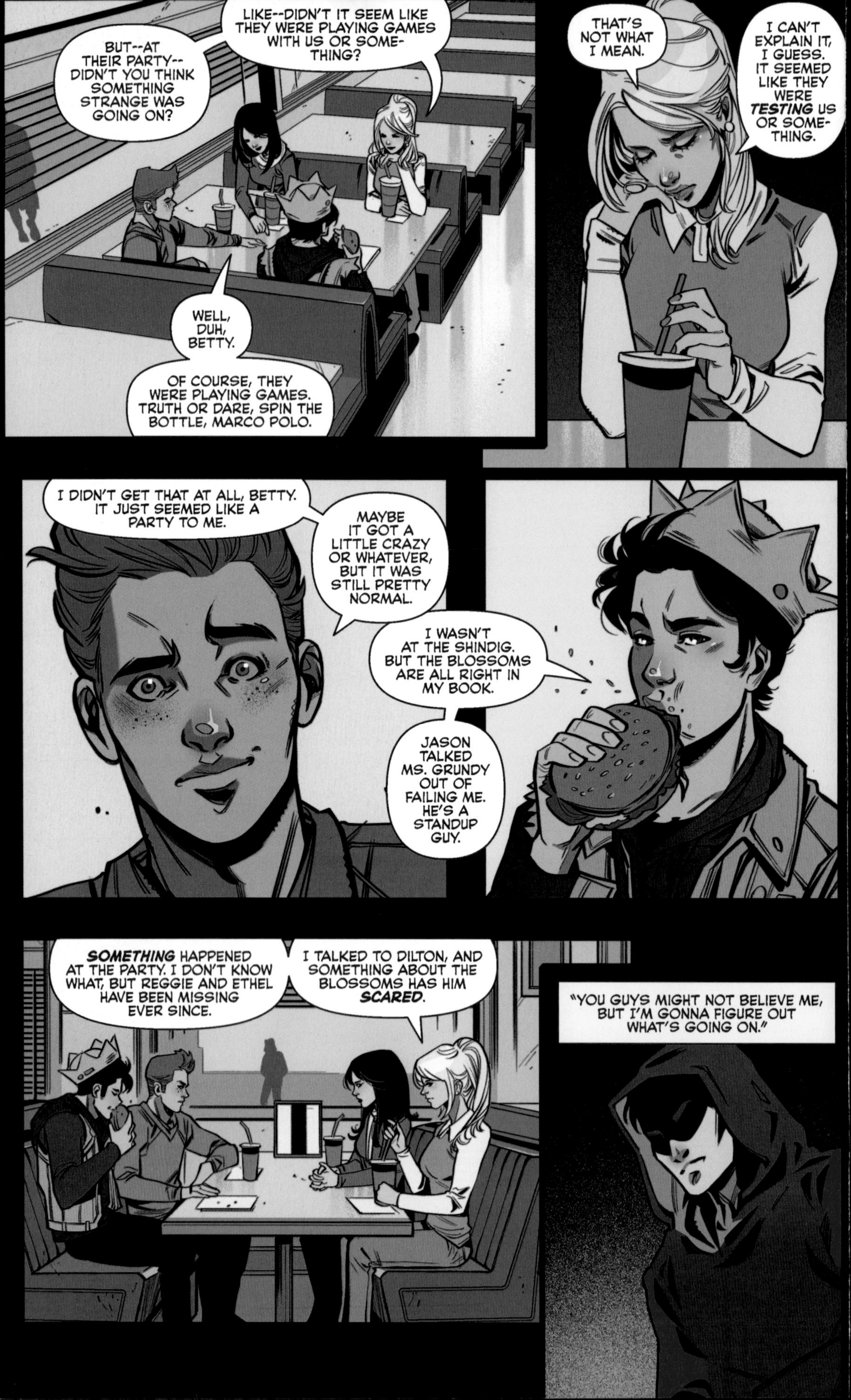
BUT--AT THEIR PARTY--DIDN'T YOU THINK SOMETHING STRANGE WAS GOING ON?
LIKE--DIDN'T IT SEEM LIKE THEY WERE PLAYING GAMES WITH US OR SOMETHING?
WELL, DUH, BETTY.
OF COURSE, THEY WERE PLAYING GAMES. TRUTH OR DARE, SPIN THE BOTTLE, MARCO POLO.
THAT'S NOT WHAT I MEAN.
I CAN'T EXPLAIN IT, I GUESS. IT SEEMED LIKE THEY WERE *TESTING* US OR SOMETHING.
I DIDN'T GET THAT AT ALL, BETTY. IT JUST SEEMED LIKE A PARTY TO ME.
MAYBE IT GOT A LITTLE CRAZY OR WHATEVER, BUT IT WAS STILL PRETTY NORMAL.
I WASN'T AT THE SHINDIG. BUT THE BLOSSOMS ARE ALL RIGHT IN MY BOOK.
JASON TALKED MS. GRUNDY OUT OF FAILING ME. HE'S A STANDUP GUY.
SOMETHING HAPPENED AT THE PARTY. I DON'T KNOW WHAT, BUT REGGIE AND ETHEL HAVE BEEN MISSING EVER SINCE.
I TALKED TO DILTON, AND SOMETHING ABOUT THE BLOSSOMS HAS HIM *SCARED*.
"YOU GUYS MIGHT NOT BELIEVE ME, BUT I'M GONNA FIGURE OUT WHAT'S GOING ON."

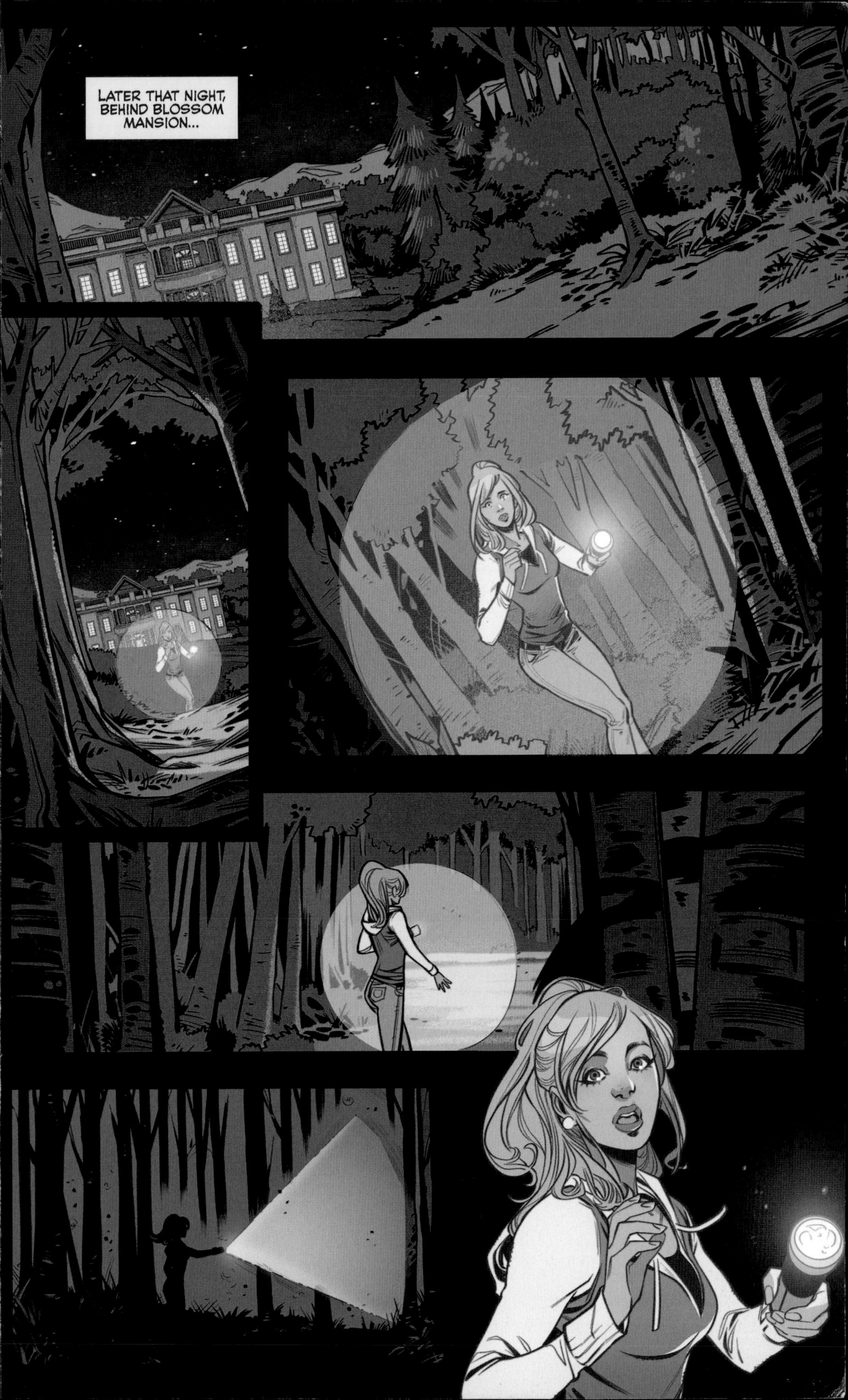
LATER THAT NIGHT, BEHIND BLOSSOM MANSION...

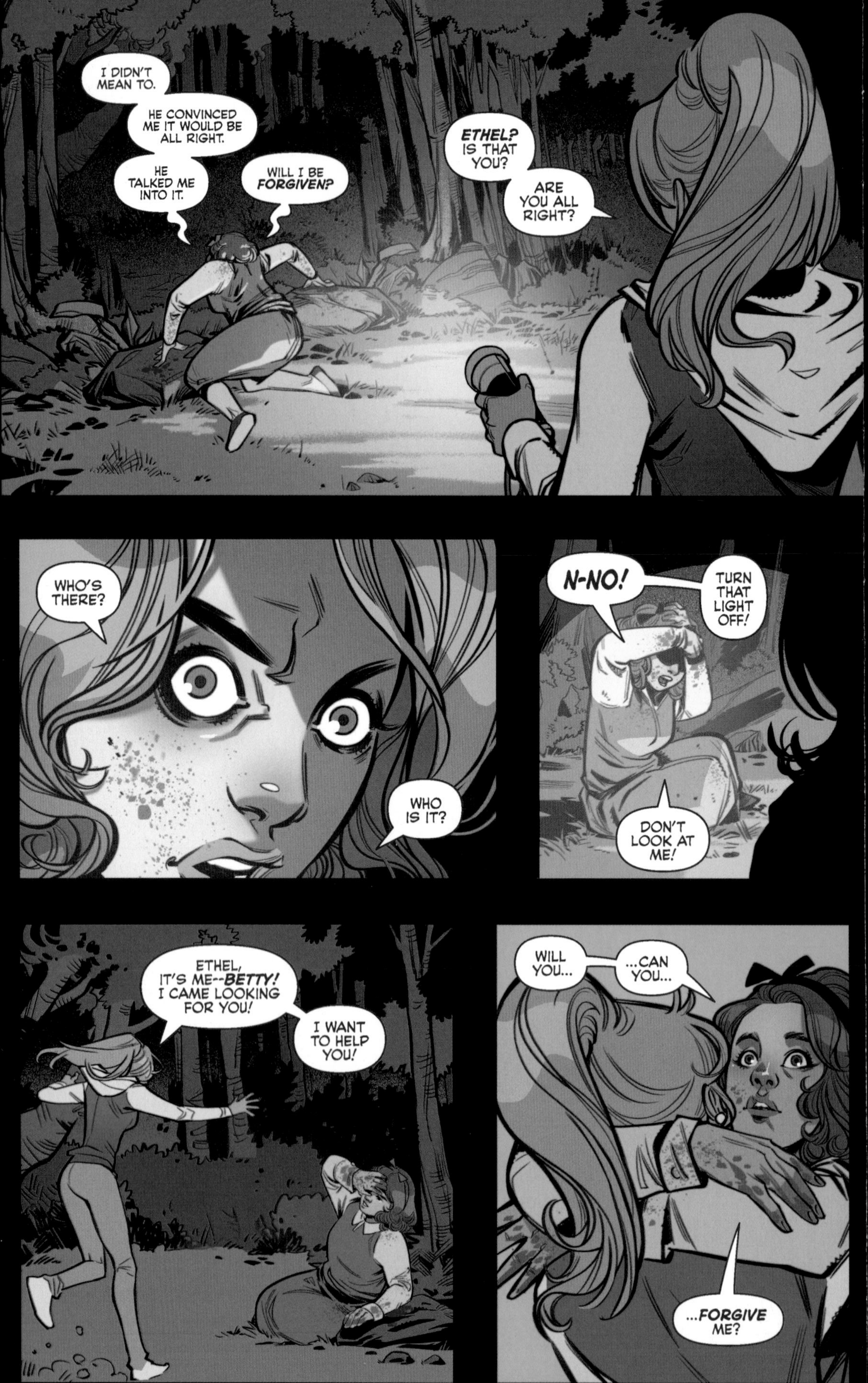
I DIDN'T MEAN TO.
HE CONVINCED ME IT WOULD BE ALL RIGHT.
HE TALKED ME INTO IT.
WILL I BE *FORGIVEN?*
ETHEL? IS THAT YOU?
ARE YOU ALL RIGHT?
WHO'S THERE?
WHO IS IT?
N-NO!
TURN THAT LIGHT OFF!
DON'T LOOK AT ME!
ETHEL, IT'S ME--*BETTY!* I CAME LOOKING FOR YOU!
I WANT TO HELP YOU!
WILL YOU...
...CAN YOU...
...*FORGIVE* ME?

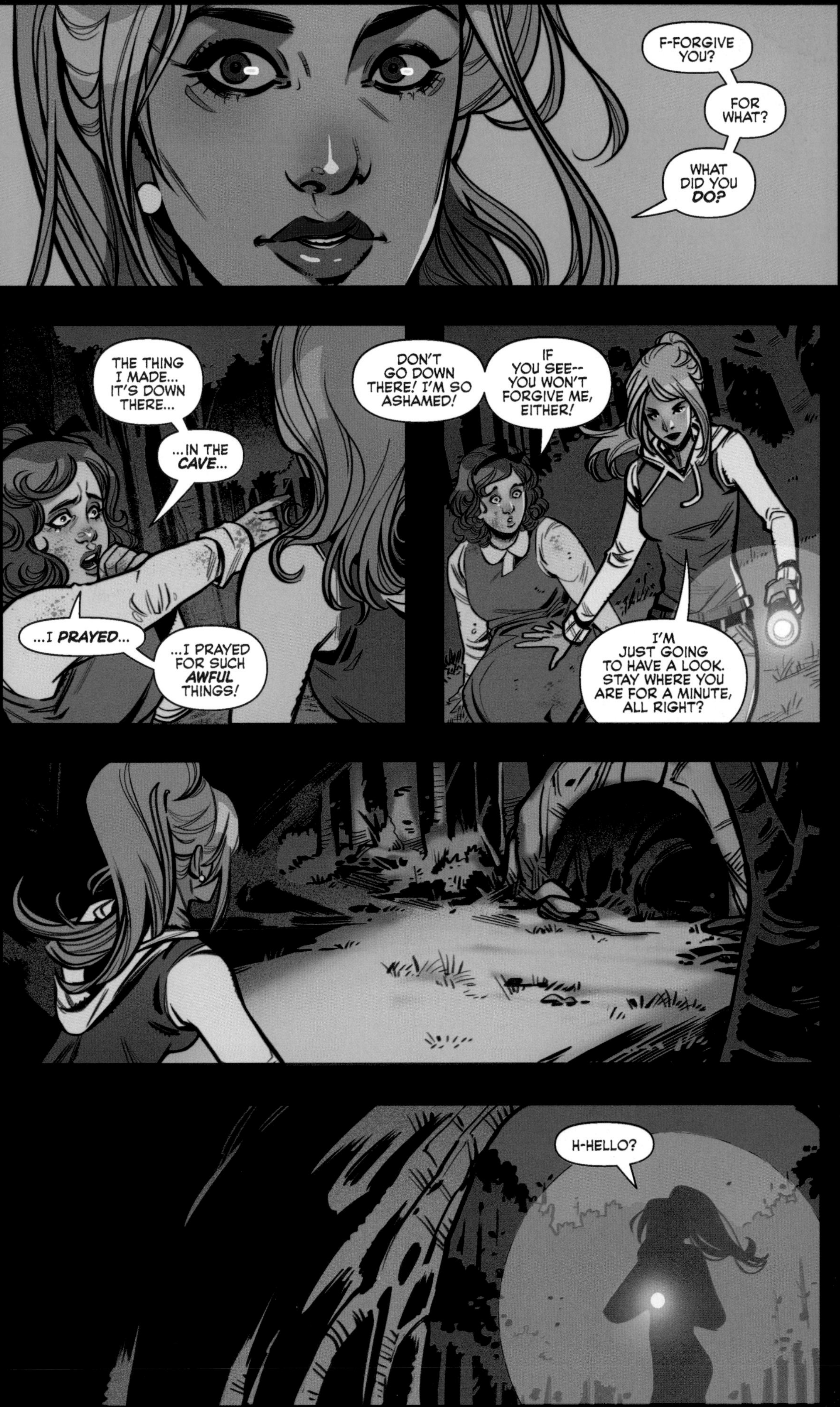
F-FORGIVE YOU?
FOR WHAT?
WHAT DID YOU *DO?*
THE THING I MADE... IT'S DOWN THERE...
...IN THE *CAVE*...
...I *PRAYED*...
...I PRAYED FOR SUCH *AWFUL* THINGS!
DON'T GO DOWN THERE! I'M SO ASHAMED!
IF YOU SEE-- YOU WON'T FORGIVE ME, EITHER!
I'M JUST GOING TO HAVE A LOOK. STAY WHERE YOU ARE FOR A MINUTE, ALL RIGHT?
H-HELLO?

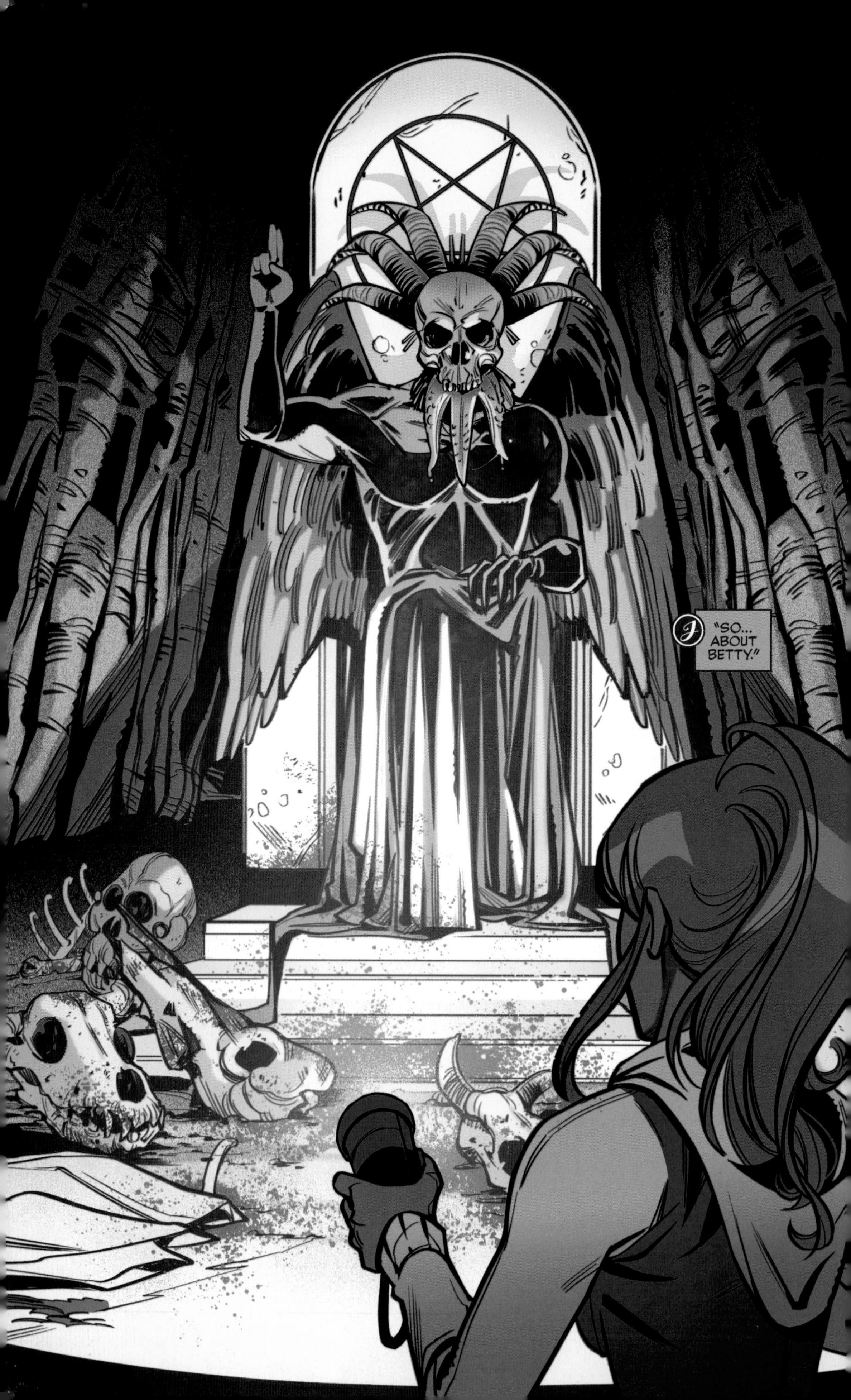
"SO... ABOUT BETTY."

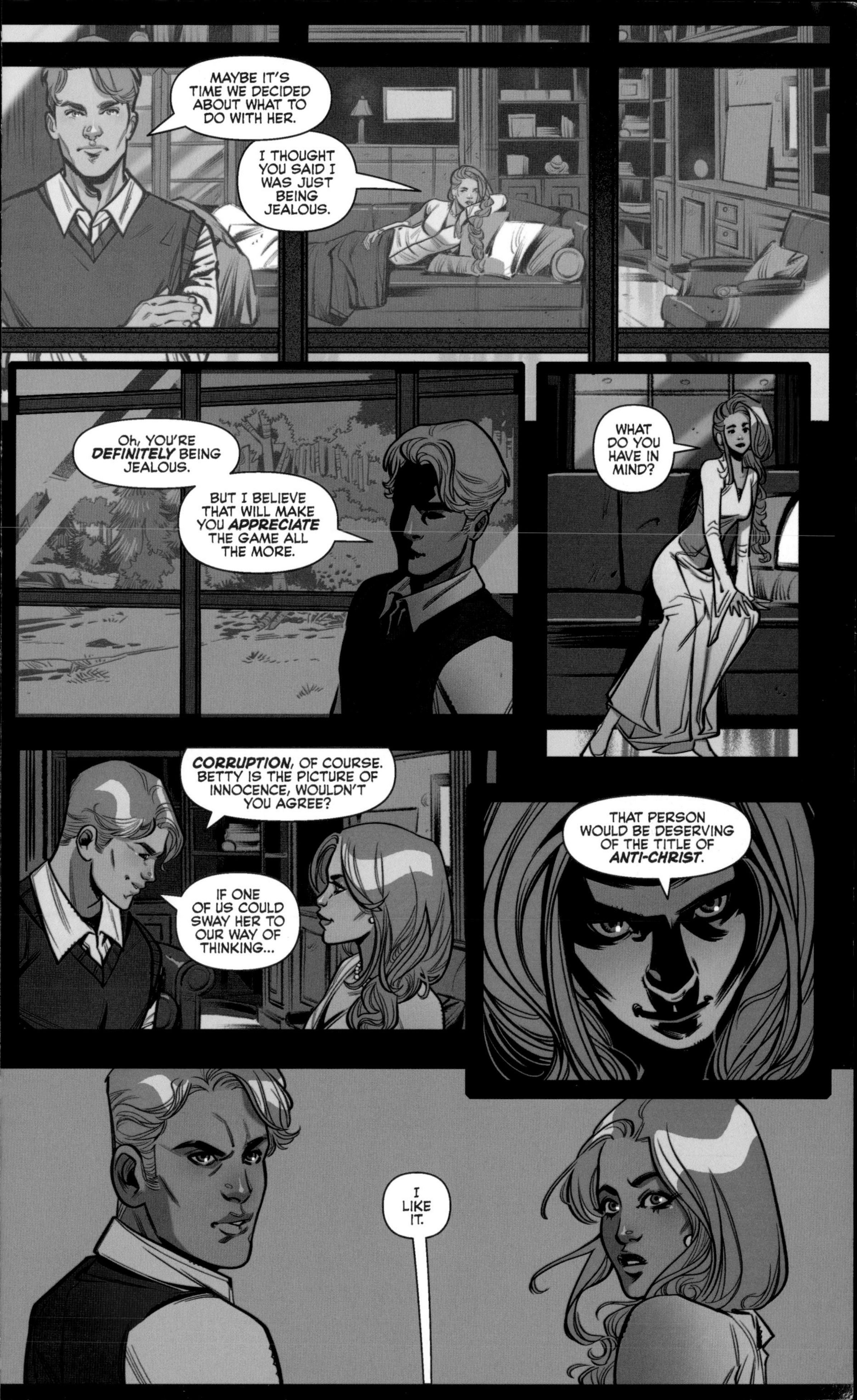
MAYBE IT'S TIME WE DECIDED ABOUT WHAT TO DO WITH HER.
I THOUGHT YOU SAID I WAS JUST BEING JEALOUS.
Oh, YOU'RE *DEFINITELY* BEING JEALOUS.
BUT I BELIEVE THAT WILL MAKE YOU *APPRECIATE* THE GAME ALL THE MORE.
WHAT DO YOU HAVE IN MIND?
CORRUPTION, OF COURSE. BETTY IS THE PICTURE OF INNOCENCE, WOULDN'T YOU AGREE?
IF ONE OF US COULD SWAY HER TO OUR WAY OF THINKING...
THAT PERSON WOULD BE DESERVING OF THE TITLE OF *ANTI-CHRIST*.
I LIKE IT.

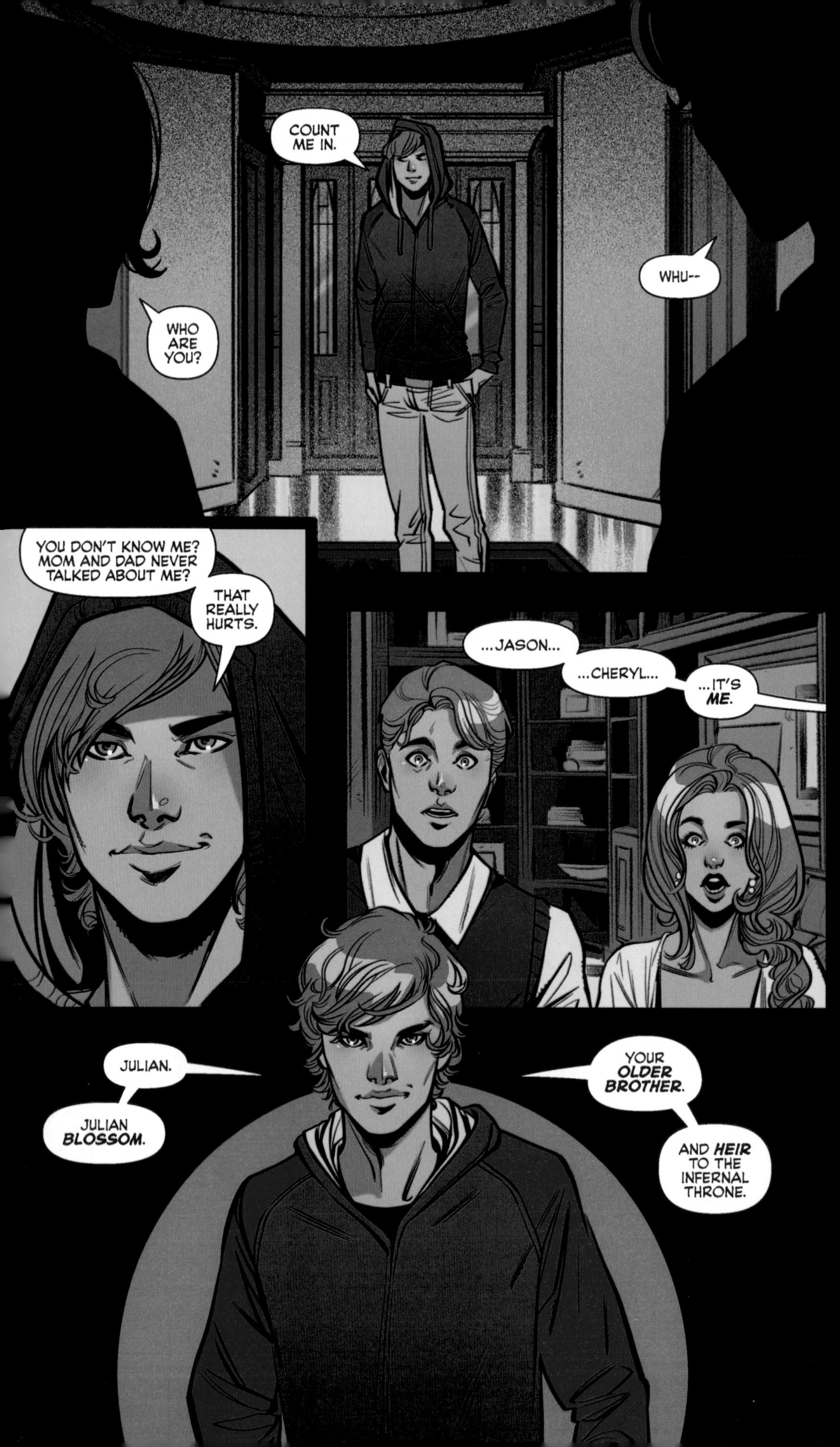
COUNT ME IN.
WHO ARE YOU?
WHU--
YOU DON'T KNOW ME? MOM AND DAD NEVER TALKED ABOUT ME?
THAT REALLY HURTS.
...JASON...
...CHERYL...
...IT'S ME.
JULIAN.
JULIAN BLOSSOM.
YOUR OLDER BROTHER.
AND HEIR TO THE INFERNAL THRONE.

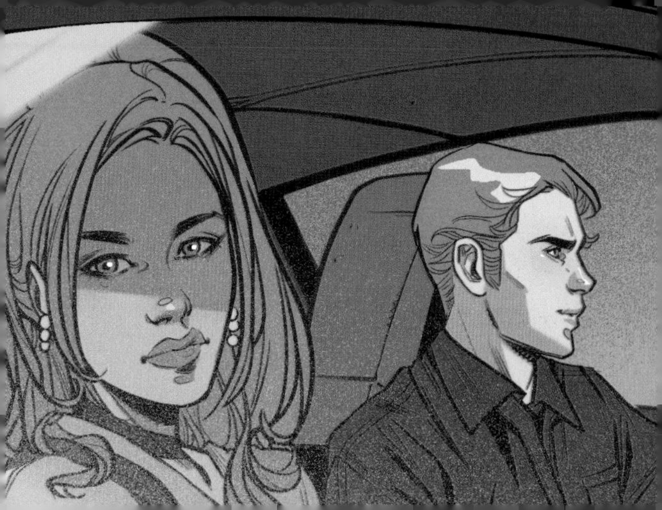

CHAPTER THREE

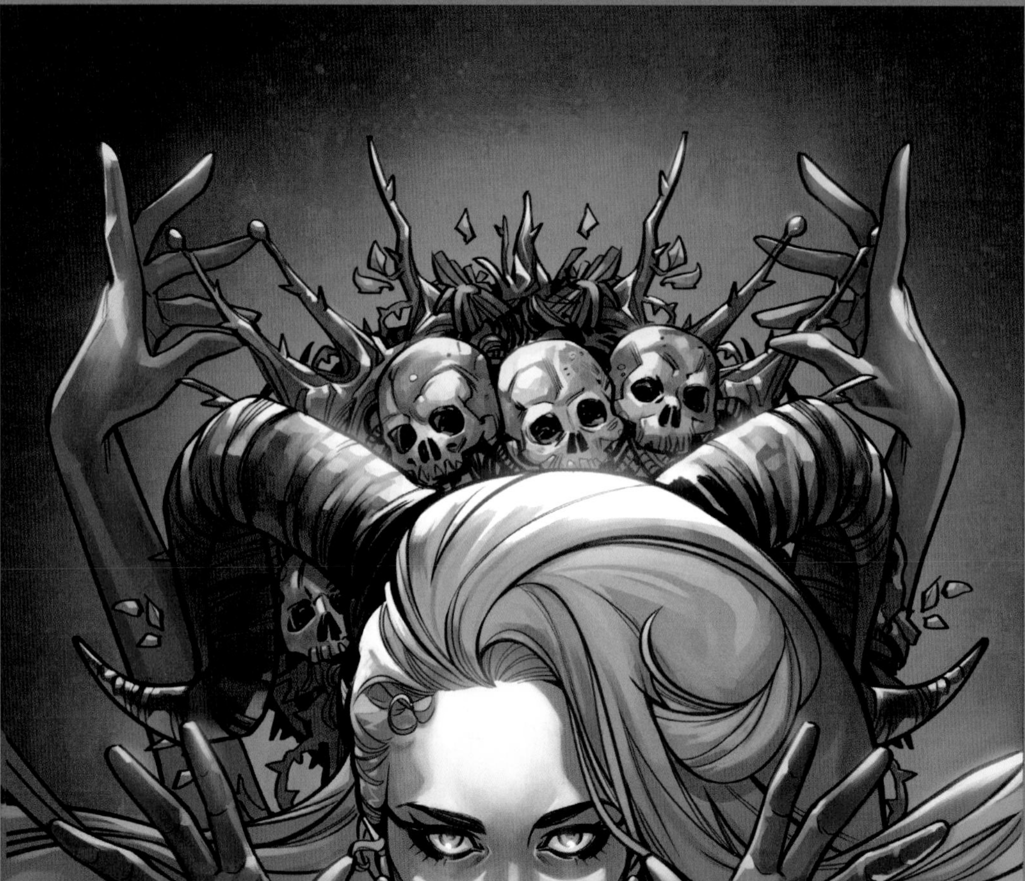

LAURA
BRAGA
2018

COVER ART BY LAURA BRAGA

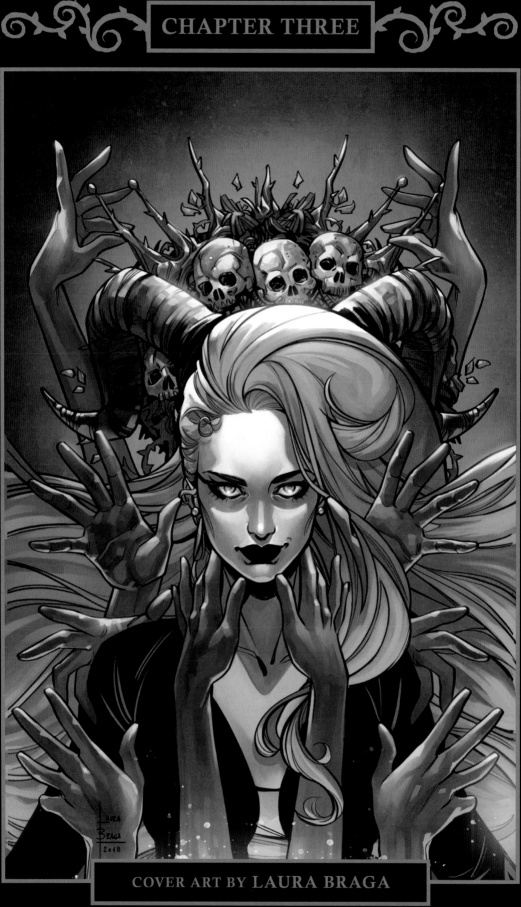

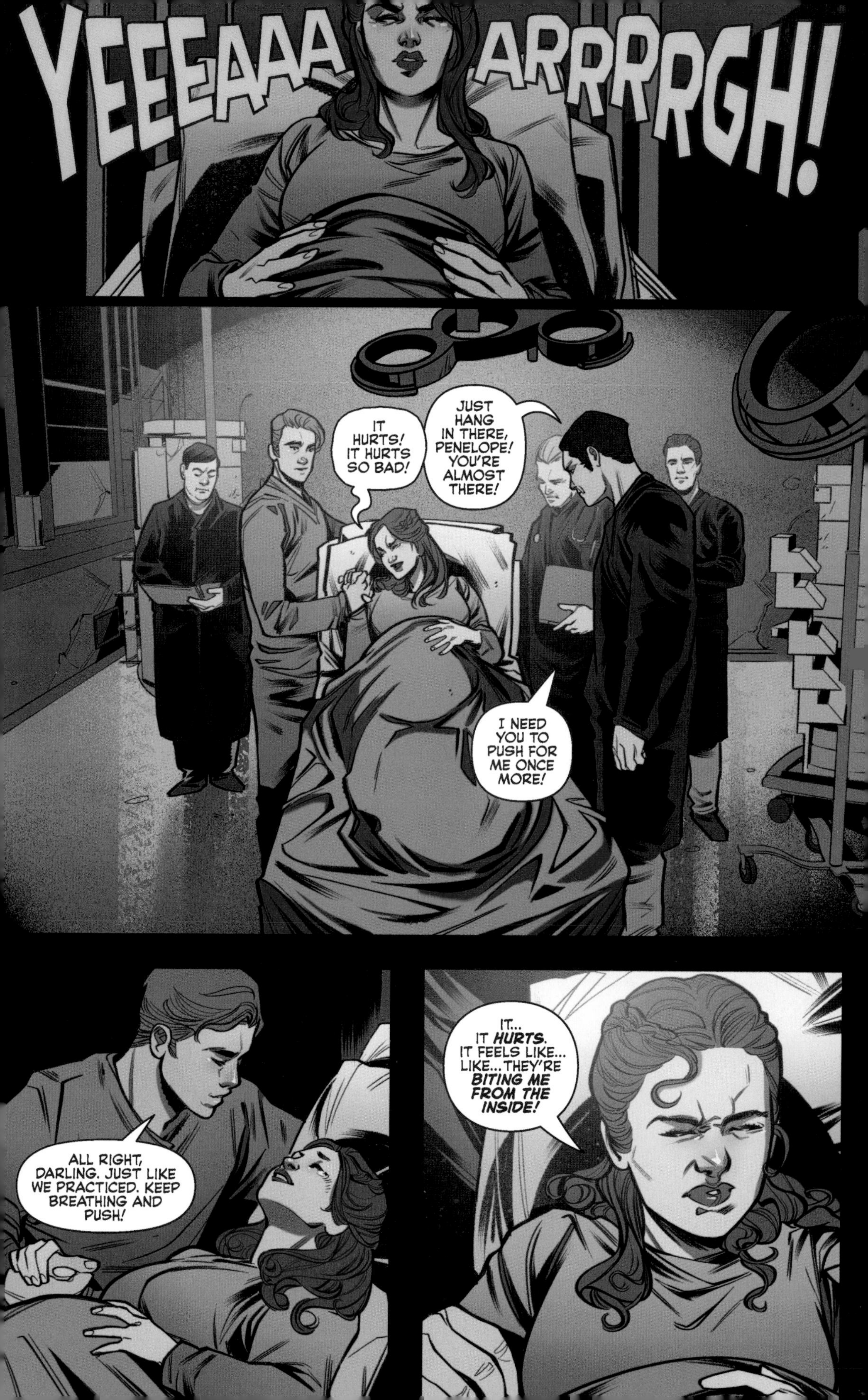
YEEEAAA ARRRRGH!
IT HURTS! IT HURTS SO BAD!
JUST HANG IN THERE, PENELOPE! YOU'RE ALMOST THERE!
I NEED YOU TO PUSH FOR ME ONCE MORE!
ALL RIGHT, DARLING. JUST LIKE WE PRACTICED. KEEP BREATHING AND PUSH!
IT... IT *HURTS*. IT FEELS LIKE... LIKE...THEY'RE ***BITING ME FROM THE INSIDE!***

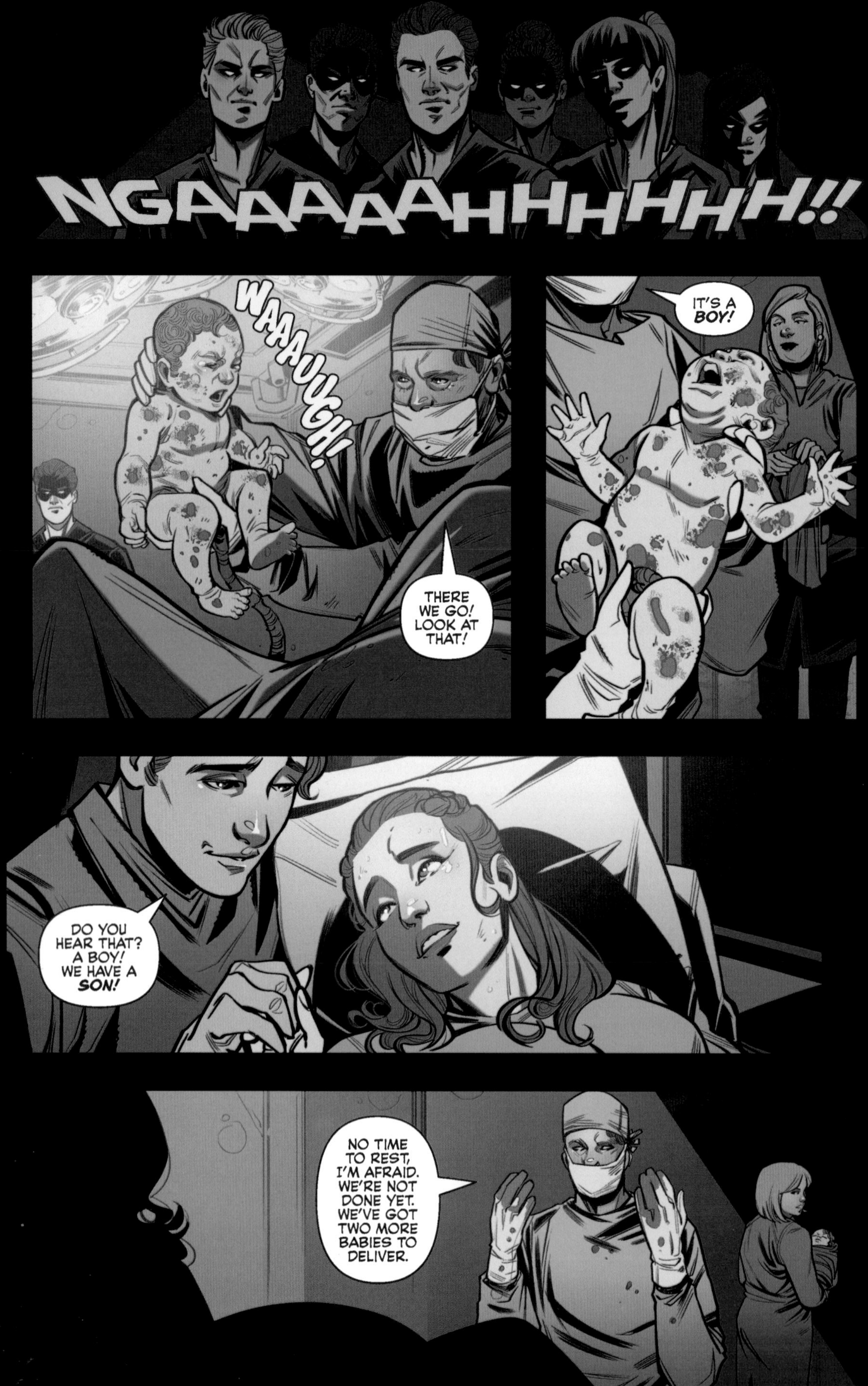
NGAAAAAHHHHHH!!
WAAAAUUGH!!
THERE WE GO! LOOK AT THAT!
IT'S A BOY!
DO YOU HEAR THAT? A BOY! WE HAVE A SON!
NO TIME TO REST, I'M AFRAID. WE'RE NOT DONE YET. WE'VE GOT TWO MORE BABIES TO DELIVER.

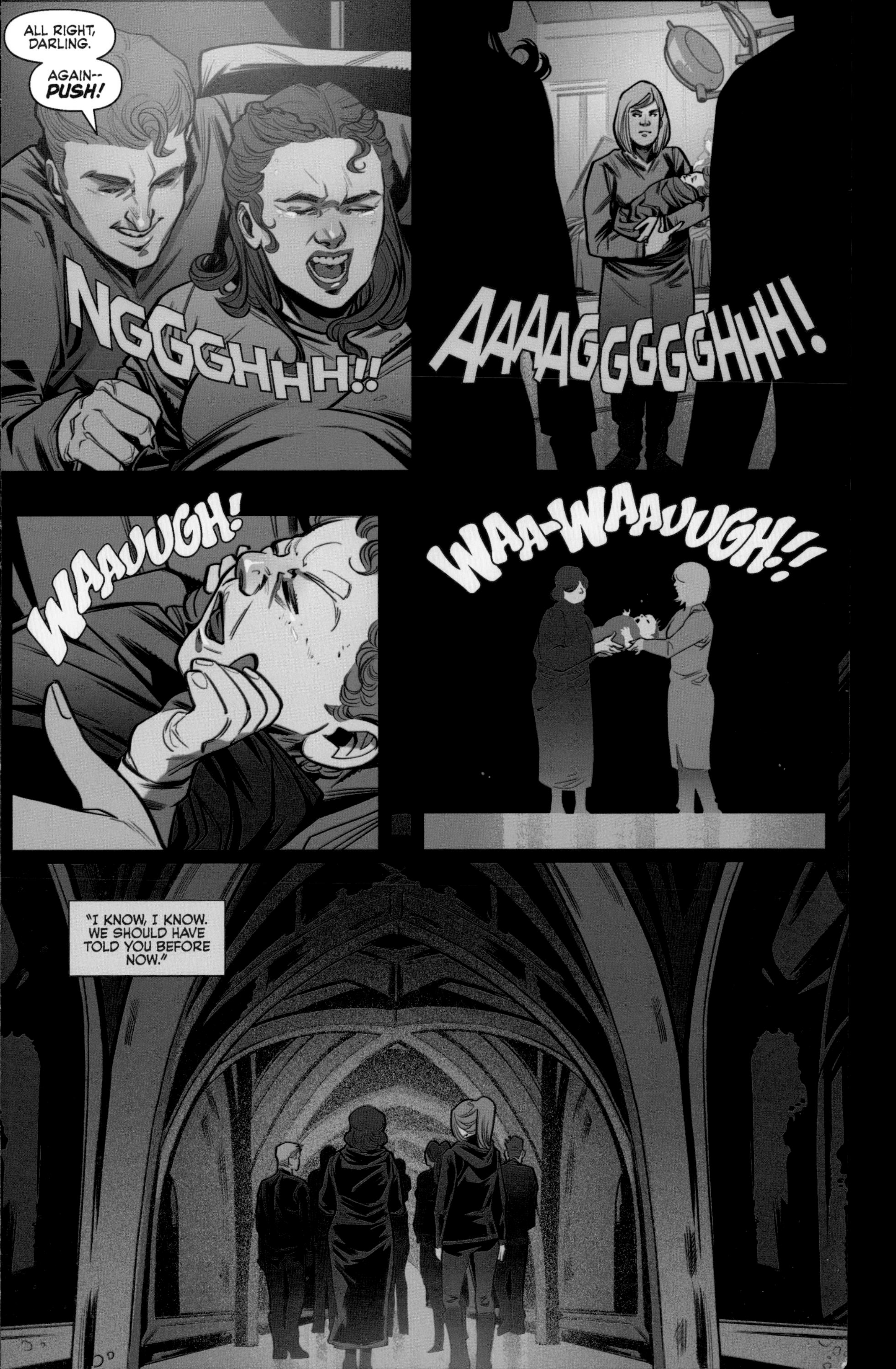
ALL RIGHT, DARLING.
AGAIN-- PUSH!
NGGGHHH!!
AAAAGGGGHHH!
WAAUUGH!
WAA-WAAUUGH!!
"I KNOW, I KNOW. WE SHOULD HAVE TOLD YOU BEFORE NOW."

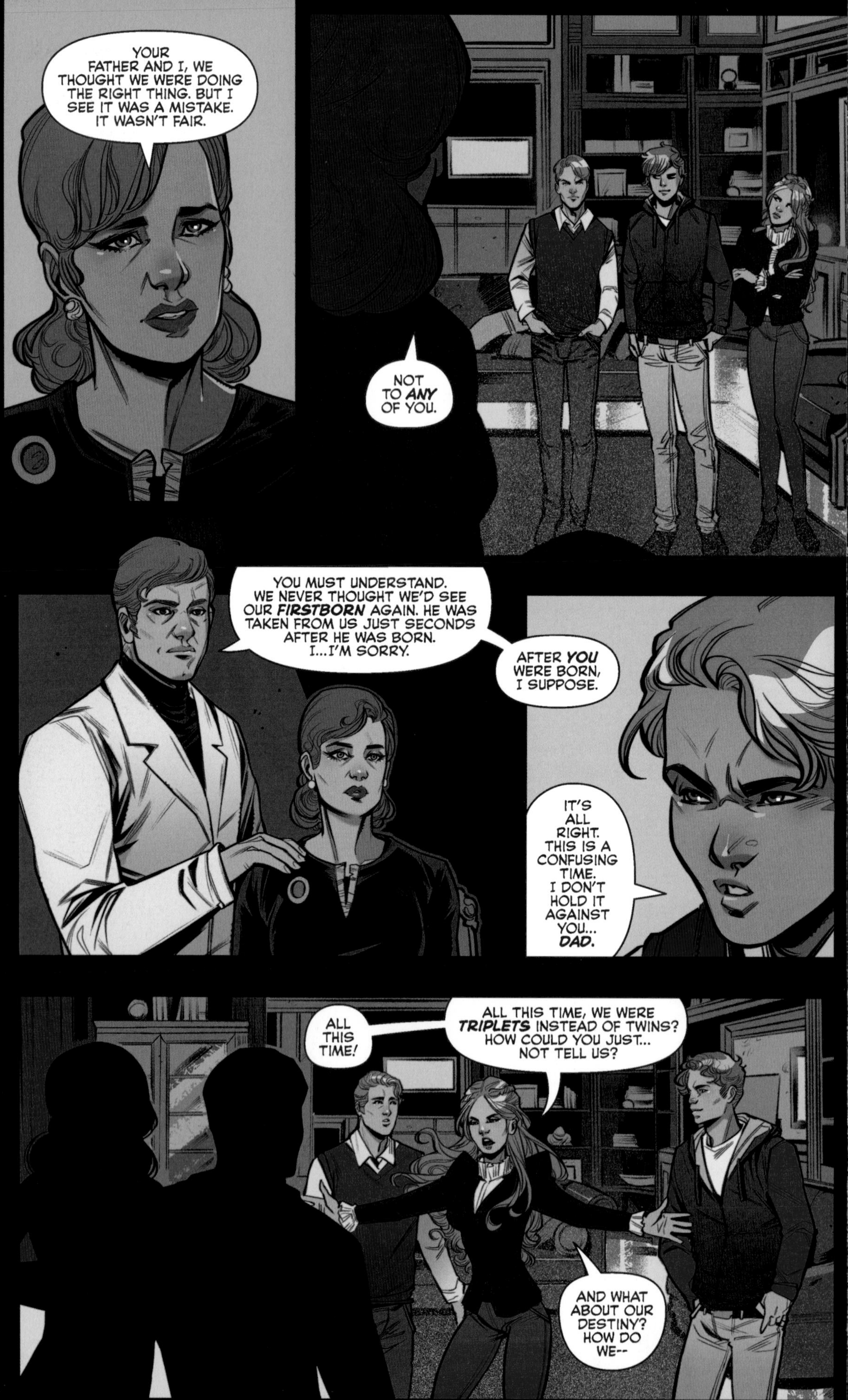
YOUR FATHER AND I, WE THOUGHT WE WERE DOING THE RIGHT THING. BUT I SEE IT WAS A MISTAKE. IT WASN'T FAIR.
NOT TO ANY OF YOU.
YOU MUST UNDERSTAND. WE NEVER THOUGHT WE'D SEE OUR FIRSTBORN AGAIN. HE WAS TAKEN FROM US JUST SECONDS AFTER HE WAS BORN. I...I'M SORRY.
AFTER YOU WERE BORN, I SUPPOSE.
IT'S ALL RIGHT. THIS IS A CONFUSING TIME. I DON'T HOLD IT AGAINST YOU... DAD.
ALL THIS TIME!
ALL THIS TIME, WE WERE TRIPLETS INSTEAD OF TWINS? HOW COULD YOU JUST... NOT TELL US?
AND WHAT ABOUT OUR DESTINY? HOW DO WE--

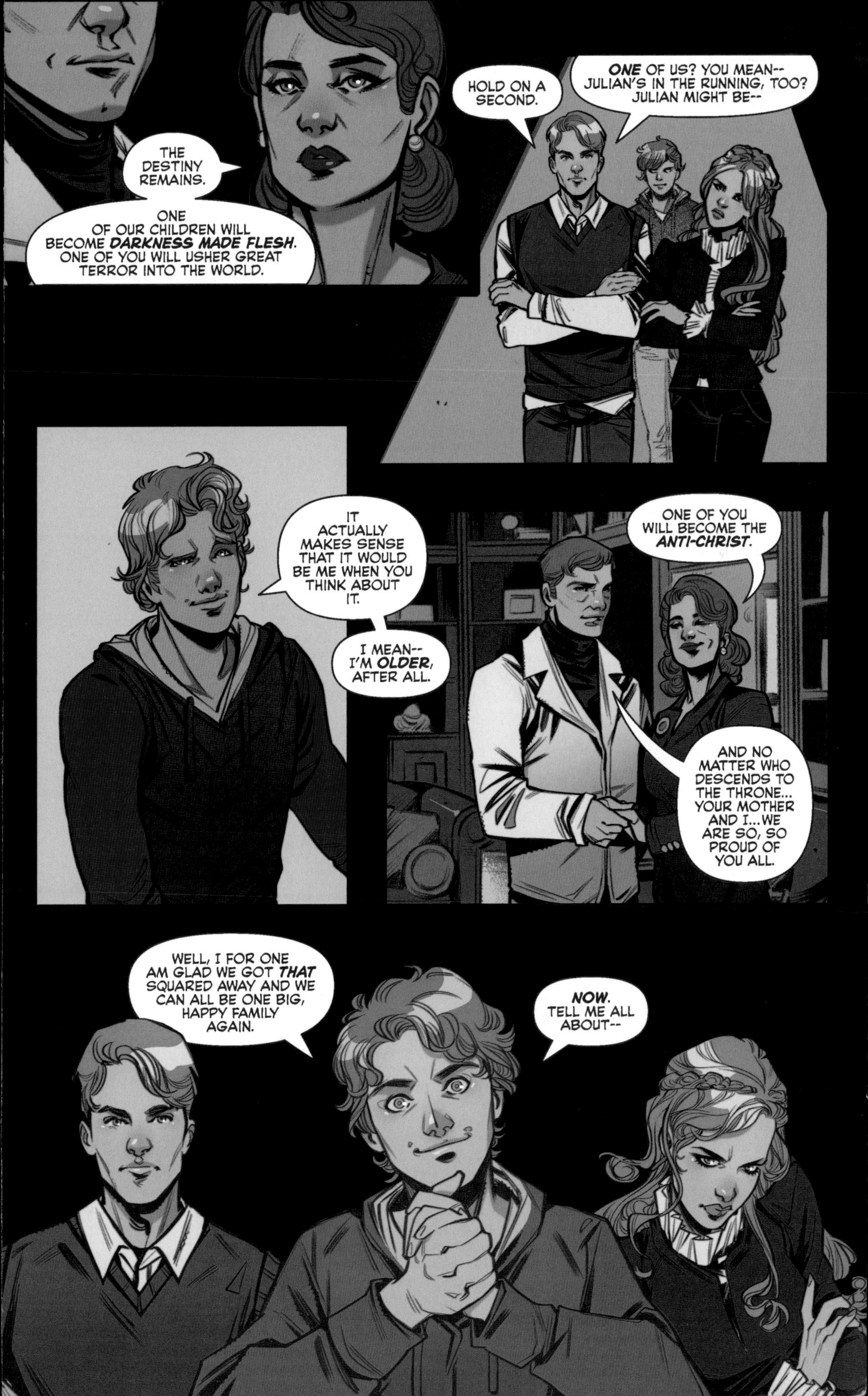
THE DESTINY REMAINS.
ONE OF OUR CHILDREN WILL BECOME DARKNESS MADE FLESH. ONE OF YOU WILL USHER GREAT TERROR INTO THE WORLD.
HOLD ON A SECOND.
ONE OF US? YOU MEAN-- JULIAN'S IN THE RUNNING, TOO? JULIAN MIGHT BE--
IT ACTUALLY MAKES SENSE THAT IT WOULD BE ME WHEN YOU THINK ABOUT IT.
I MEAN-- I'M OLDER, AFTER ALL.
ONE OF YOU WILL BECOME THE ANTI-CHRIST.
AND NO MATTER WHO DESCENDS TO THE THRONE... YOUR MOTHER AND I...WE ARE SO, SO PROUD OF YOU ALL.
WELL, I FOR ONE AM GLAD WE GOT THAT SQUARED AWAY AND WE CAN ALL BE ONE BIG, HAPPY FAMILY AGAIN.
NOW. TELL ME ALL ABOUT--

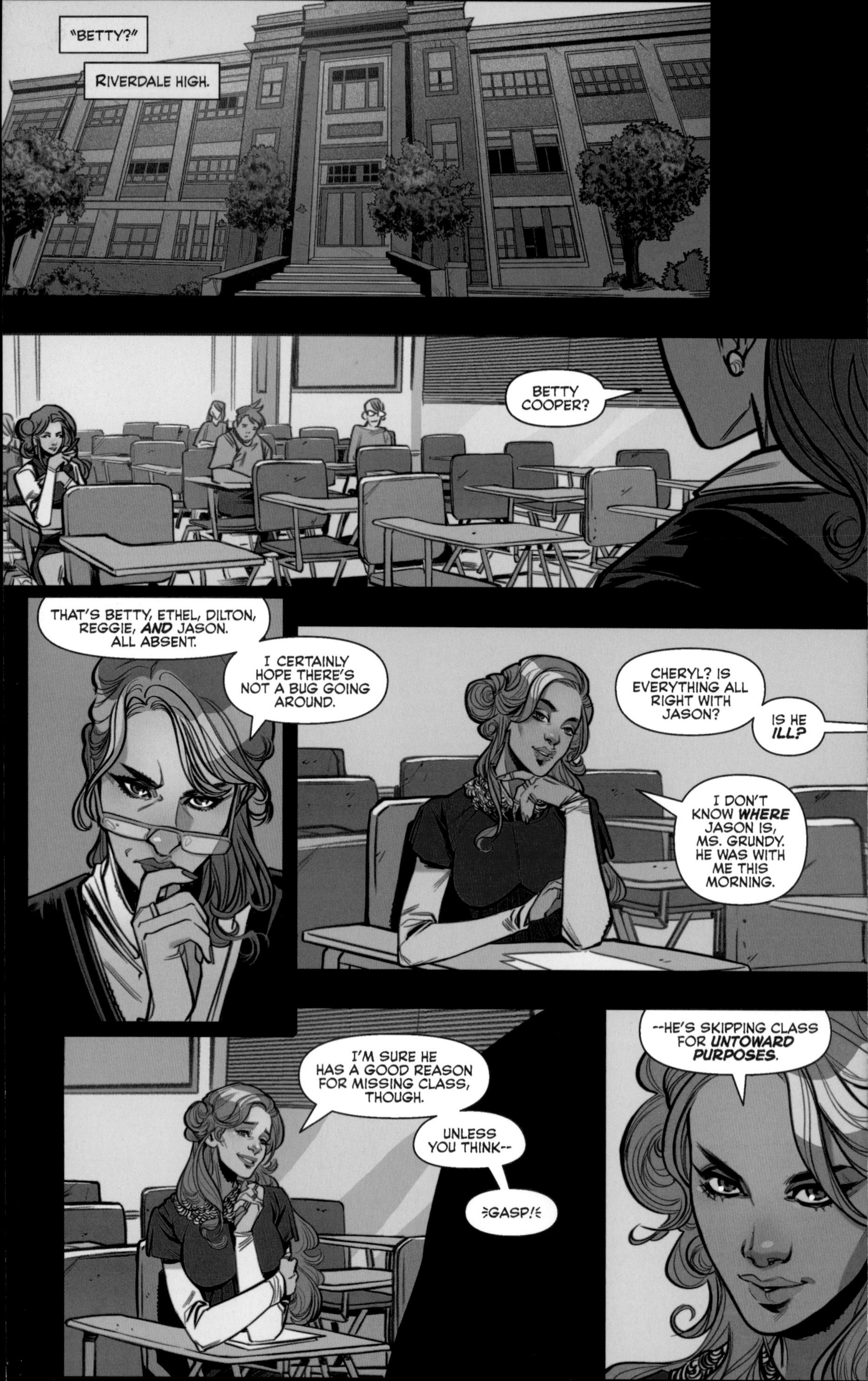
"BETTY?"
RIVERDALE HIGH.
BETTY COOPER?
THAT'S BETTY, ETHEL, DILTON, REGGIE, AND JASON. ALL ABSENT.
I CERTAINLY HOPE THERE'S NOT A BUG GOING AROUND.
CHERYL? IS EVERYTHING ALL RIGHT WITH JASON?
IS HE ILL?
I DON'T KNOW WHERE JASON IS, MS. GRUNDY. HE WAS WITH ME THIS MORNING.
I'M SURE HE HAS A GOOD REASON FOR MISSING CLASS, THOUGH.
UNLESS YOU THINK--
GASP!
--HE'S SKIPPING CLASS FOR UNTOWARD PURPOSES.

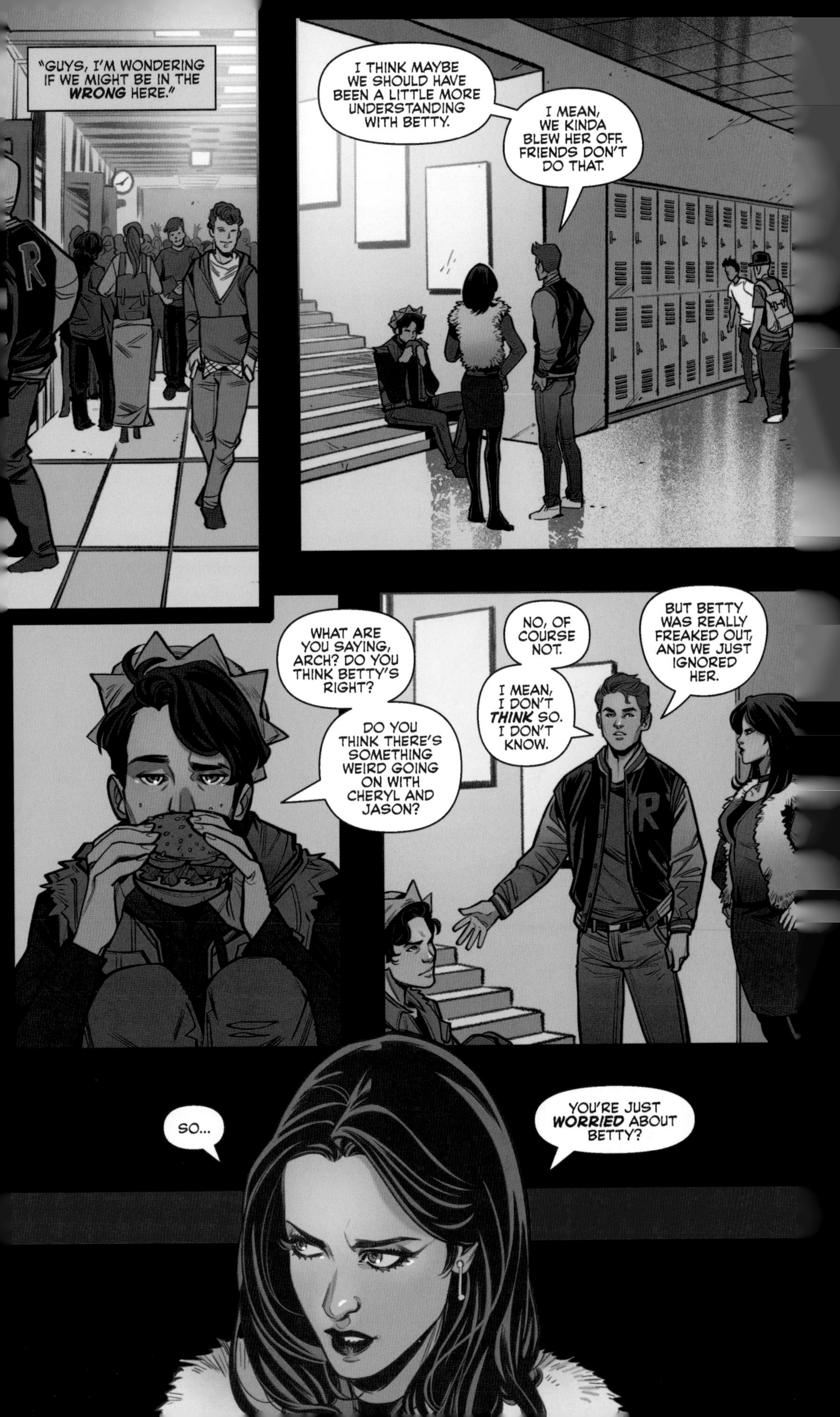
"GUYS, I'M WONDERING IF WE MIGHT BE IN THE **WRONG** HERE."
I THINK MAYBE WE SHOULD HAVE BEEN A LITTLE MORE UNDERSTANDING WITH BETTY.
I MEAN, WE KINDA BLEW HER OFF. FRIENDS DON'T DO THAT.
WHAT ARE YOU SAYING, ARCH? DO YOU THINK BETTY'S RIGHT?
DO YOU THINK THERE'S SOMETHING WEIRD GOING ON WITH CHERYL AND JASON?
NO, OF COURSE NOT.
I MEAN, I DON'T **THINK** SO. I DON'T KNOW.
BUT BETTY WAS REALLY FREAKED OUT, AND WE JUST IGNORED HER.
SO...
YOU'RE JUST **WORRIED** ABOUT BETTY?

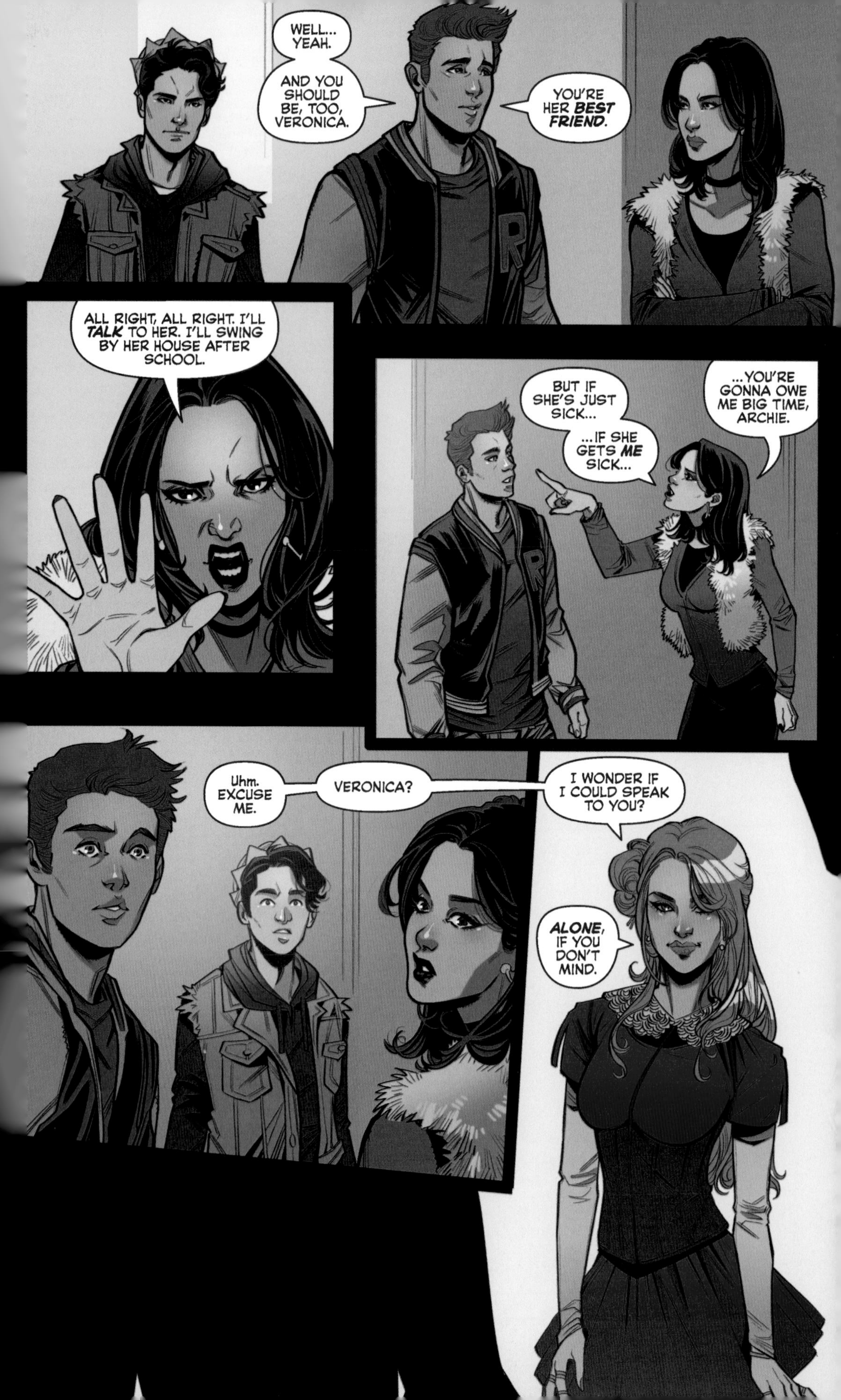
WELL... YEAH.
AND YOU SHOULD BE, TOO, VERONICA.
YOU'RE HER **BEST FRIEND**.
ALL RIGHT, ALL RIGHT. I'LL ***TALK*** TO HER. I'LL SWING BY HER HOUSE AFTER SCHOOL.
BUT IF SHE'S JUST SICK...
...IF SHE GETS ***ME*** SICK...
...YOU'RE GONNA OWE ME BIG TIME, ARCHIE.
Uhm. EXCUSE ME.
VERONICA?
I WONDER IF I COULD SPEAK TO YOU?
ALONE, IF YOU DON'T MIND.

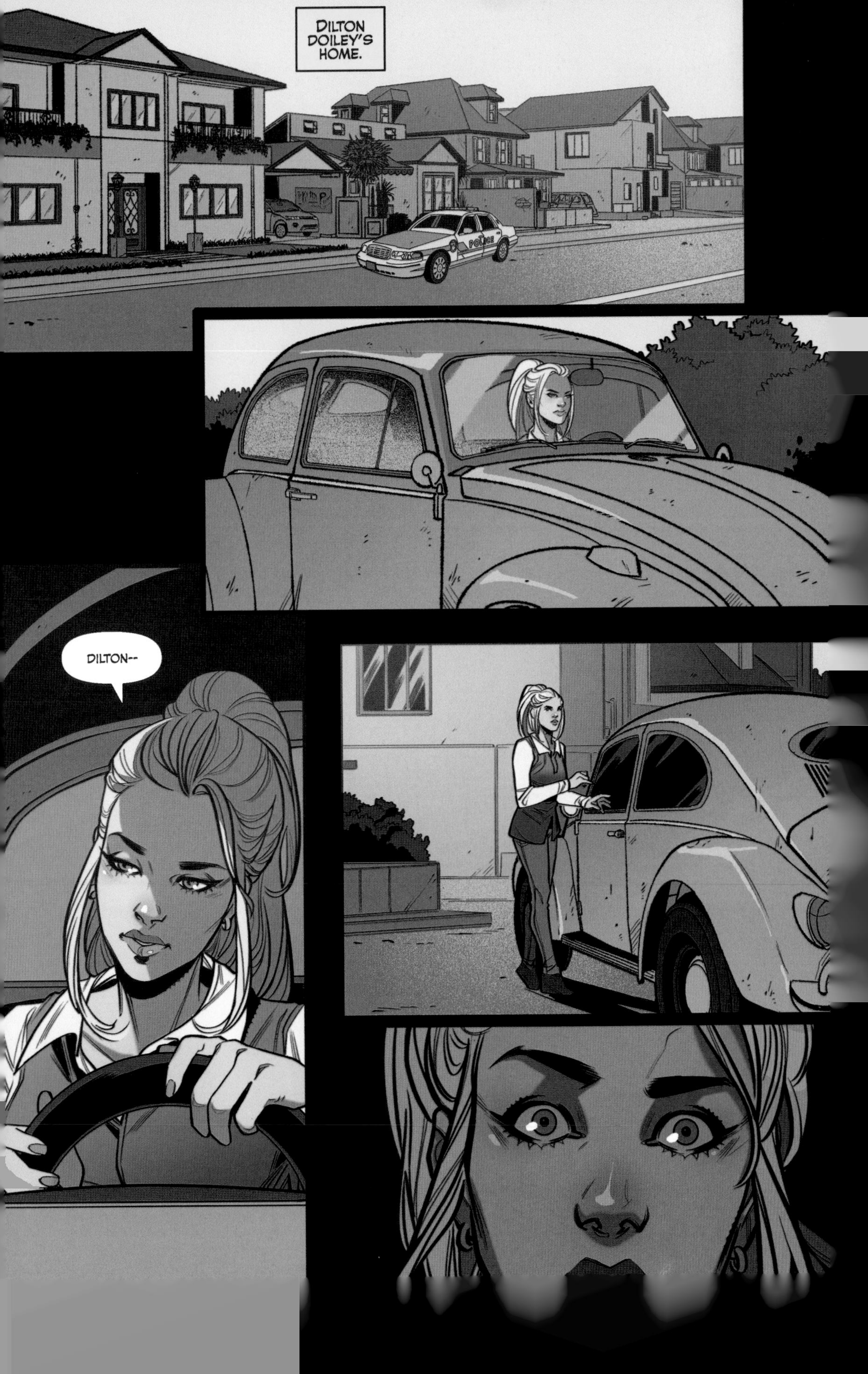
DILTON DOILEY'S HOME.
DILTON--

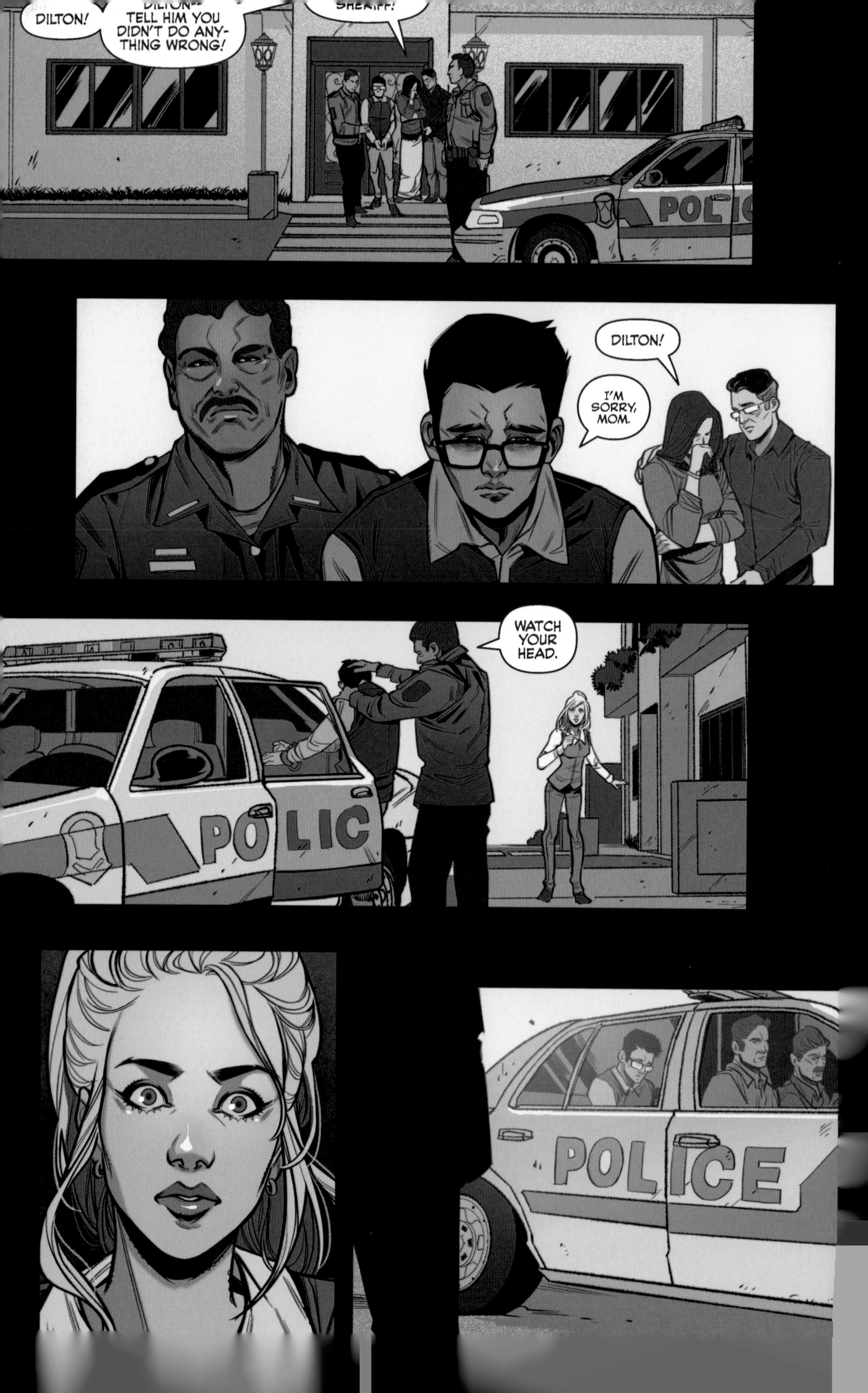
DILTON!
TELL HIM YOU DIDN'T DO ANY-THING WRONG!
DILTON!
I'M SORRY, MOM.
WATCH YOUR HEAD.
POLICE

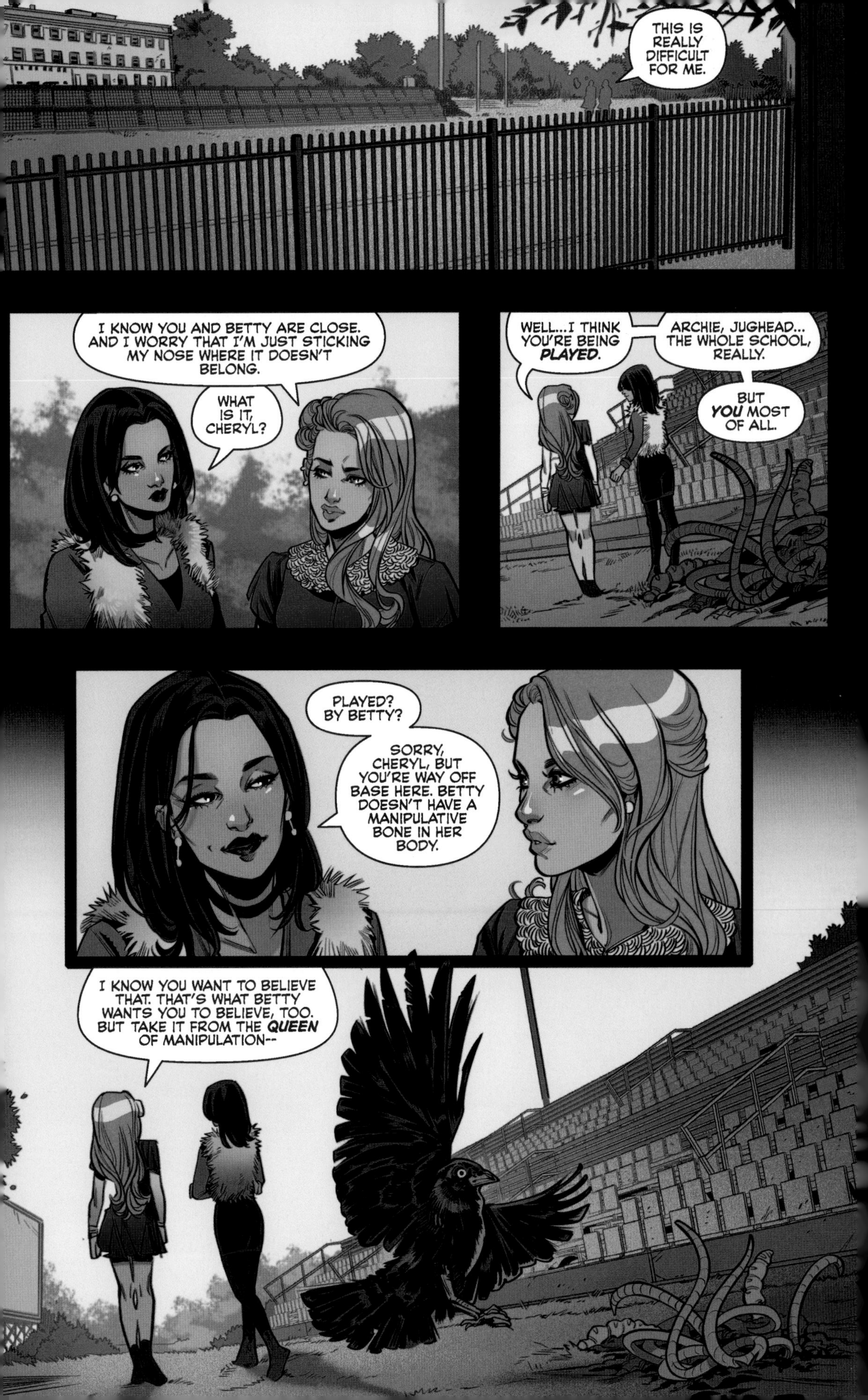
THIS IS REALLY DIFFICULT FOR ME.
I KNOW YOU AND BETTY ARE CLOSE. AND I WORRY THAT I'M JUST STICKING MY NOSE WHERE IT DOESN'T BELONG.
WHAT IS IT, CHERYL?
WELL...I THINK YOU'RE BEING *PLAYED*.
ARCHIE, JUGHEAD... THE WHOLE SCHOOL, REALLY.
BUT *YOU* MOST OF ALL.
PLAYED? BY BETTY?
SORRY, CHERYL, BUT YOU'RE WAY OFF BASE HERE. BETTY DOESN'T HAVE A MANIPULATIVE BONE IN HER BODY.
I KNOW YOU WANT TO BELIEVE THAT. THAT'S WHAT BETTY WANTS YOU TO BELIEVE, TOO. BUT TAKE IT FROM THE *QUEEN* OF MANIPULATION--

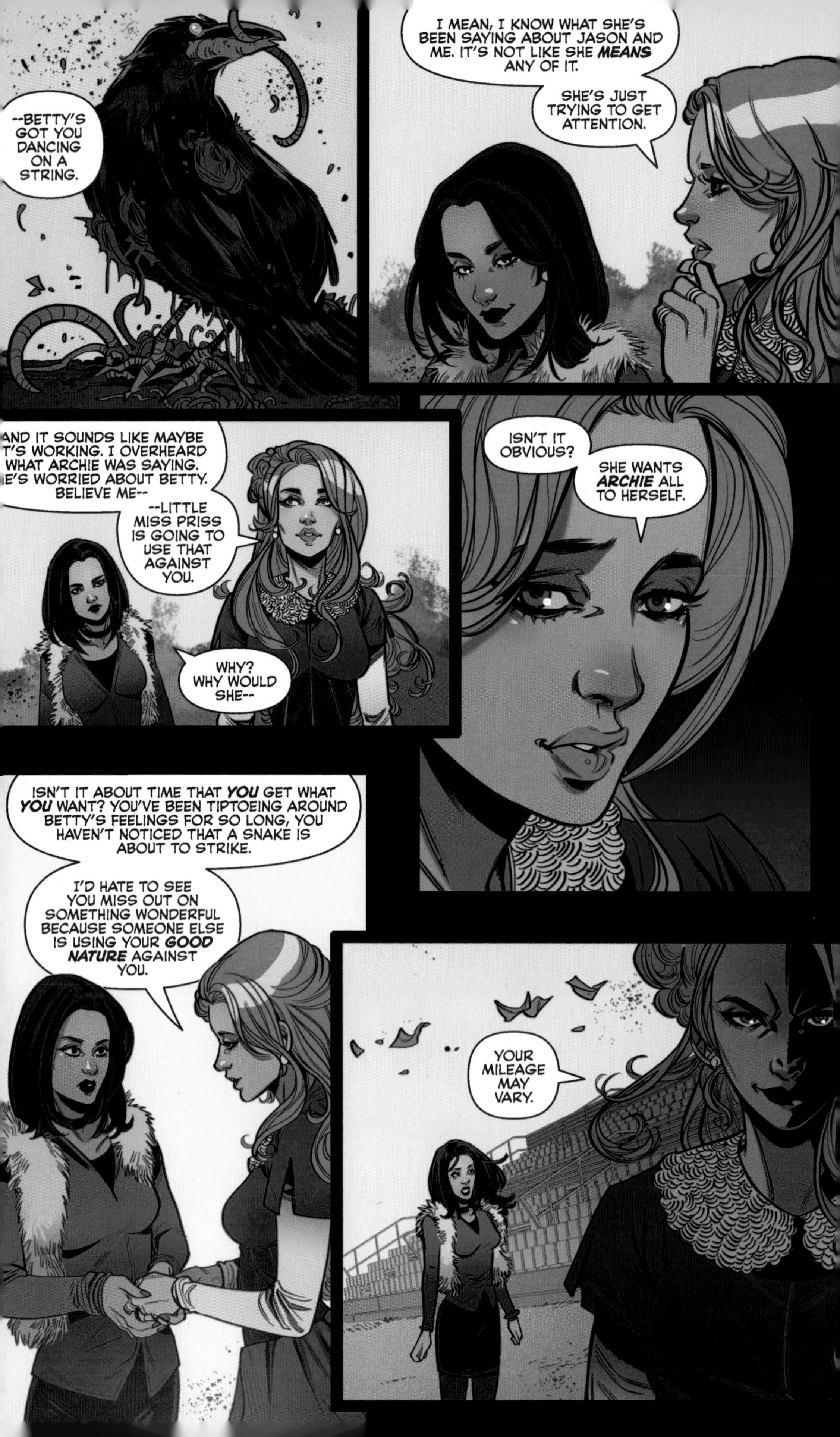
--BETTY'S GOT YOU DANCING ON A STRING.
I MEAN, I KNOW WHAT SHE'S BEEN SAYING ABOUT JASON AND ME. IT'S NOT LIKE SHE MEANS ANY OF IT.
SHE'S JUST TRYING TO GET ATTENTION.
AND IT SOUNDS LIKE MAYBE T'S WORKING. I OVERHEARD WHAT ARCHIE WAS SAYING. E'S WORRIED ABOUT BETTY. BELIEVE ME--
--LITTLE MISS PRISS IS GOING TO USE THAT AGAINST YOU.
WHY? WHY WOULD SHE--
ISN'T IT OBVIOUS?
SHE WANTS ARCHIE ALL TO HERSELF.
ISN'T IT ABOUT TIME THAT YOU GET WHAT YOU WANT? YOU'VE BEEN TIPTOEING AROUND BETTY'S FEELINGS FOR SO LONG, YOU HAVEN'T NOTICED THAT A SNAKE IS ABOUT TO STRIKE.
I'D HATE TO SEE YOU MISS OUT ON SOMETHING WONDERFUL BECAUSE SOMEONE ELSE IS USING YOUR GOOD NATURE AGAINST YOU.
YOUR MILEAGE MAY VARY.

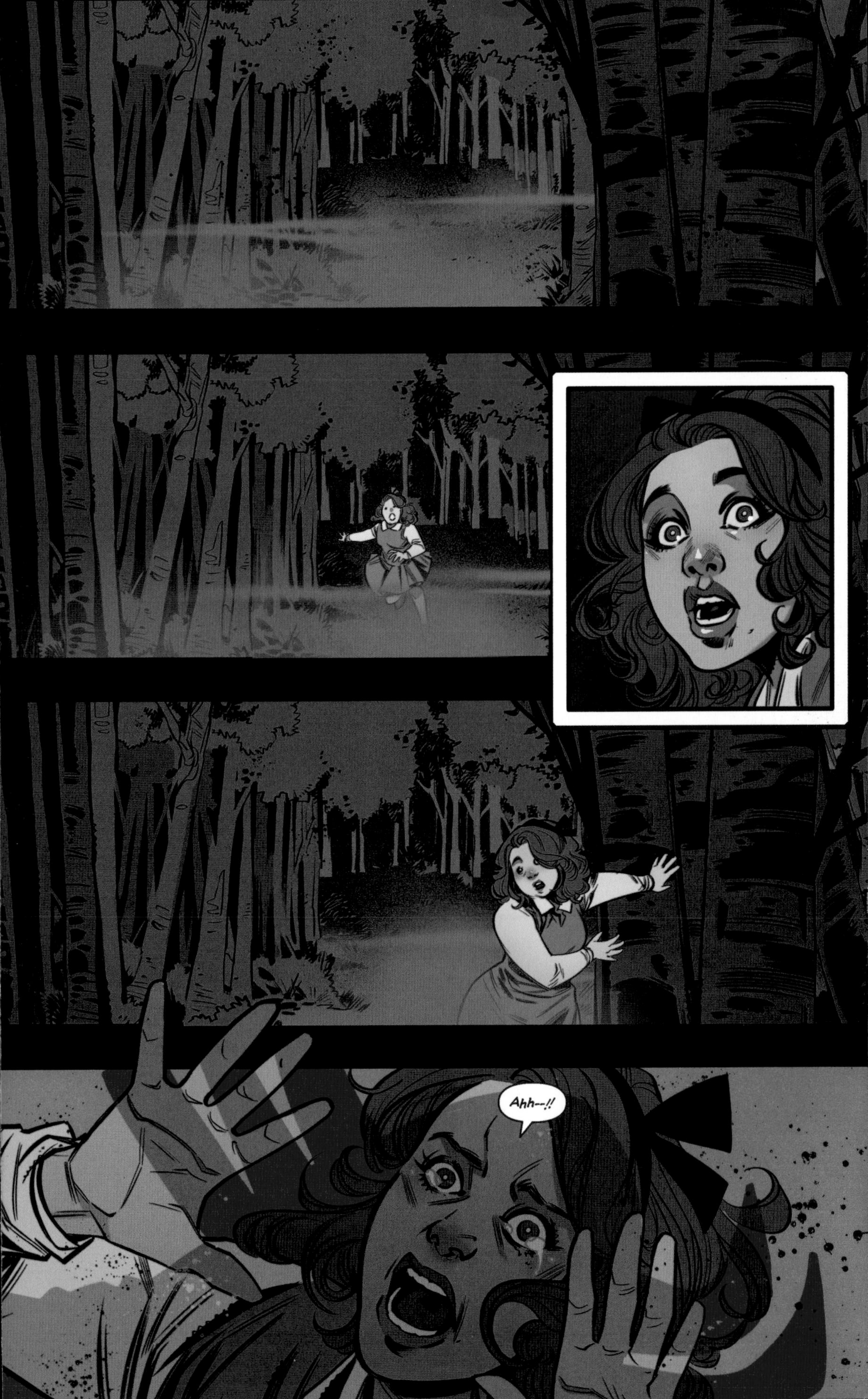
Ahh--!!

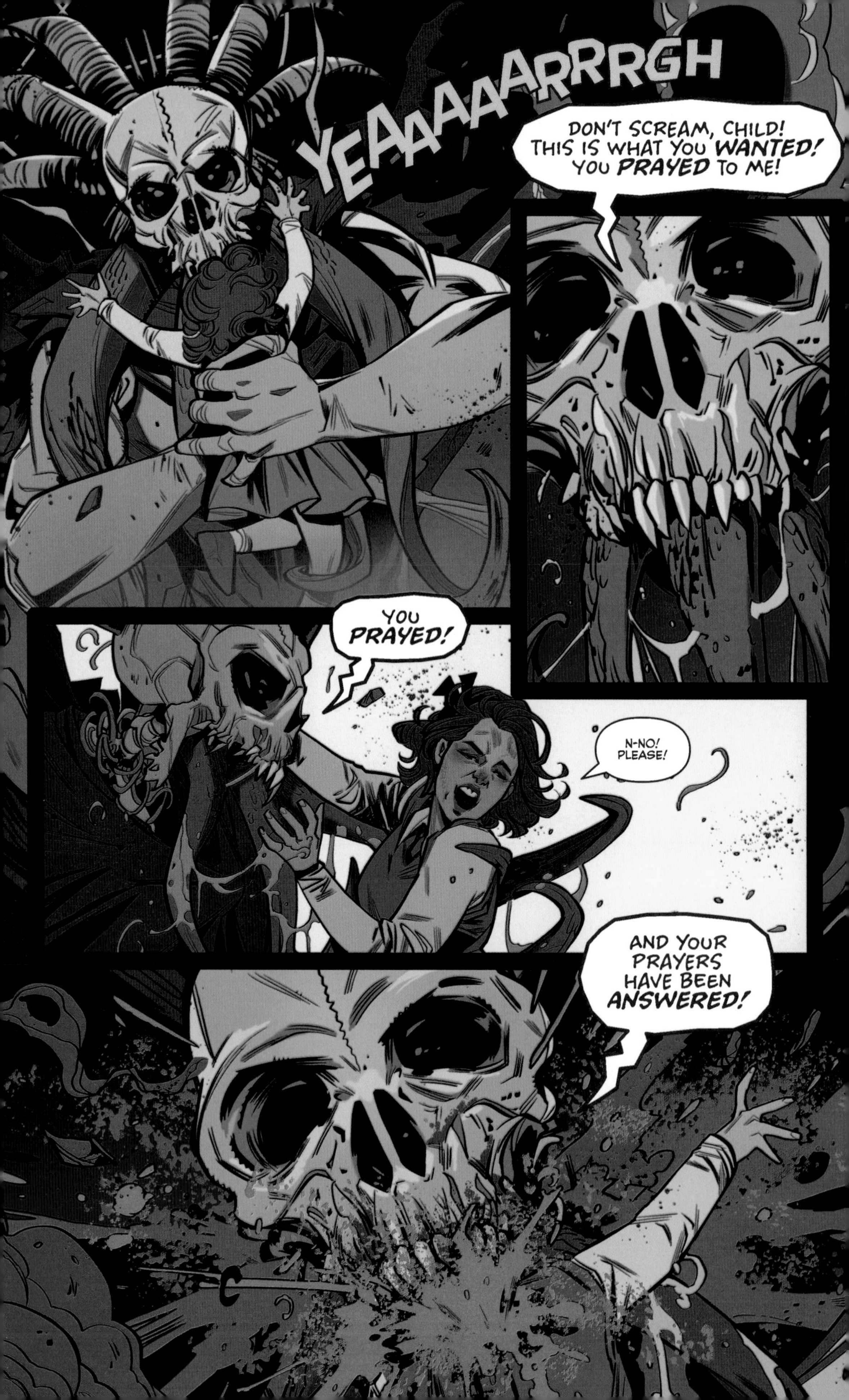
YEAAAAARRRGH
DON'T SCREAM, CHILD! THIS IS WHAT YOU WANTED! YOU PRAYED TO ME!
YOU PRAYED!
N-NO! PLEASE!
AND YOUR PRAYERS HAVE BEEN ANSWERED!

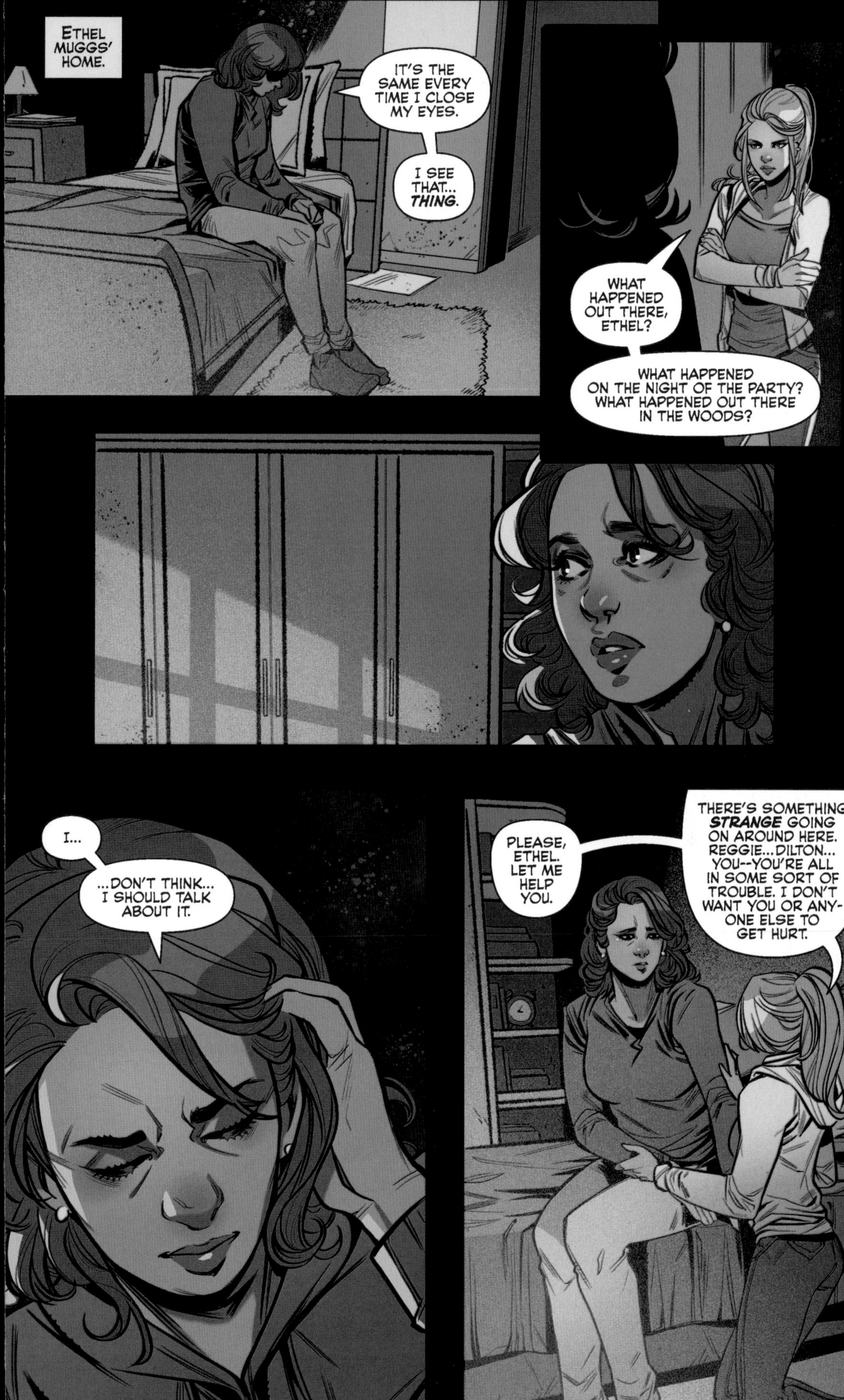
ETHEL MUGGS' HOME.
IT'S THE SAME EVERY TIME I CLOSE MY EYES.
I SEE THAT... THING.
WHAT HAPPENED OUT THERE, ETHEL?
WHAT HAPPENED ON THE NIGHT OF THE PARTY? WHAT HAPPENED OUT THERE IN THE WOODS?
I...
...DON'T THINK... I SHOULD TALK ABOUT IT.
PLEASE, ETHEL. LET ME HELP YOU.
THERE'S SOMETHING STRANGE GOING ON AROUND HERE. REGGIE...DILTON... YOU--YOU'RE ALL IN SOME SORT OF TROUBLE. I DON'T WANT YOU OR ANY-ONE ELSE TO GET HURT.

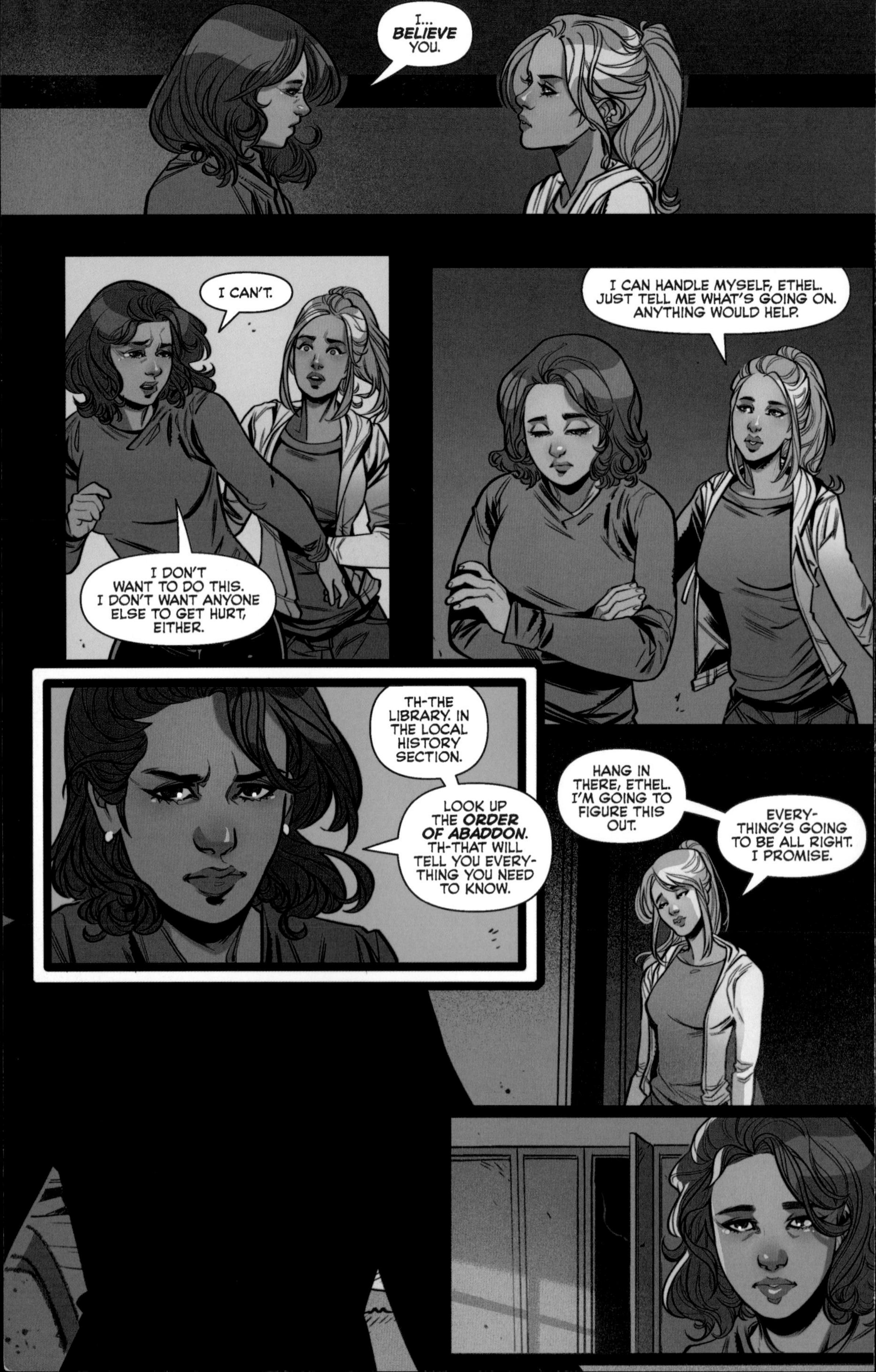
I... BELIEVE YOU.
I CAN'T.
I DON'T WANT TO DO THIS. I DON'T WANT ANYONE ELSE TO GET HURT, EITHER.
I CAN HANDLE MYSELF, ETHEL. JUST TELL ME WHAT'S GOING ON. ANYTHING WOULD HELP.
TH-THE LIBRARY. IN THE LOCAL HISTORY SECTION.
LOOK UP THE ORDER OF ABADDON. TH-THAT WILL TELL YOU EVERYTHING YOU NEED TO KNOW.
HANG IN THERE, ETHEL. I'M GOING TO FIGURE THIS OUT.
EVERYTHING'S GOING TO BE ALL RIGHT. I PROMISE.

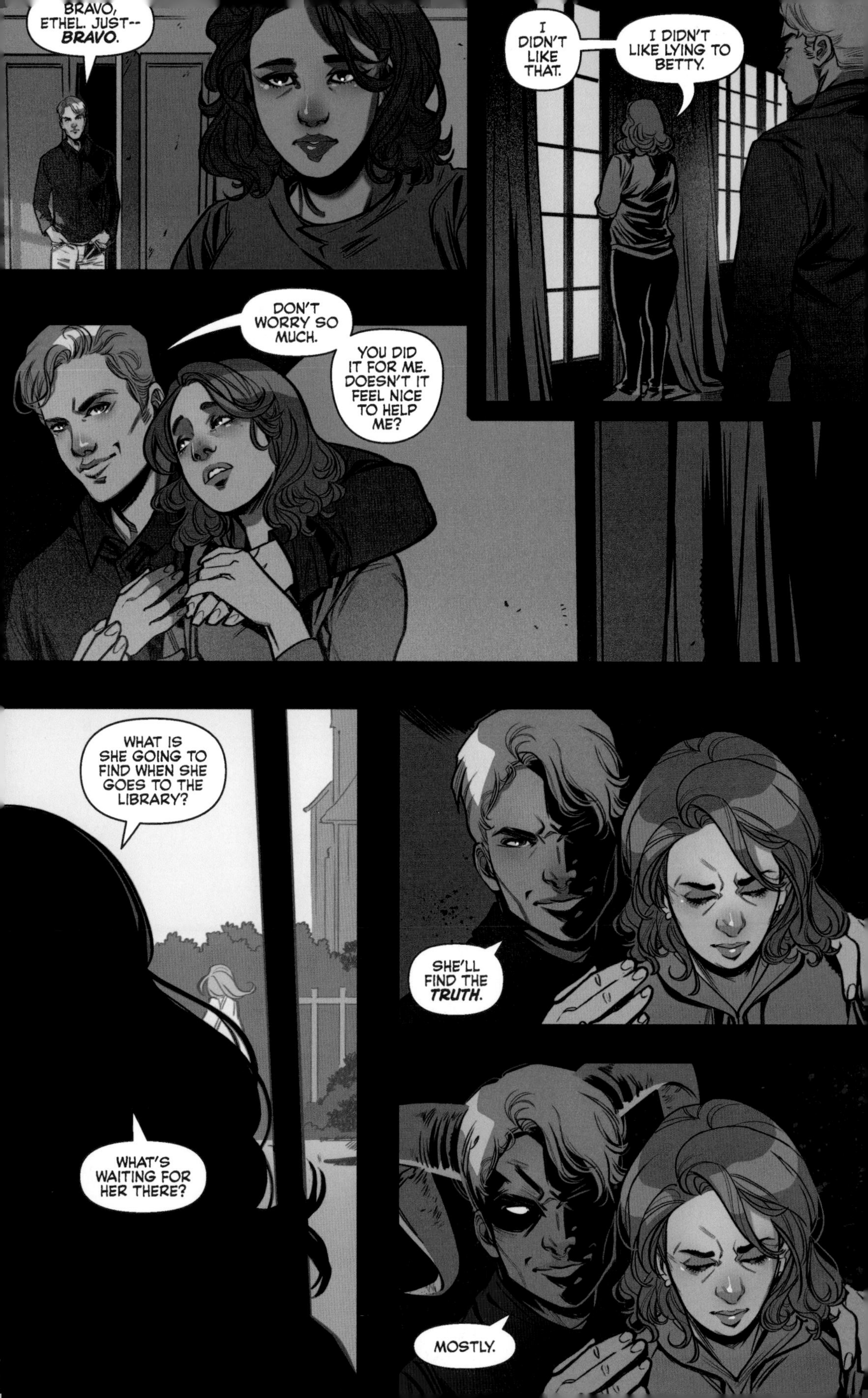
BRAVO, ETHEL. JUST-- BRAVO.
I DIDN'T LIKE THAT.
I DIDN'T LIKE LYING TO BETTY.
DON'T WORRY SO MUCH.
YOU DID IT FOR ME. DOESN'T IT FEEL NICE TO HELP ME?
WHAT IS SHE GOING TO FIND WHEN SHE GOES TO THE LIBRARY?
SHE'LL FIND THE TRUTH.
WHAT'S WAITING FOR HER THERE?
MOSTLY.

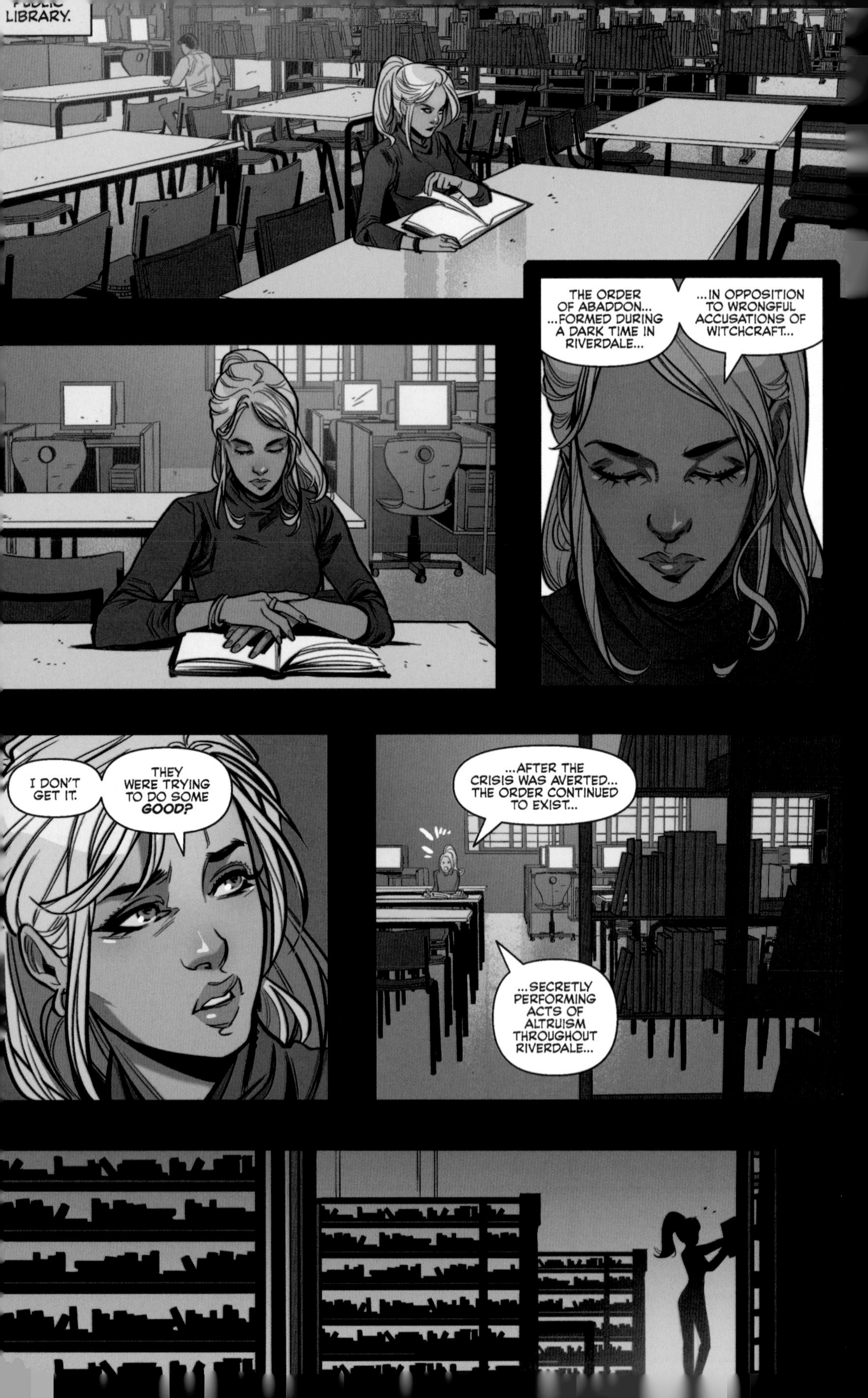
PUBLIC LIBRARY.
THE ORDER OF ABADDON... ...FORMED DURING A DARK TIME IN RIVERDALE...
...IN OPPOSITION TO WRONGFUL ACCUSATIONS OF WITCHCRAFT...
I DON'T GET IT.
THEY WERE TRYING TO DO SOME GOOD?
...AFTER THE CRISIS WAS AVERTED... THE ORDER CONTINUED TO EXIST...
...SECRETLY PERFORMING ACTS OF ALTRUISM THROUGHOUT RIVERDALE...

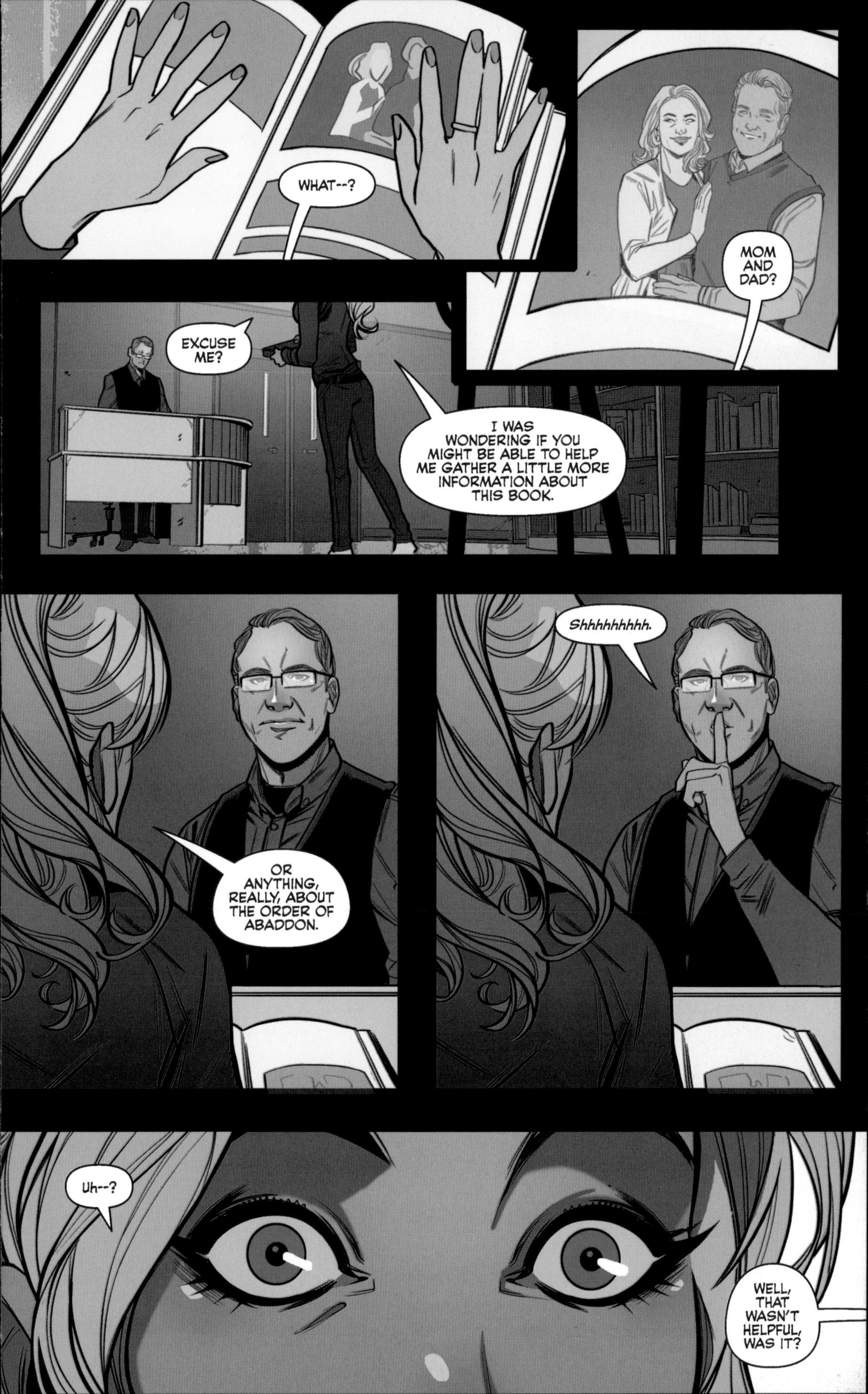
WHAT--?
MOM AND DAD?
EXCUSE ME?
I WAS WONDERING IF YOU MIGHT BE ABLE TO HELP ME GATHER A LITTLE MORE INFORMATION ABOUT THIS BOOK.
OR ANYTHING, REALLY, ABOUT THE ORDER OF ABADDON.
Shhhhhhhhh.
Uh--?
WELL, THAT WASN'T HELPFUL, WAS IT?

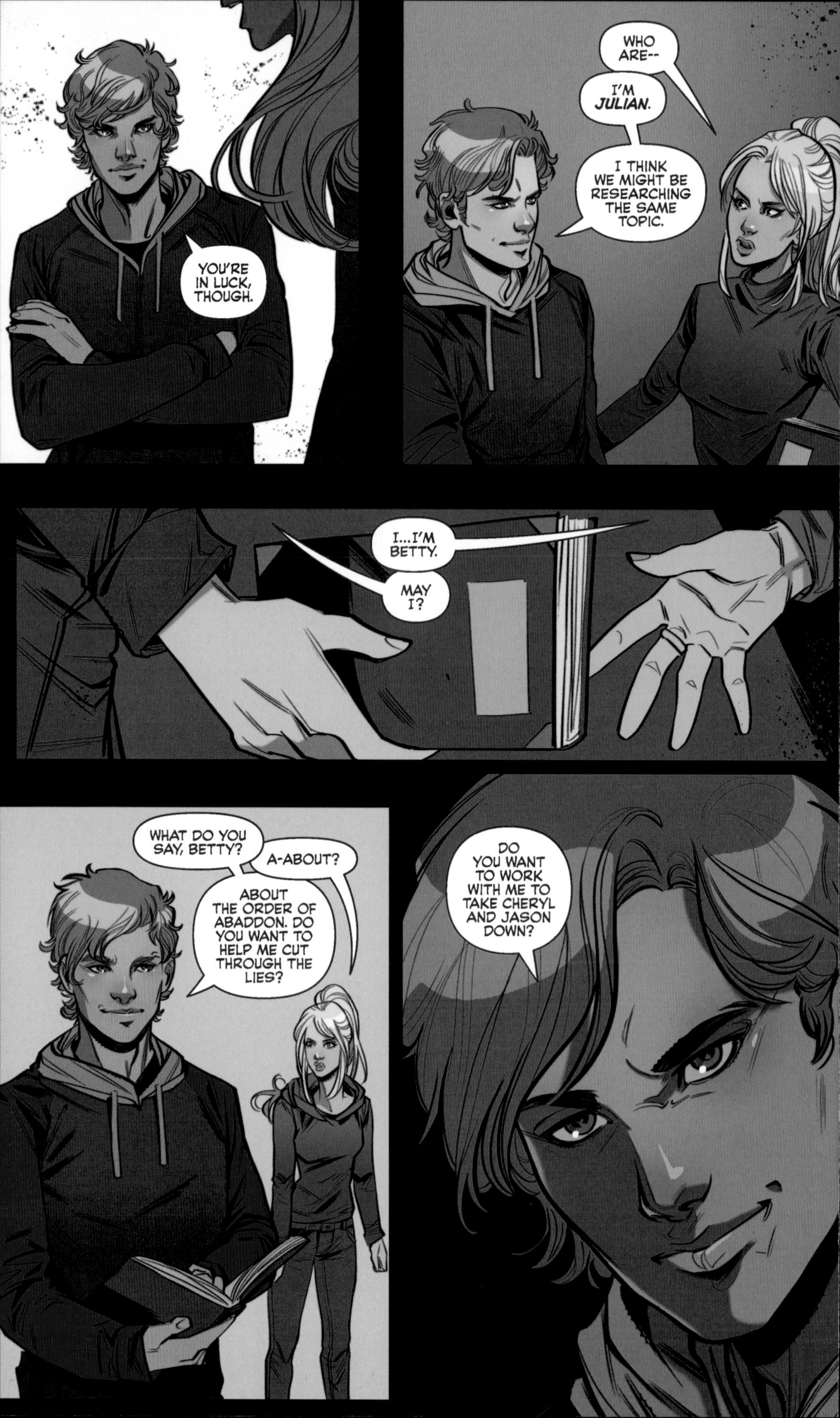
YOU'RE IN LUCK, THOUGH.
WHO ARE--
I'M JULIAN.
I THINK WE MIGHT BE RESEARCHING THE SAME TOPIC.
I...I'M BETTY.
MAY I?
WHAT DO YOU SAY, BETTY?
A-ABOUT?
ABOUT THE ORDER OF ABADDON. DO YOU WANT TO HELP ME CUT THROUGH THE LIES?
DO YOU WANT TO WORK WITH ME TO TAKE CHERYL AND JASON DOWN?

TO BE CONTINUED...

CHAPTER FOUR

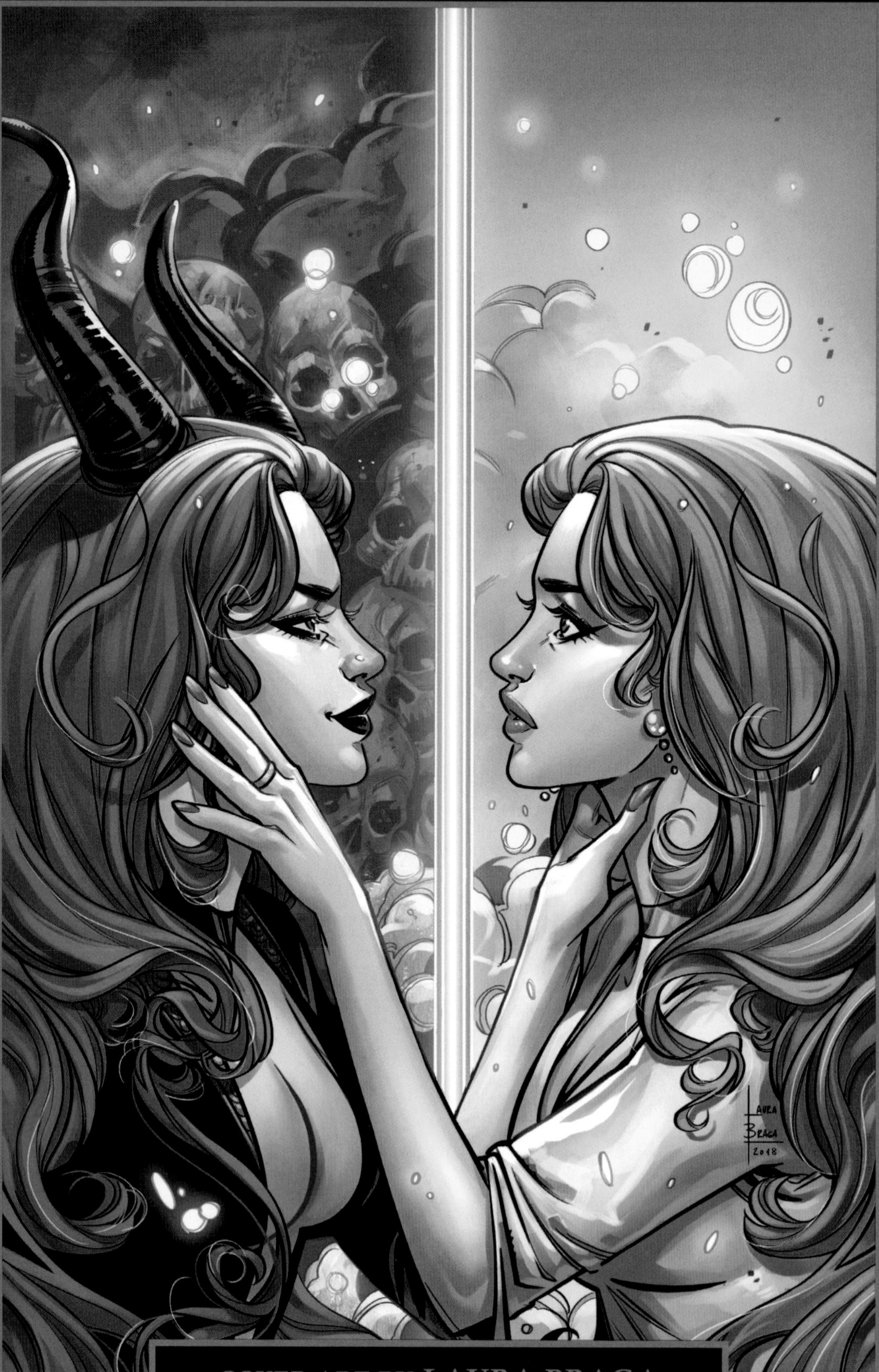
LAURA BRAGA 2018

COVER ART BY LAURA BRAGA

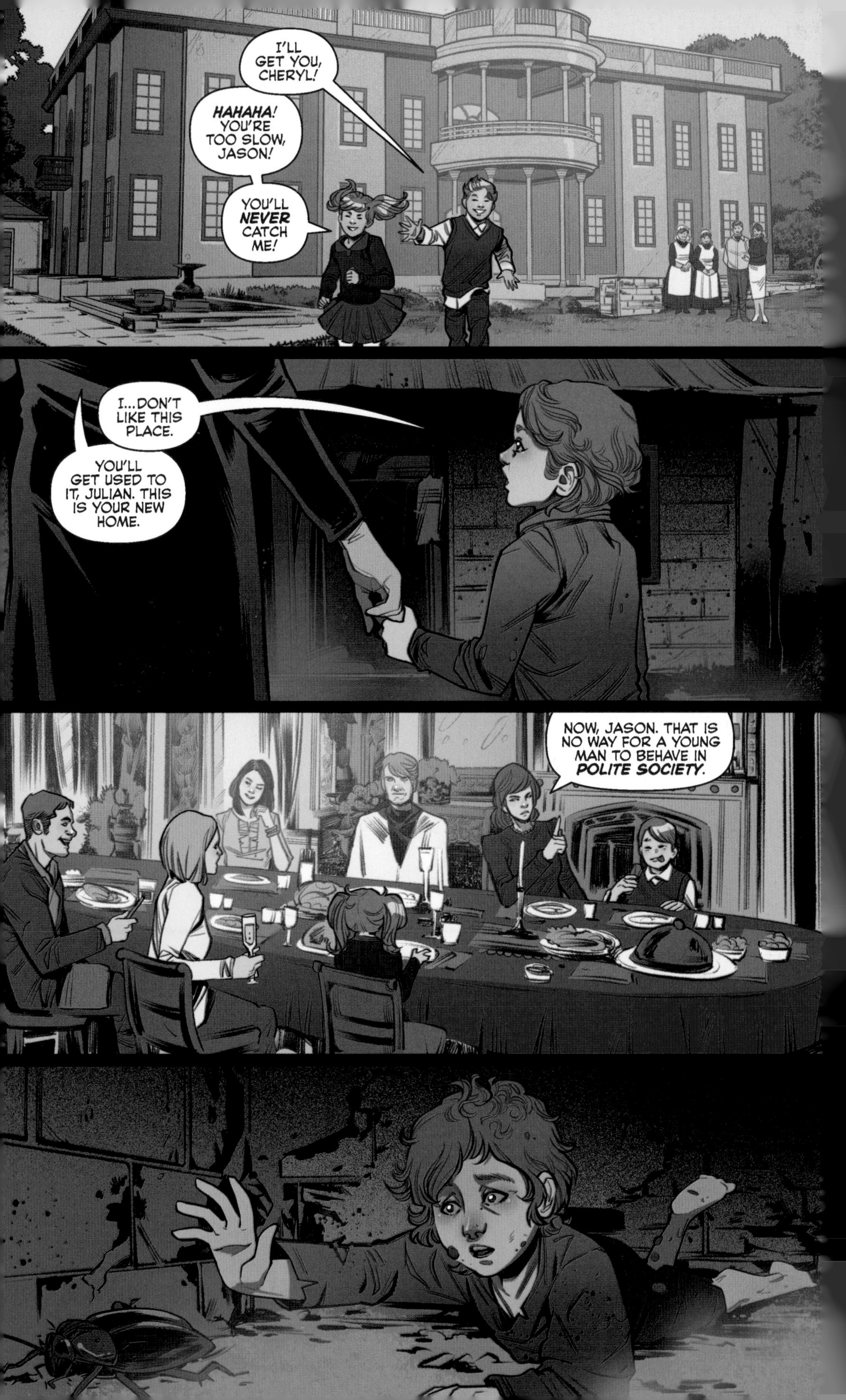

I'LL GET YOU, CHERYL!
HAHAHA! YOU'RE TOO SLOW, JASON!
YOU'LL NEVER CATCH ME!
I...DON'T LIKE THIS PLACE.
YOU'LL GET USED TO IT, JULIAN. THIS IS YOUR NEW HOME.
NOW, JASON. THAT IS NO WAY FOR A YOUNG MAN TO BEHAVE IN POLITE SOCIETY.

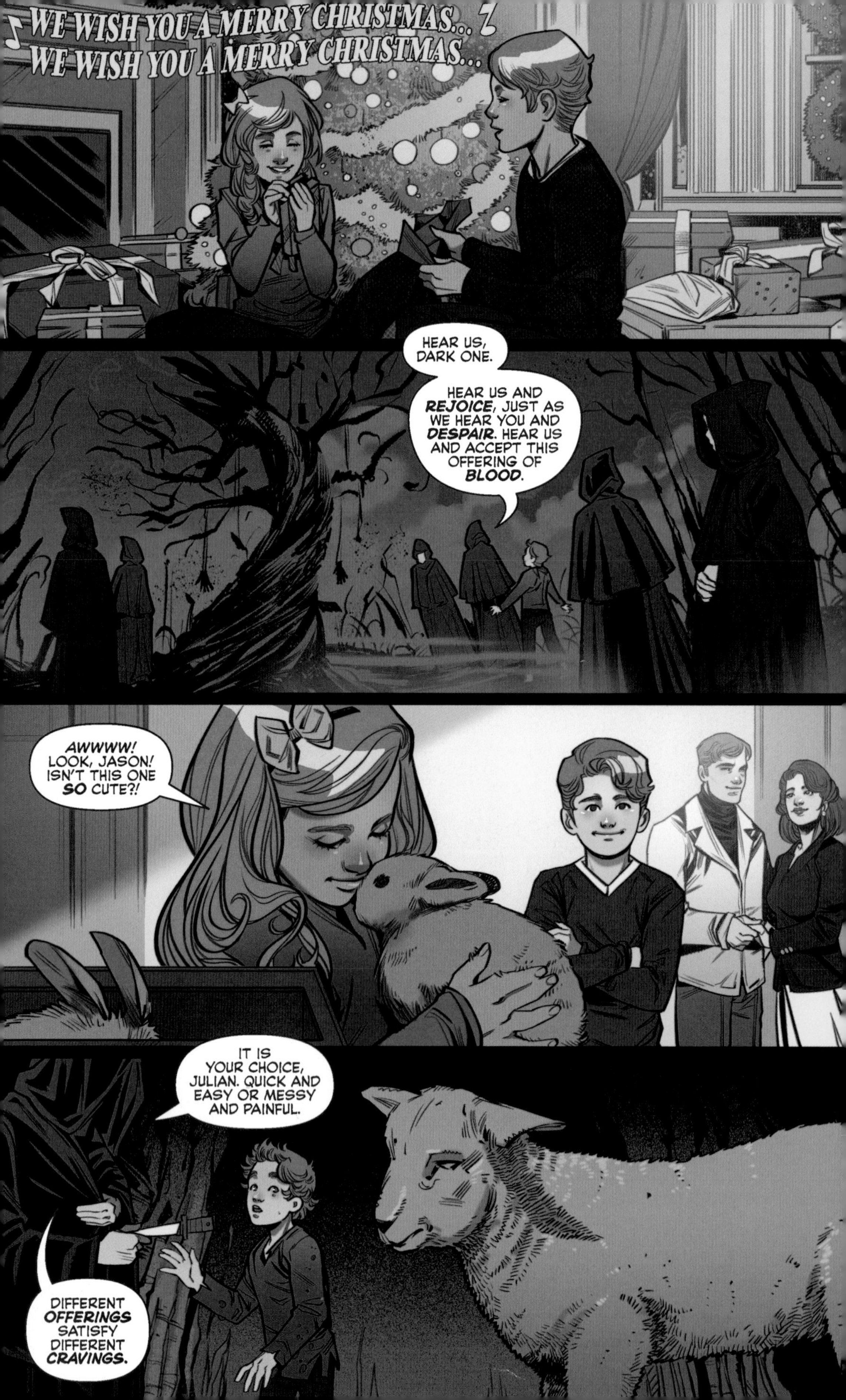

WE WISH YOU A MERRY CHRISTMAS...
WE WISH YOU A MERRY CHRISTMAS...
HEAR US, DARK ONE.
HEAR US AND REJOICE, JUST AS WE HEAR YOU AND DESPAIR. HEAR US AND ACCEPT THIS OFFERING OF BLOOD.
AWWWW! LOOK, JASON! ISN'T THIS ONE SO CUTE?!
IT IS YOUR CHOICE, JULIAN. QUICK AND EASY OR MESSY AND PAINFUL.
DIFFERENT OFFERINGS SATISFY DIFFERENT CRAVINGS.

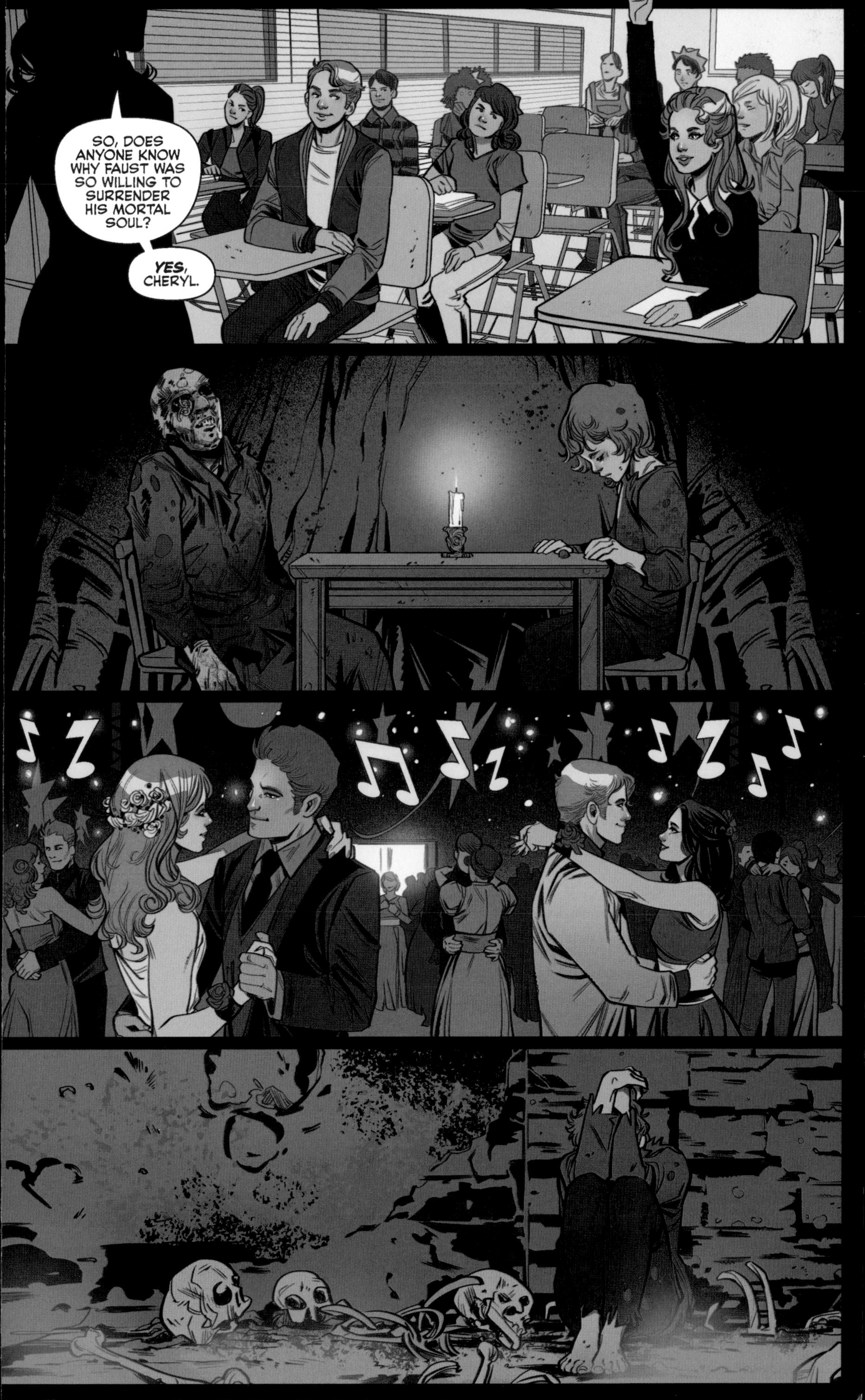
SO, DOES ANYONE KNOW WHY FAUST WAS SO WILLING TO SURRENDER HIS MORTAL SOUL?
YES, CHERYL.

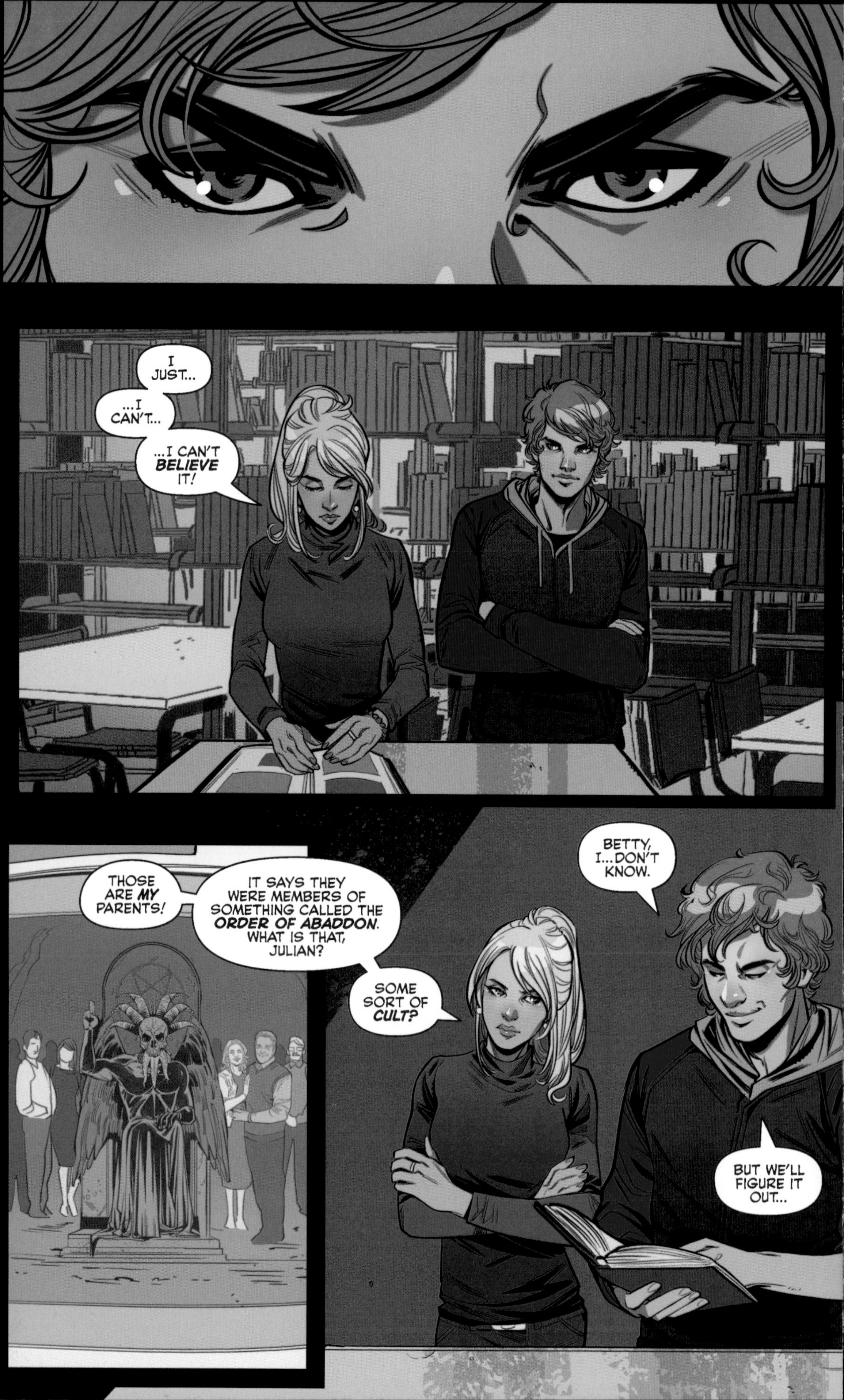
I JUST...
...I CAN'T...
...I CAN'T BELIEVE IT!
THOSE ARE MY PARENTS!
IT SAYS THEY WERE MEMBERS OF SOMETHING CALLED THE ORDER OF ABADDON. WHAT IS THAT, JULIAN?
SOME SORT OF CULT?
BETTY, I...DON'T KNOW.
BUT WE'LL FIGURE IT OUT...

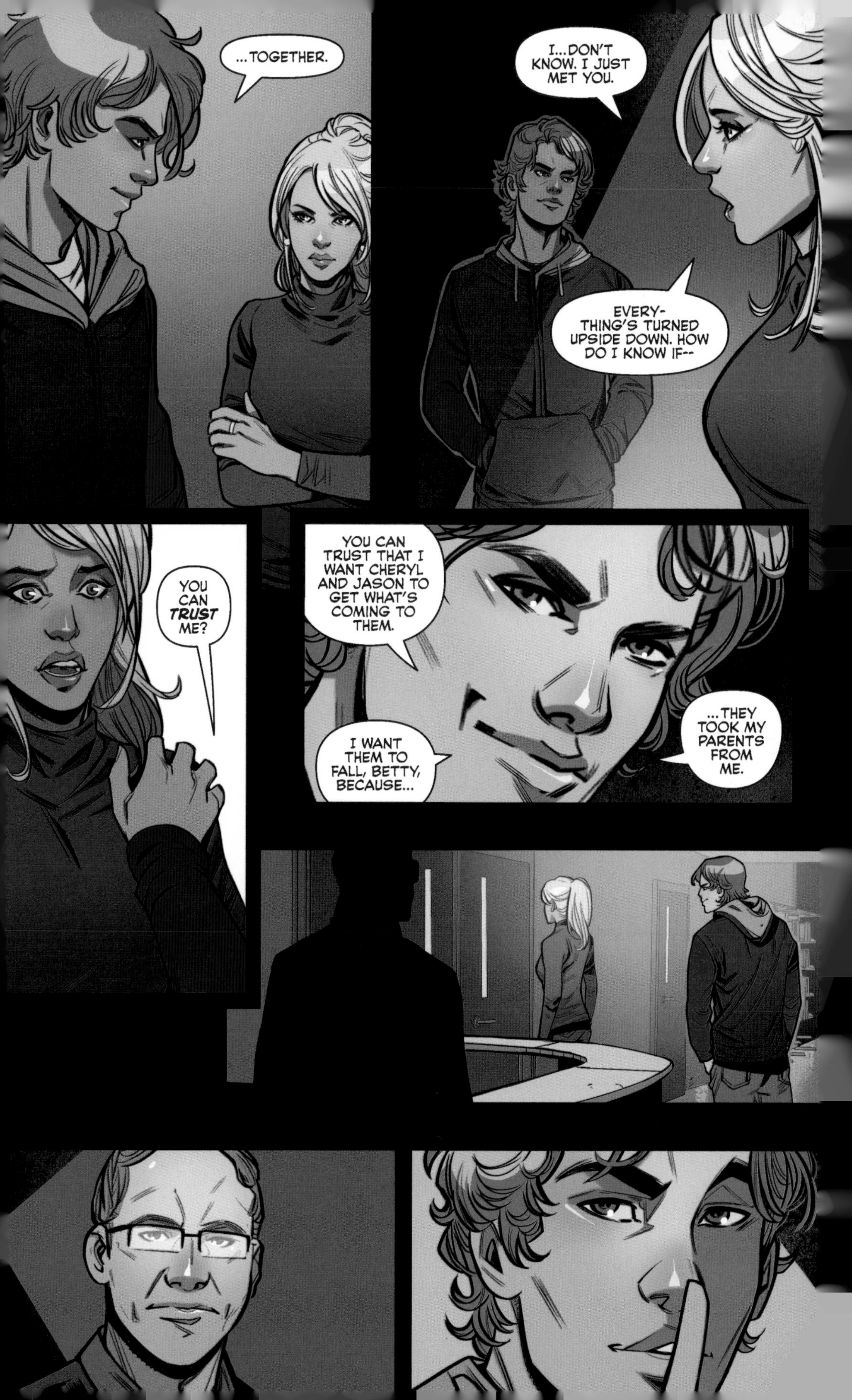
...TOGETHER.
I...DON'T KNOW. I JUST MET YOU.
EVERY-THING'S TURNED UPSIDE DOWN. HOW DO I KNOW IF--
YOU CAN TRUST ME?
YOU CAN TRUST THAT I WANT CHERYL AND JASON TO GET WHAT'S COMING TO THEM.
I WANT THEM TO FALL, BETTY, BECAUSE...
...THEY TOOK MY PARENTS FROM ME.

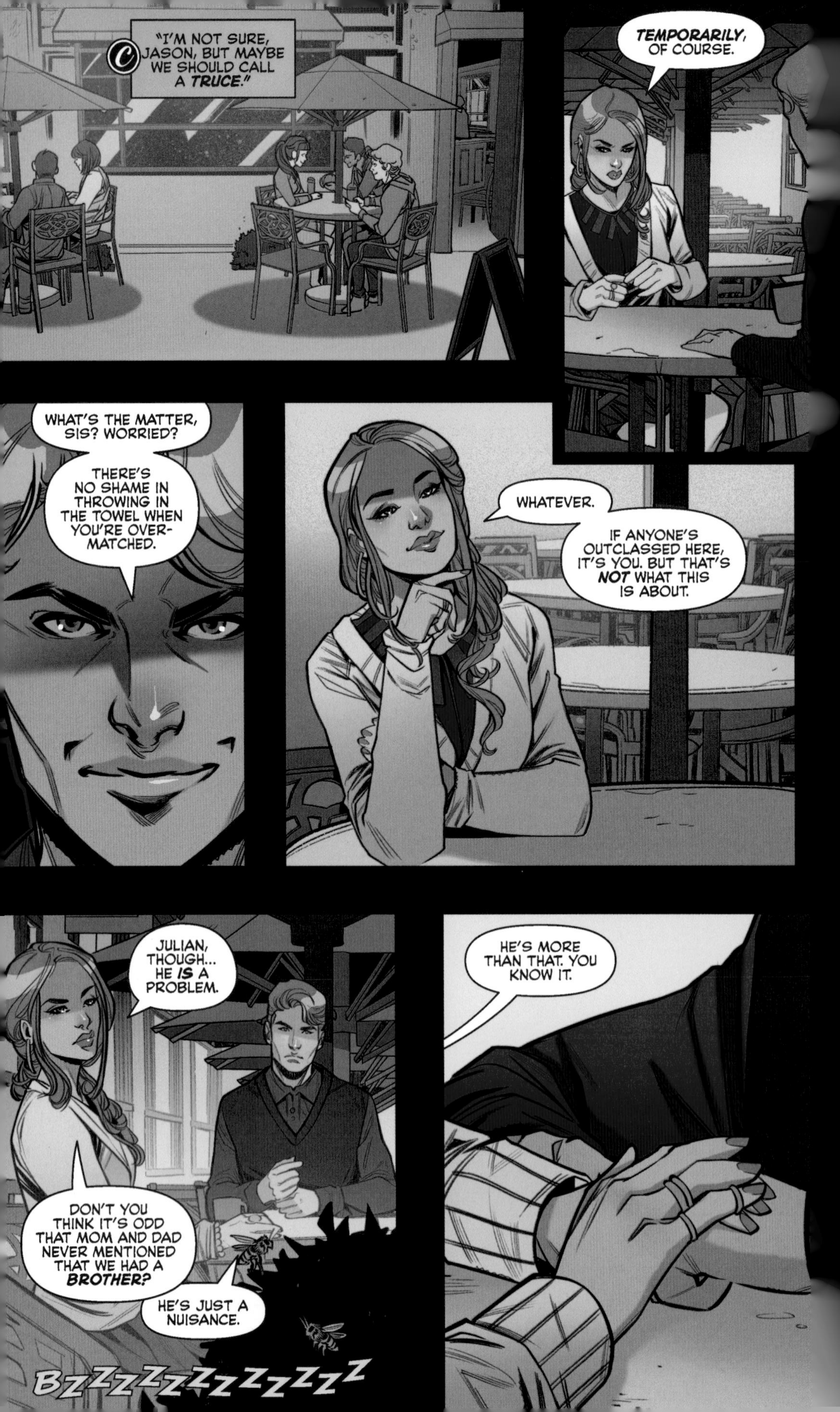
"I'M NOT SURE, JASON, BUT MAYBE WE SHOULD CALL A TRUCE."
TEMPORARILY, OF COURSE.
WHAT'S THE MATTER, SIS? WORRIED?
THERE'S NO SHAME IN THROWING IN THE TOWEL WHEN YOU'RE OVER-MATCHED.
WHATEVER.
IF ANYONE'S OUTCLASSED HERE, IT'S YOU. BUT THAT'S NOT WHAT THIS IS ABOUT.
JULIAN, THOUGH... HE IS A PROBLEM.
DON'T YOU THINK IT'S ODD THAT MOM AND DAD NEVER MENTIONED THAT WE HAD A BROTHER?
HE'S JUST A NUISANCE.
BZZZZZZZZZZZZZZ
HE'S MORE THAN THAT. YOU KNOW IT.

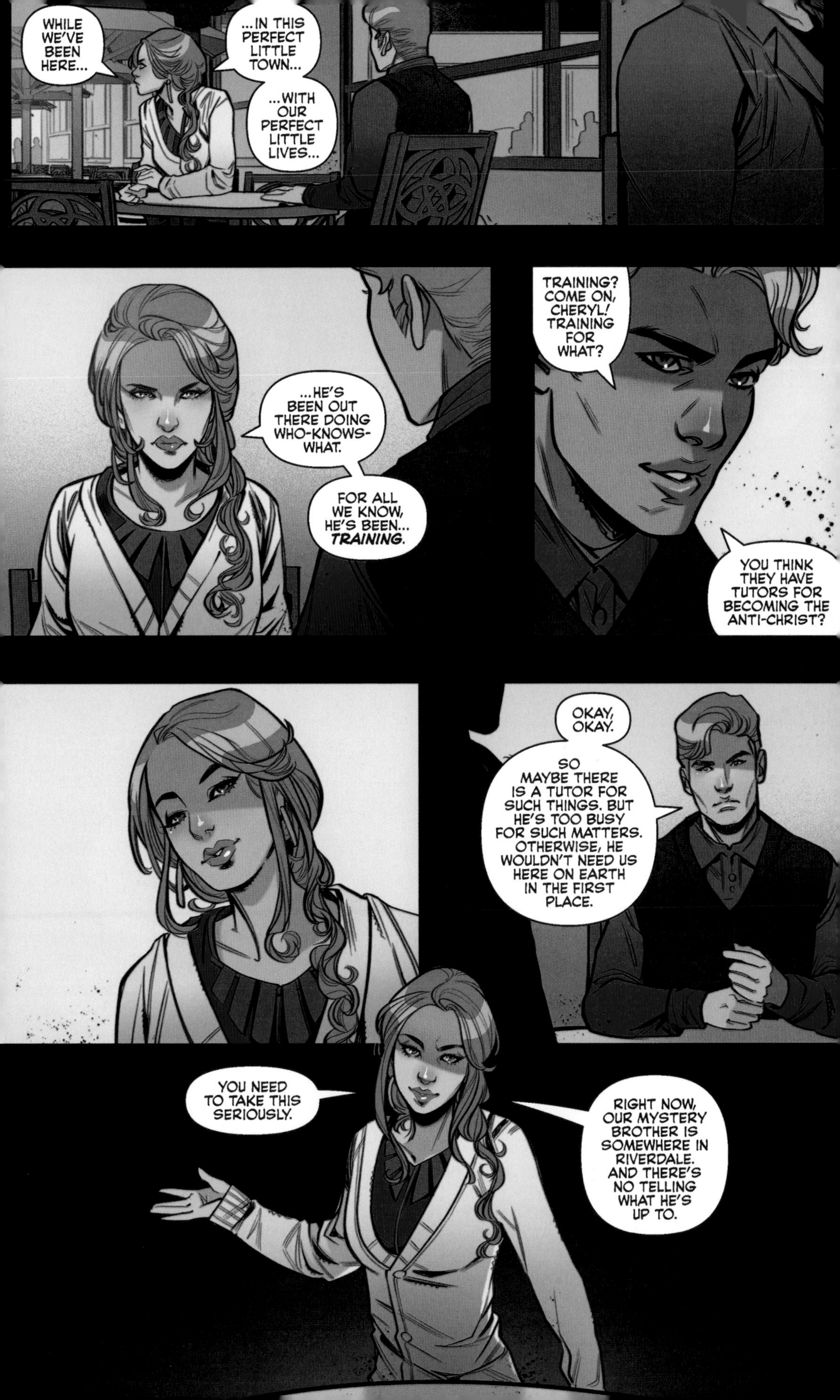

WHILE WE'VE BEEN HERE...
...IN THIS PERFECT LITTLE TOWN...
...WITH OUR PERFECT LITTLE LIVES...
...HE'S BEEN OUT THERE DOING WHO-KNOWS-WHAT.
FOR ALL WE KNOW, HE'S BEEN... *TRAINING*.
TRAINING? COME ON, CHERYL! TRAINING FOR WHAT?
YOU THINK THEY HAVE TUTORS FOR BECOMING THE ANTI-CHRIST?
OKAY, OKAY.
SO MAYBE THERE IS A TUTOR FOR SUCH THINGS. BUT HE'S TOO BUSY FOR SUCH MATTERS. OTHERWISE, HE WOULDN'T NEED US HERE ON EARTH IN THE FIRST PLACE.
YOU NEED TO TAKE THIS SERIOUSLY.
RIGHT NOW, OUR MYSTERY BROTHER IS SOMEWHERE IN RIVERDALE. AND THERE'S NO TELLING WHAT HE'S UP TO.

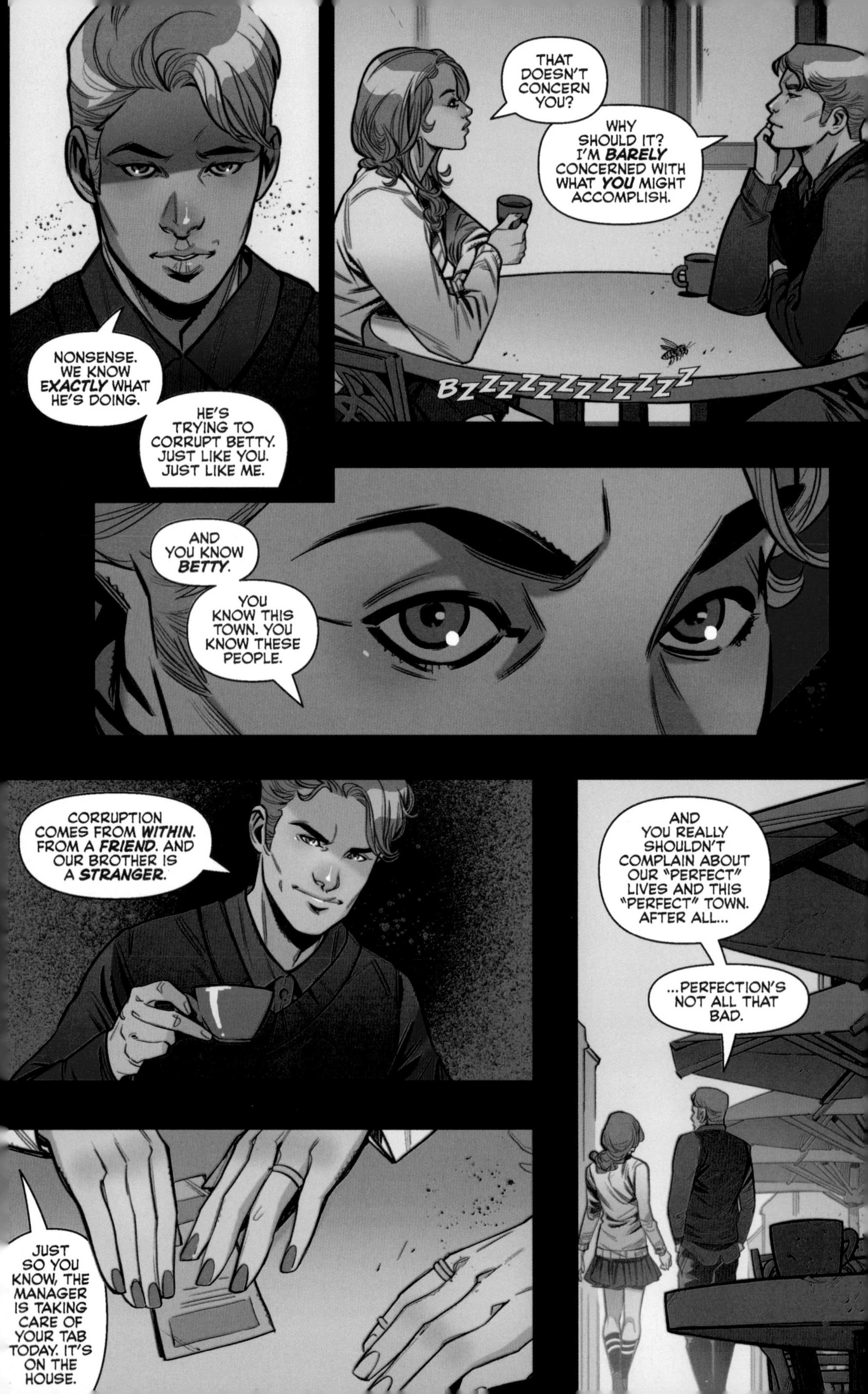
THAT DOESN'T CONCERN YOU?
WHY SHOULD IT? I'M BARELY CONCERNED WITH WHAT YOU MIGHT ACCOMPLISH.
BZZZZZZZZZZZZZ
NONSENSE. WE KNOW EXACTLY WHAT HE'S DOING.
HE'S TRYING TO CORRUPT BETTY. JUST LIKE YOU. JUST LIKE ME.
AND YOU KNOW BETTY.
YOU KNOW THIS TOWN. YOU KNOW THESE PEOPLE.
CORRUPTION COMES FROM WITHIN. FROM A FRIEND. AND OUR BROTHER IS A STRANGER.
JUST SO YOU KNOW, THE MANAGER IS TAKING CARE OF YOUR TAB TODAY. IT'S ON THE HOUSE.
AND YOU REALLY SHOULDN'T COMPLAIN ABOUT OUR "PERFECT" LIVES AND THIS "PERFECT" TOWN. AFTER ALL...
...PERFECTION'S NOT ALL THAT BAD.

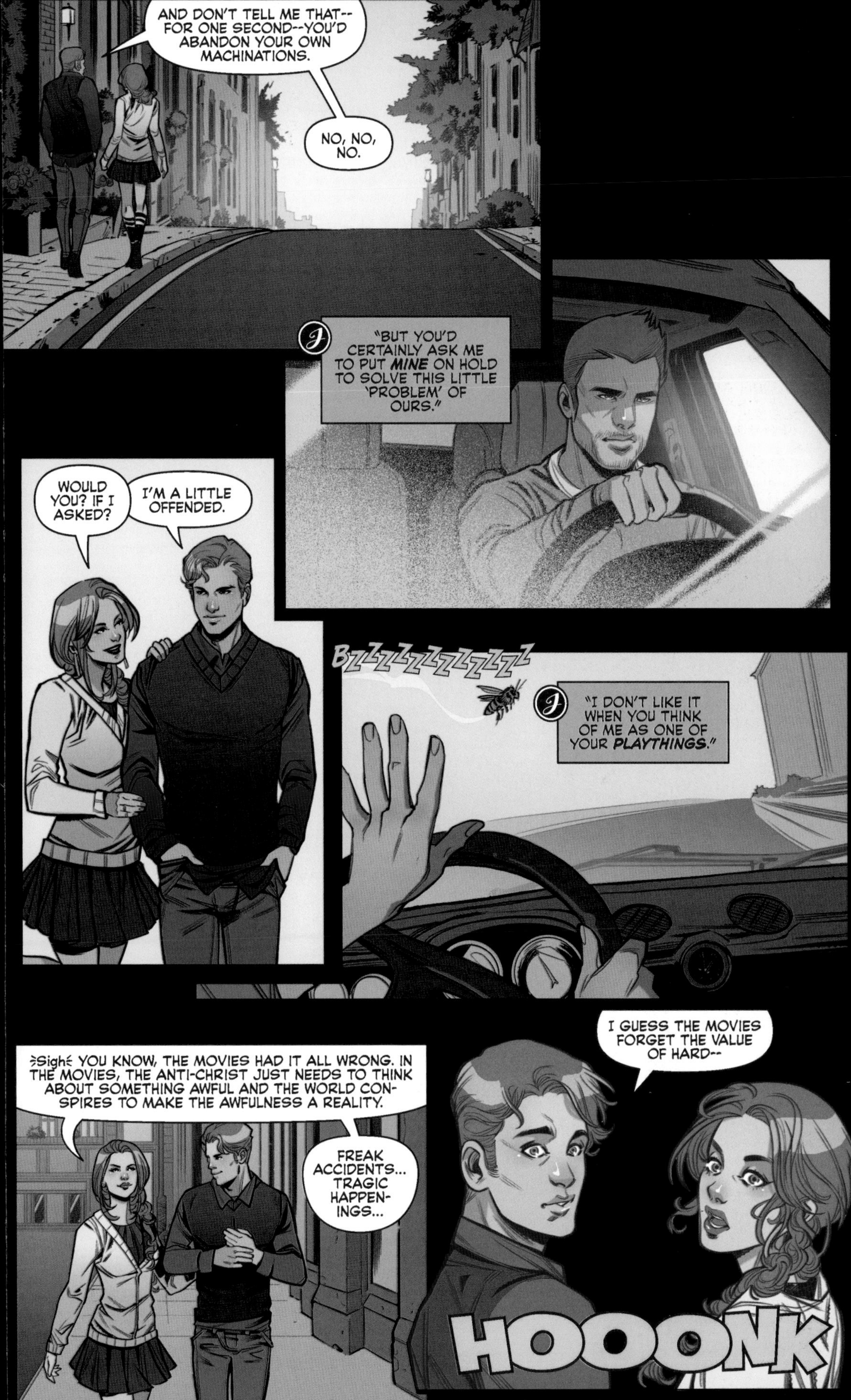
AND DON'T TELL ME THAT--FOR ONE SECOND--YOU'D ABANDON YOUR OWN MACHINATIONS.
NO, NO, NO.
"BUT YOU'D CERTAINLY ASK ME TO PUT MINE ON HOLD TO SOLVE THIS LITTLE 'PROBLEM' OF OURS."
WOULD YOU? IF I ASKED?
I'M A LITTLE OFFENDED.
BZZZZZZZZZZZZ
"I DON'T LIKE IT WHEN YOU THINK OF ME AS ONE OF YOUR PLAYTHINGS."
ƸSighƷ YOU KNOW, THE MOVIES HAD IT ALL WRONG. IN THE MOVIES, THE ANTI-CHRIST JUST NEEDS TO THINK ABOUT SOMETHING AWFUL AND THE WORLD CONSPIRES TO MAKE THE AWFULNESS A REALITY.
FREAK ACCIDENTS... TRAGIC HAPPENINGS...
I GUESS THE MOVIES FORGET THE VALUE OF HARD--
HOOONK

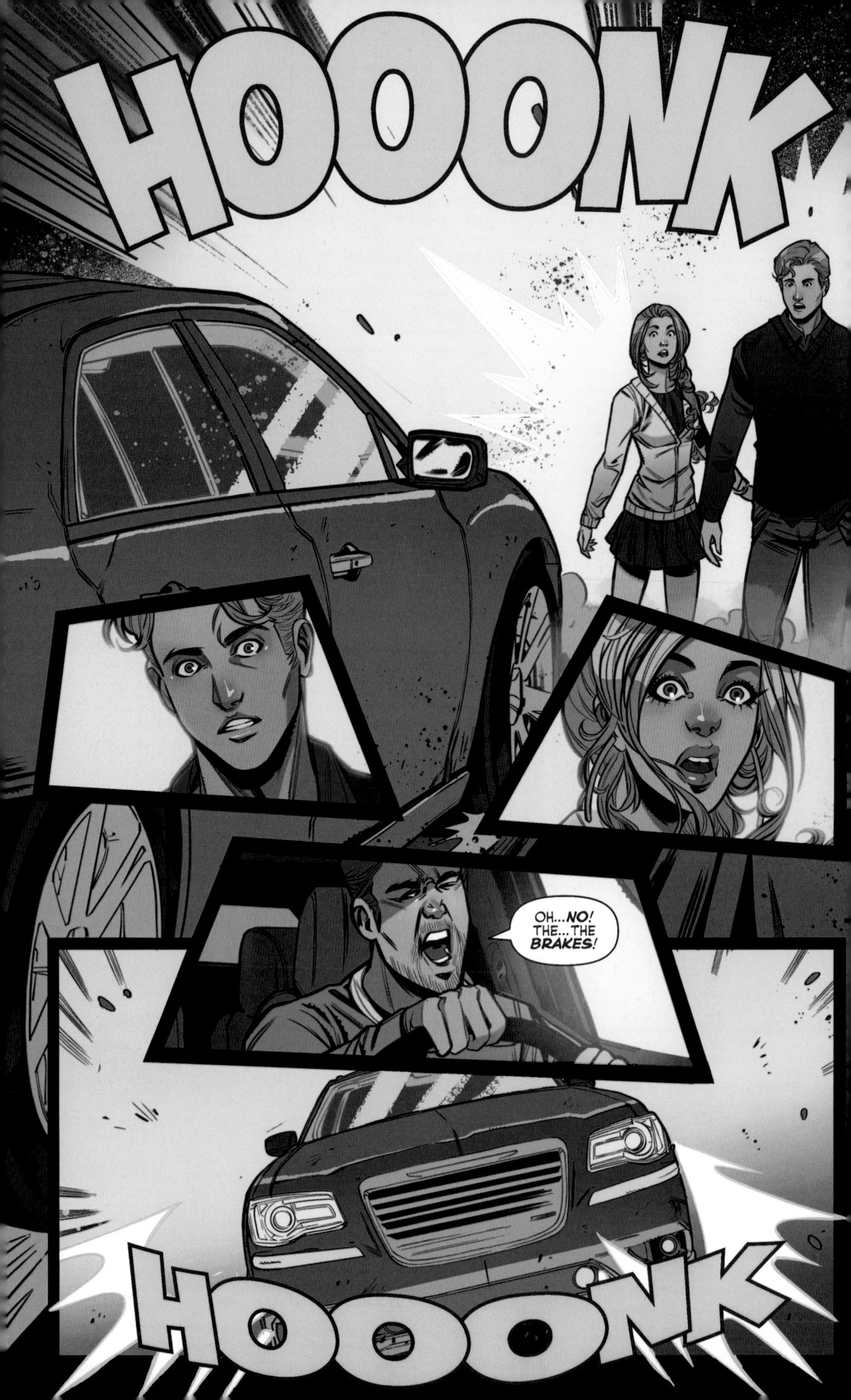
HOOONK
OH...NO! THE...THE BRAKES!
HOOONK

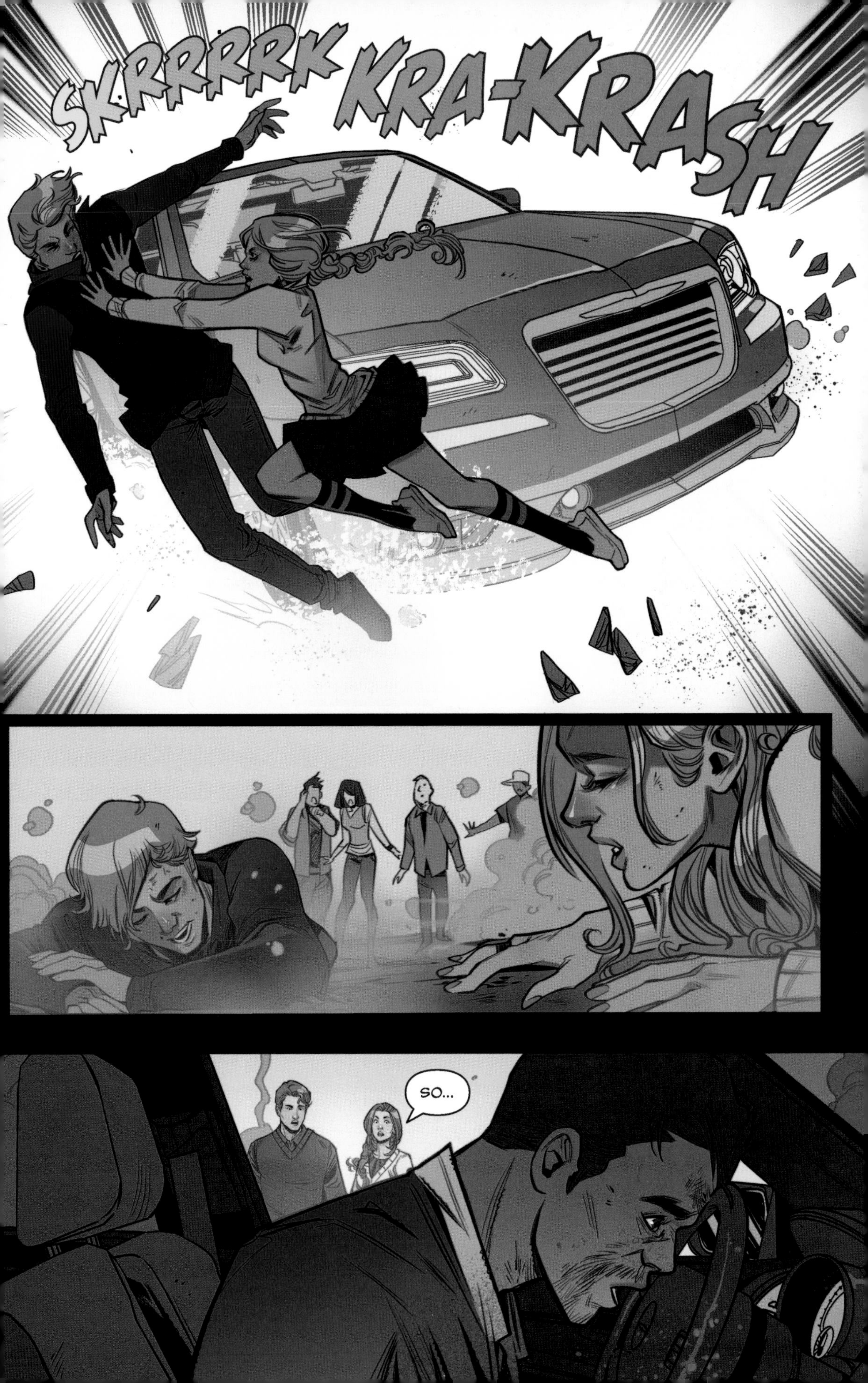
SKRRRRK KRA-KRASH
SO...

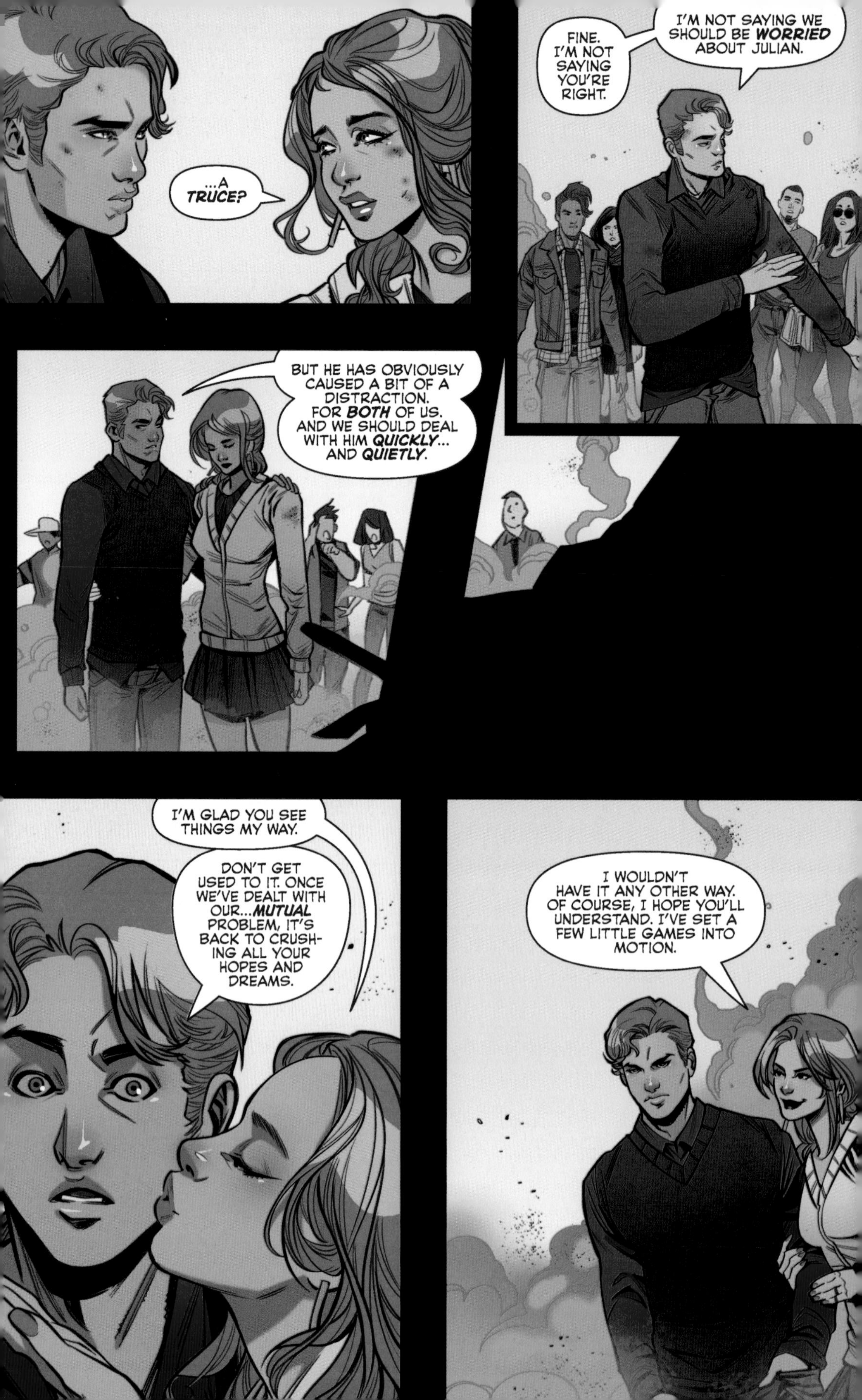
...A TRUCE?
I'M NOT SAYING WE SHOULD BE WORRIED ABOUT JULIAN.
FINE. I'M NOT SAYING YOU'RE RIGHT.
BUT HE HAS OBVIOUSLY CAUSED A BIT OF A DISTRACTION. FOR BOTH OF US. AND WE SHOULD DEAL WITH HIM QUICKLY... AND QUIETLY.
I'M GLAD YOU SEE THINGS MY WAY.
DON'T GET USED TO IT. ONCE WE'VE DEALT WITH OUR...MUTUAL PROBLEM, IT'S BACK TO CRUSHING ALL YOUR HOPES AND DREAMS.
I WOULDN'T HAVE IT ANY OTHER WAY. OF COURSE, I HOPE YOU'LL UNDERSTAND. I'VE SET A FEW LITTLE GAMES INTO MOTION.

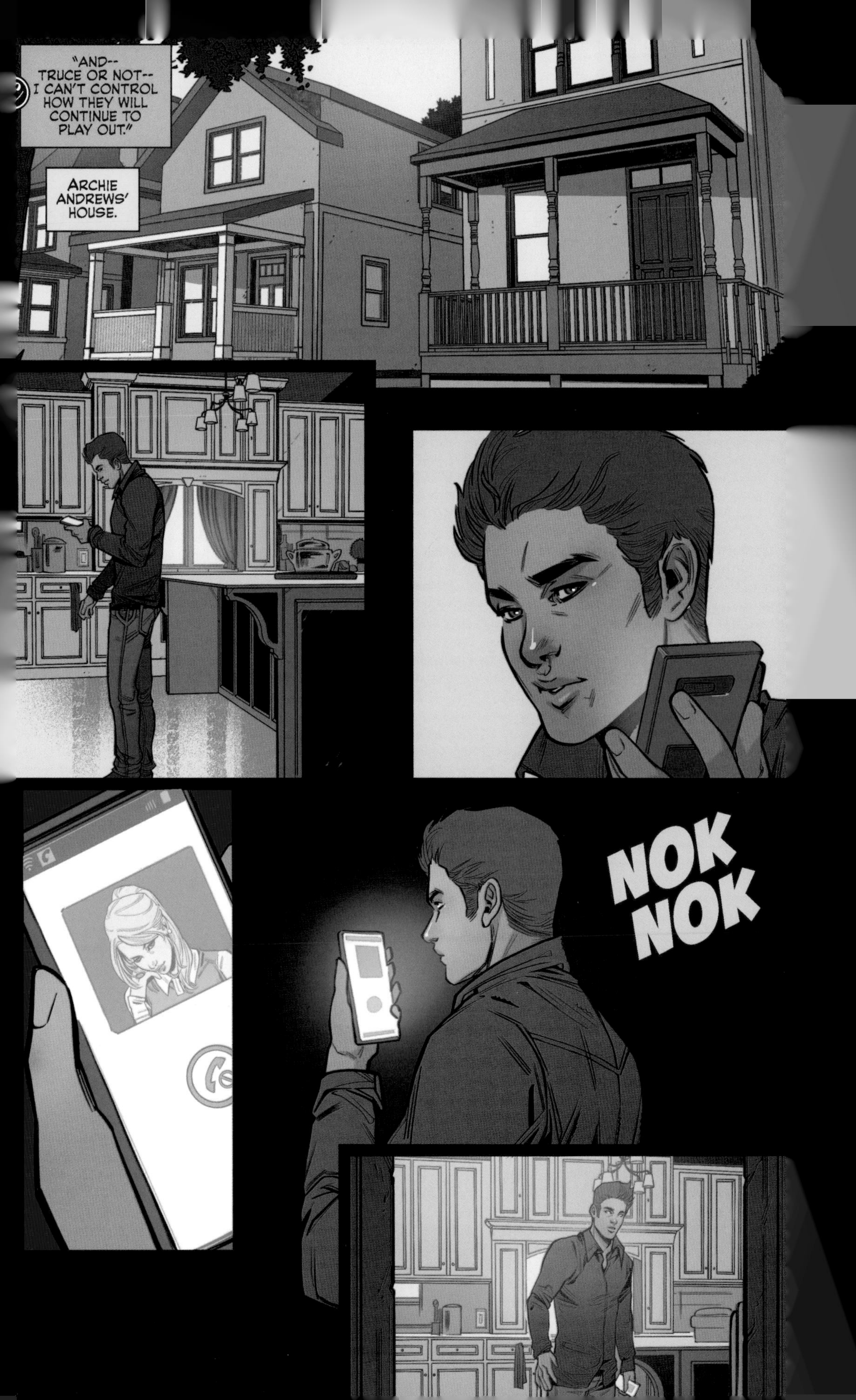
"AND-- TRUCE OR NOT-- I CAN'T CONTROL HOW THEY WILL CONTINUE TO PLAY OUT."
ARCHIE ANDREWS' HOUSE.
NOK NOK

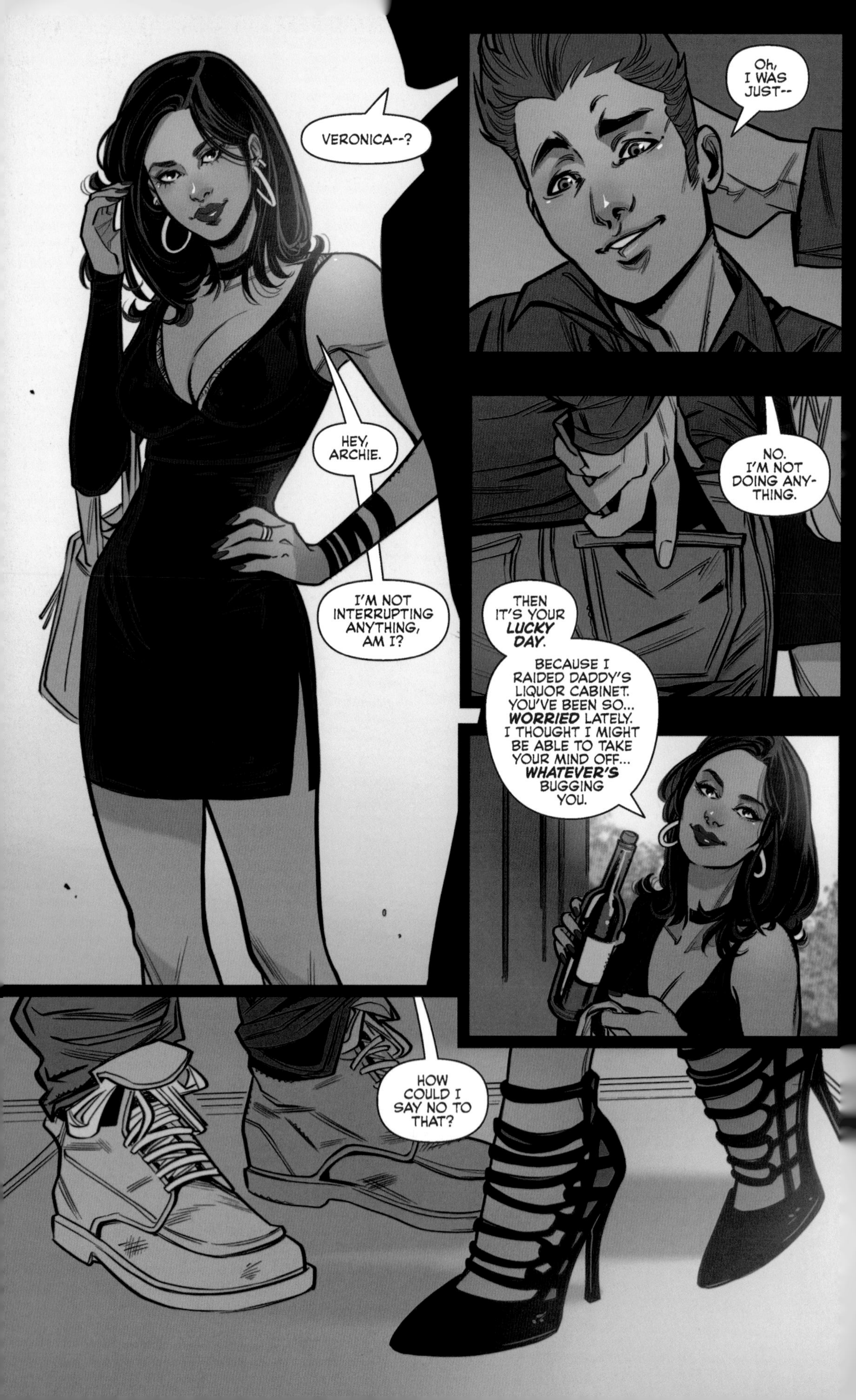
VERONICA--?
Oh, I WAS JUST--
HEY, ARCHIE.
I'M NOT INTERRUPTING ANYTHING, AM I?
NO. I'M NOT DOING ANY-THING.
THEN IT'S YOUR *LUCKY DAY*.
BECAUSE I RAIDED DADDY'S LIQUOR CABINET. YOU'VE BEEN SO... *WORRIED* LATELY. I THOUGHT I MIGHT BE ABLE TO TAKE YOUR MIND OFF... *WHATEVER'S* BUGGING YOU.
HOW COULD I SAY NO TO THAT?

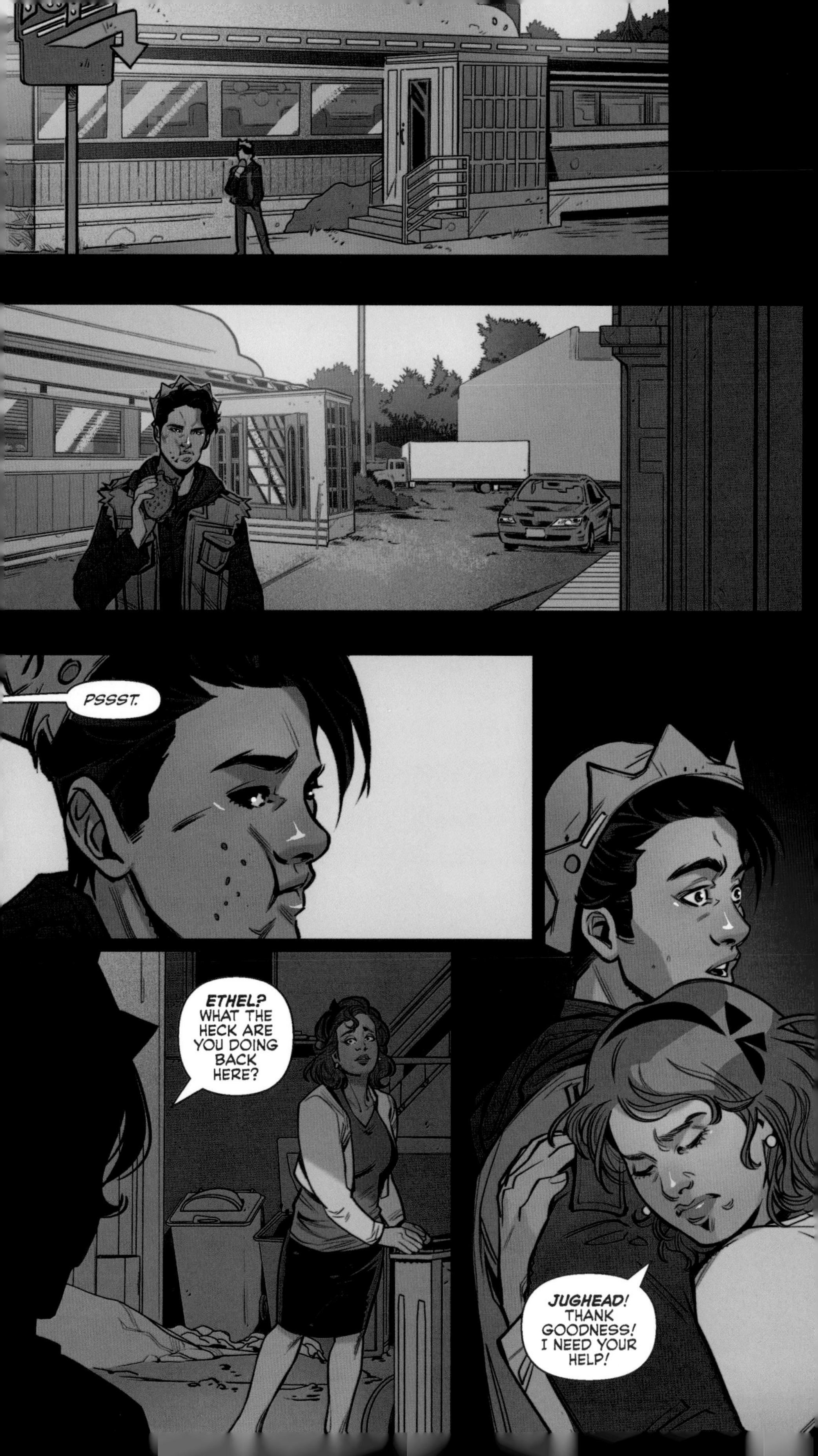

PSSST.
ETHEL? WHAT THE HECK ARE YOU DOING BACK HERE?
JUGHEAD! THANK GOODNESS! I NEED YOUR HELP!

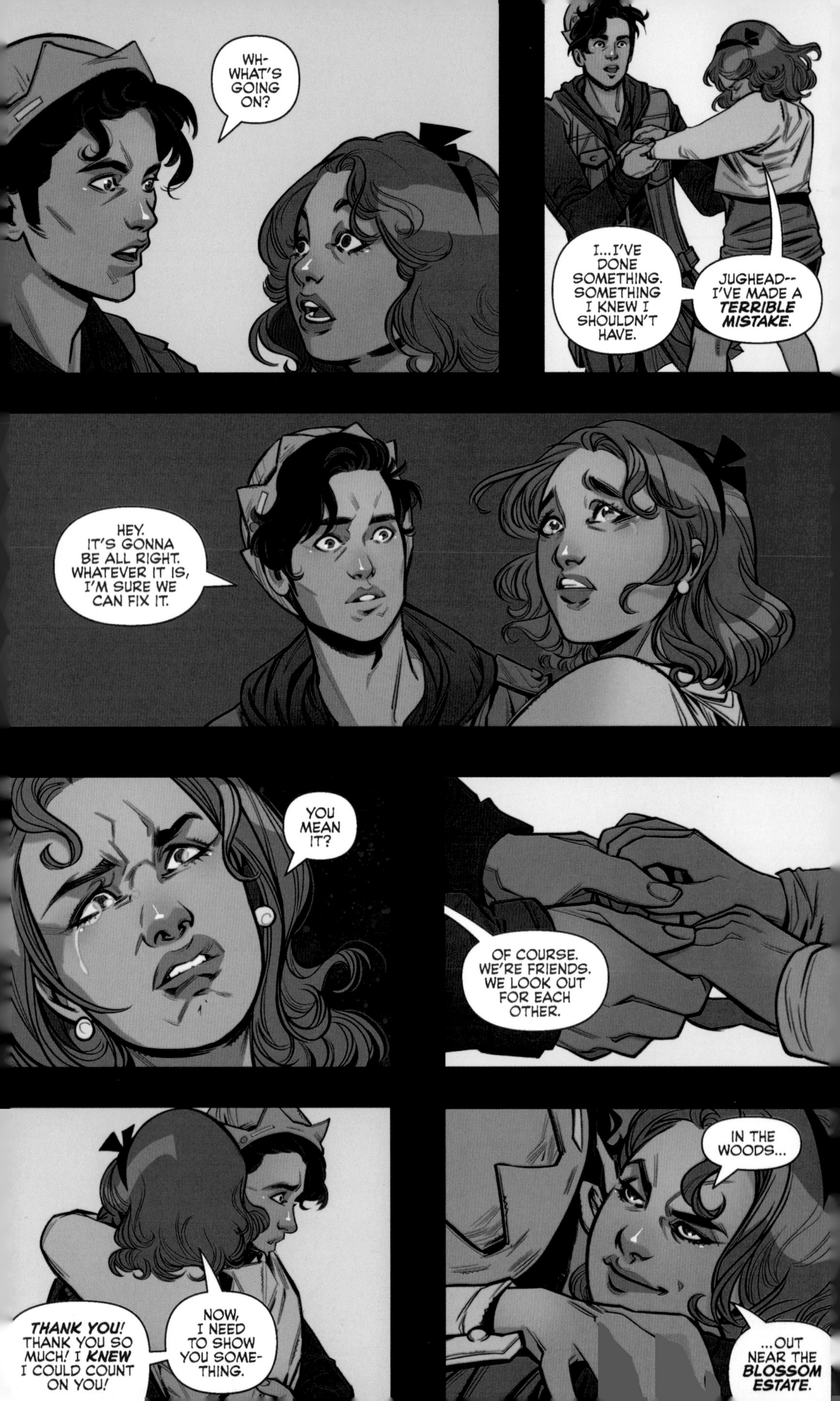
WH-WHAT'S GOING ON?
JUGHEAD-- I'VE MADE A *TERRIBLE MISTAKE*.
I...I'VE DONE SOMETHING. SOMETHING I KNEW I SHOULDN'T HAVE.
HEY. IT'S GONNA BE ALL RIGHT. WHATEVER IT IS, I'M SURE WE CAN FIX IT.
YOU MEAN IT?
OF COURSE. WE'RE FRIENDS. WE LOOK OUT FOR EACH OTHER.
THANK YOU! THANK YOU SO MUCH! I ***KNEW*** I COULD COUNT ON YOU!
NOW, I NEED TO SHOW YOU SOME-THING.
IN THE WOODS...
...OUT NEAR THE ***BLOSSOM ESTATE***.

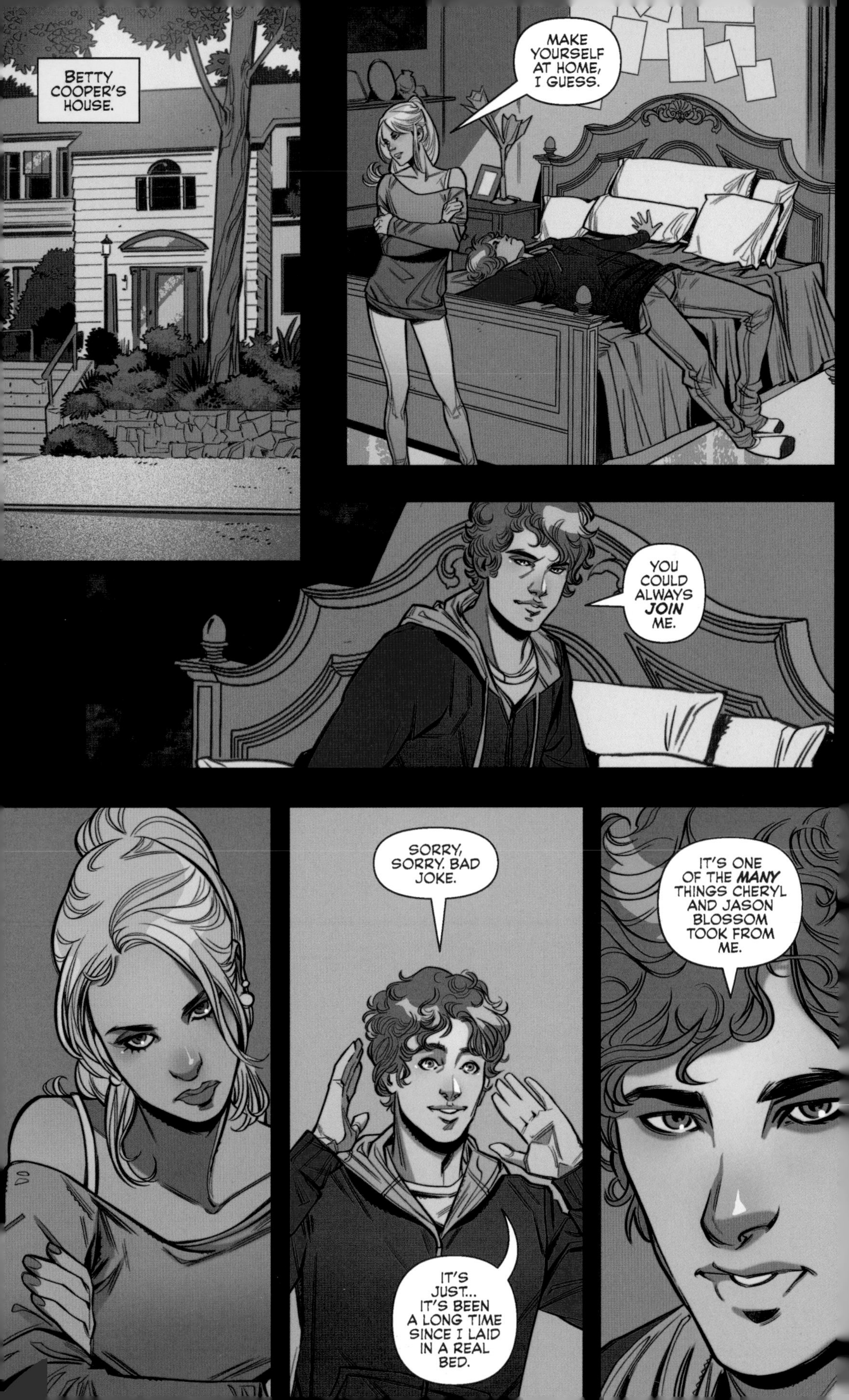
BETTY COOPER'S HOUSE.
MAKE YOURSELF AT HOME, I GUESS.
YOU COULD ALWAYS *JOIN* ME.
SORRY, SORRY. BAD JOKE.
IT'S JUST... IT'S BEEN A LONG TIME SINCE I LAID IN A REAL BED.
IT'S ONE OF THE *MANY* THINGS CHERYL AND JASON BLOSSOM TOOK FROM ME.

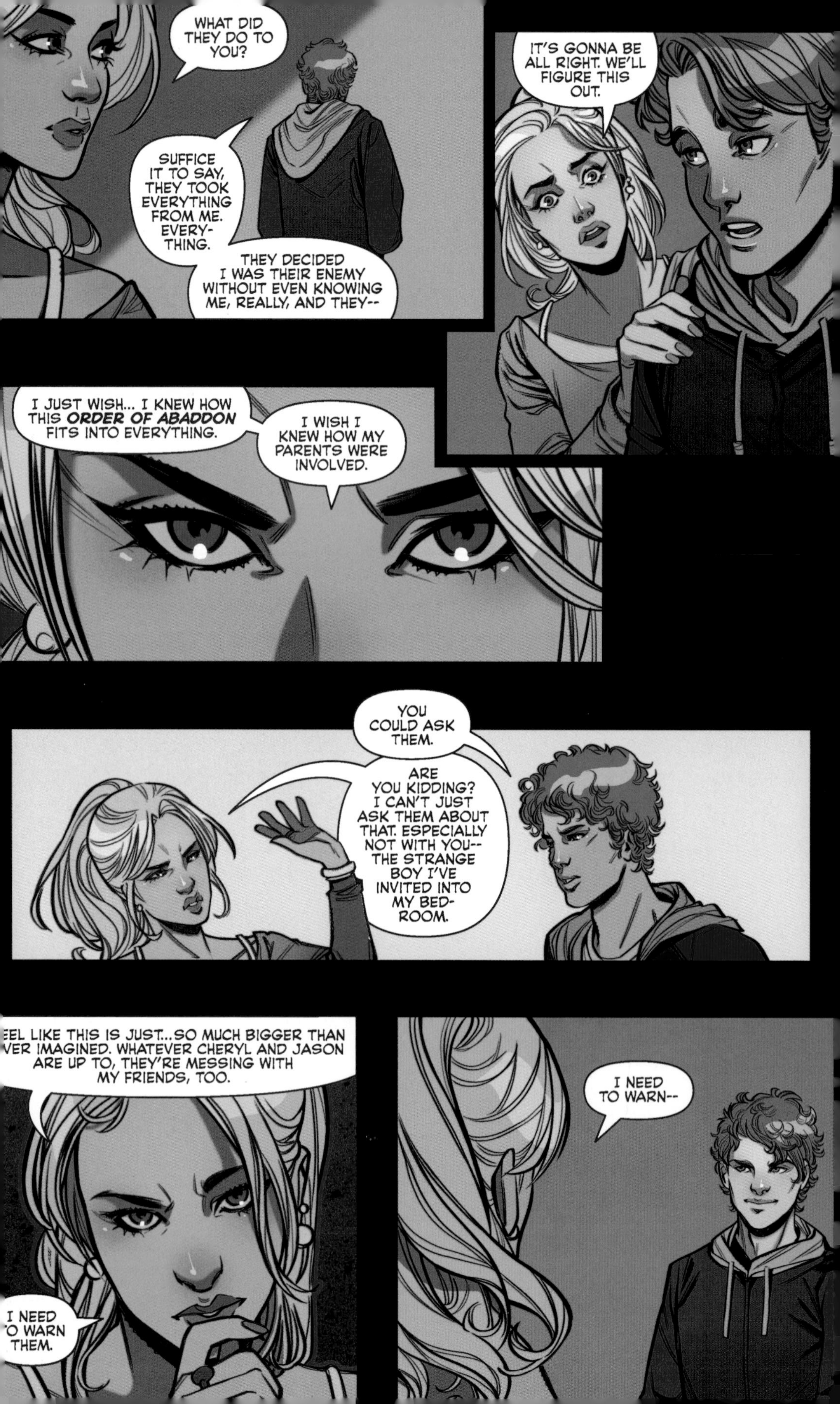
WHAT DID THEY DO TO YOU?
SUFFICE IT TO SAY, THEY TOOK EVERYTHING FROM ME. EVERY-THING.
THEY DECIDED I WAS THEIR ENEMY WITHOUT EVEN KNOWING ME, REALLY, AND THEY--
IT'S GONNA BE ALL RIGHT. WE'LL FIGURE THIS OUT.
I JUST WISH... I KNEW HOW THIS ORDER OF ABADDON FITS INTO EVERYTHING.
I WISH I KNEW HOW MY PARENTS WERE INVOLVED.
YOU COULD ASK THEM.
ARE YOU KIDDING? I CAN'T JUST ASK THEM ABOUT THAT. ESPECIALLY NOT WITH YOU-- THE STRANGE BOY I'VE INVITED INTO MY BED-ROOM.
EEL LIKE THIS IS JUST...SO MUCH BIGGER THAN VER IMAGINED. WHATEVER CHERYL AND JASON ARE UP TO, THEY'RE MESSING WITH MY FRIENDS, TOO.
I NEED O WARN THEM.
I NEED TO WARN--

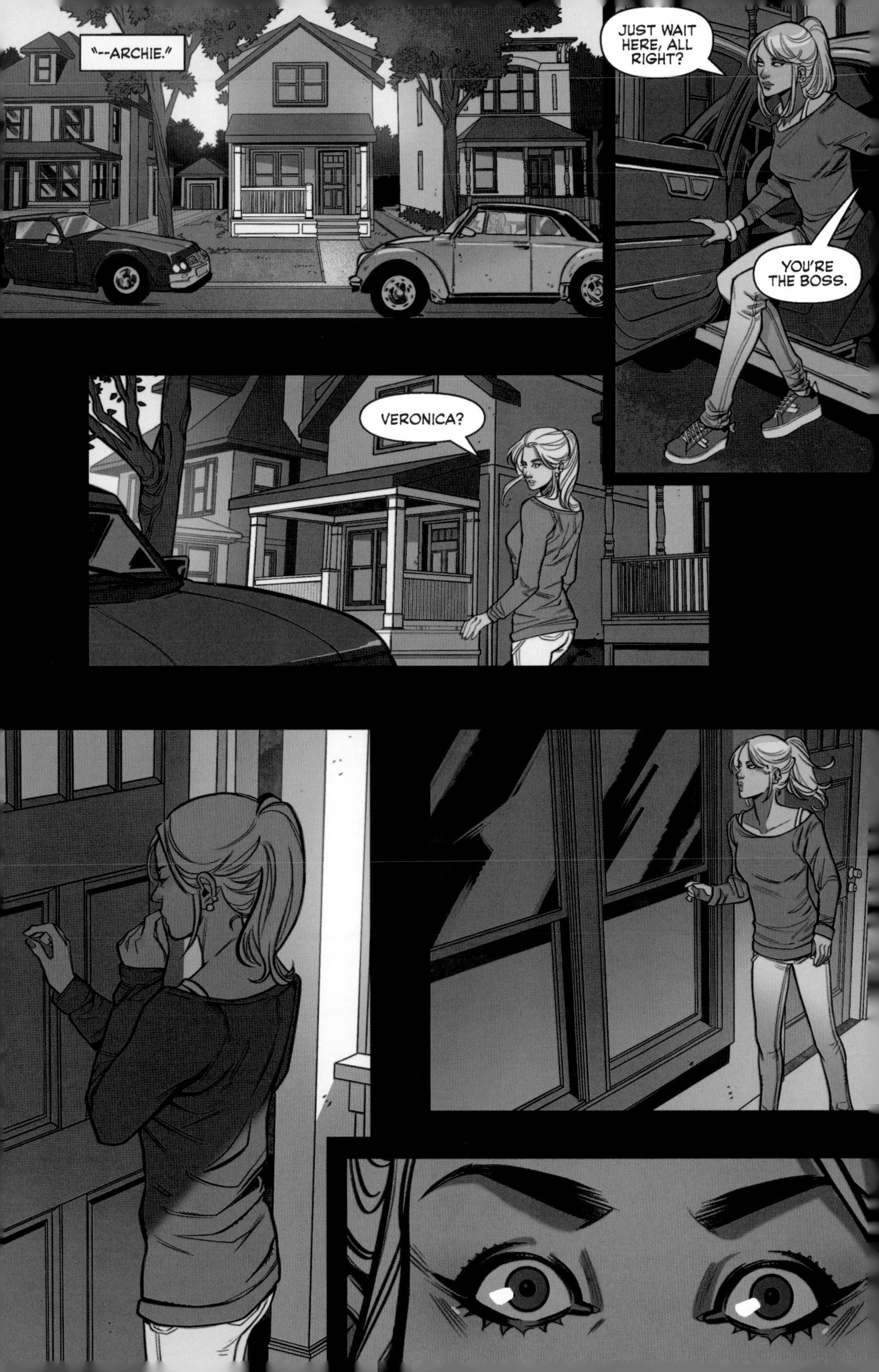
"--ARCHIE."
JUST WAIT HERE, ALL RIGHT?
YOU'RE THE BOSS.
VERONICA?

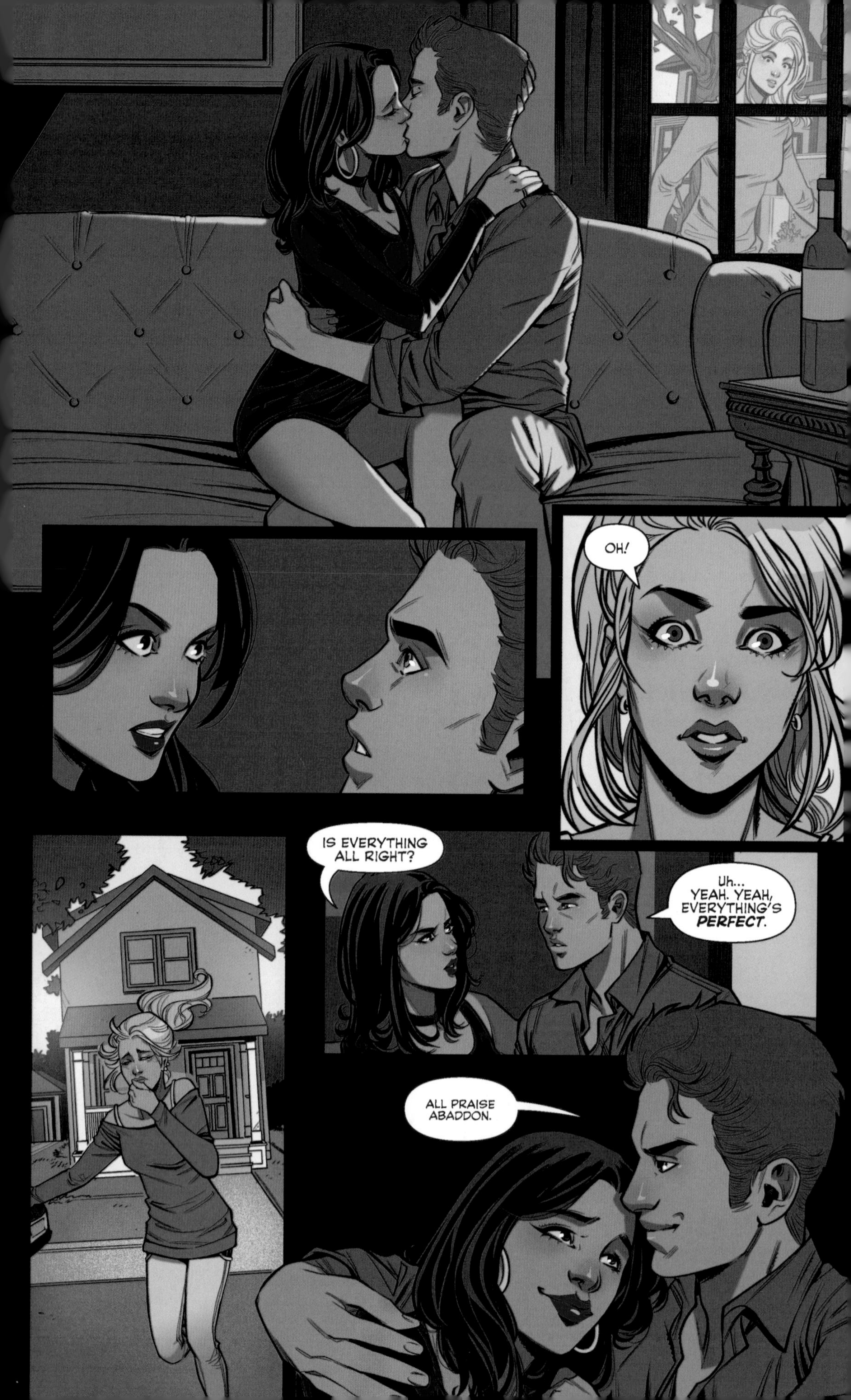
OH!
IS EVERYTHING ALL RIGHT?
Uh... YEAH. YEAH, EVERYTHING'S *PERFECT*.
ALL PRAISE ABADDON.

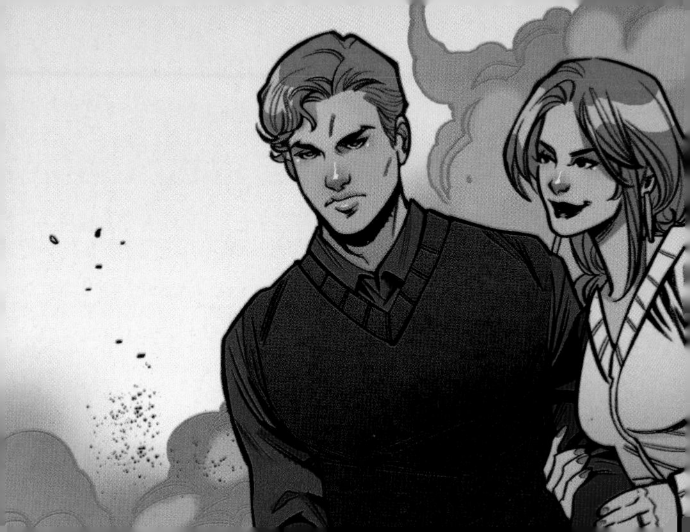

CHAPTER FIVE

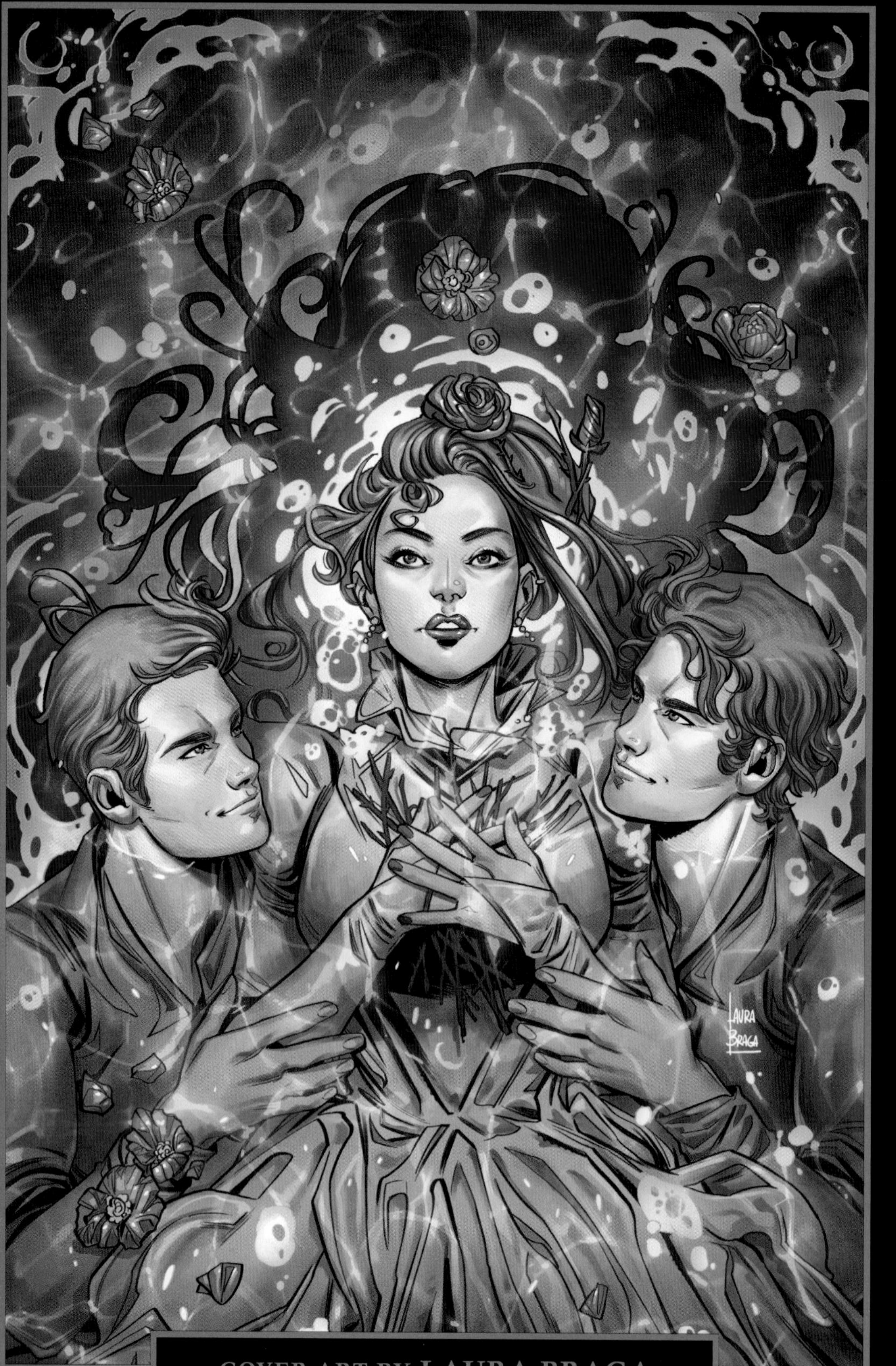
LAURA BRAGA

COVER ART BY LAURA BRAGA

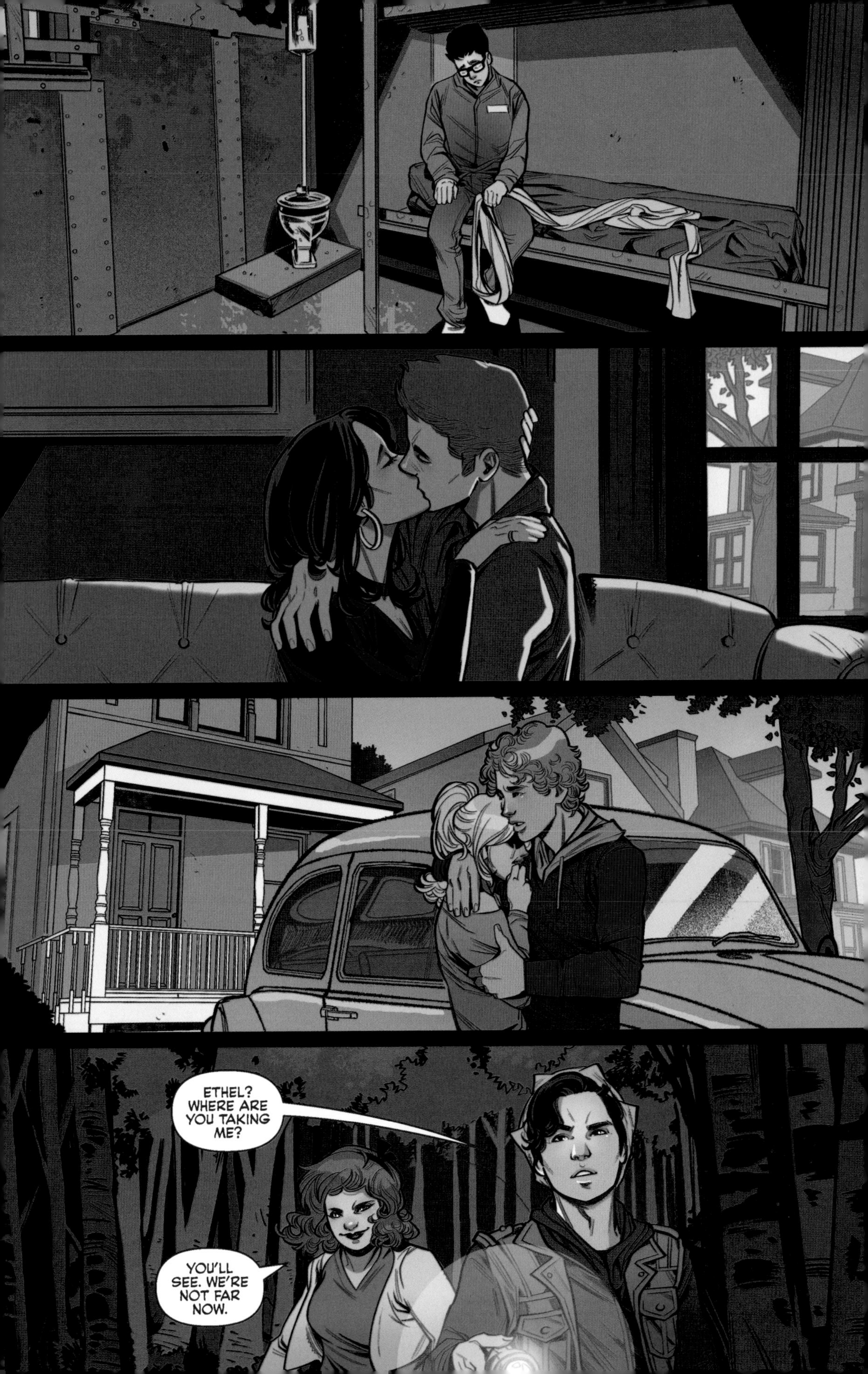
ETHEL? WHERE ARE YOU TAKING ME?
YOU'LL SEE. WE'RE NOT FAR NOW.

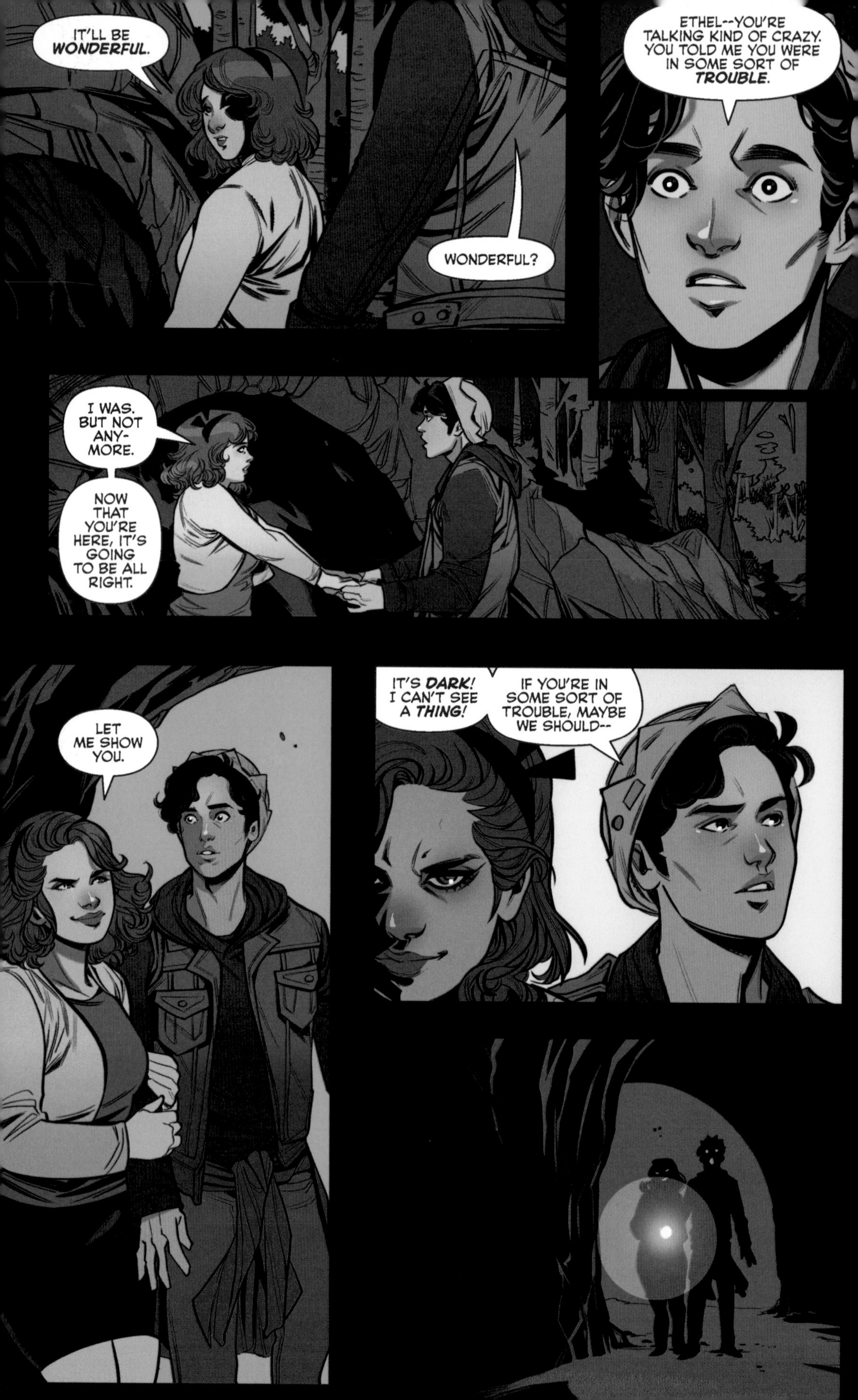
IT'LL BE **WONDERFUL**.
WONDERFUL?
ETHEL--YOU'RE TALKING KIND OF CRAZY. YOU TOLD ME YOU WERE IN SOME SORT OF **TROUBLE**.
I WAS. BUT NOT ANY-MORE.
NOW THAT YOU'RE HERE, IT'S GOING TO BE ALL RIGHT.
LET ME SHOW YOU.
IT'S **DARK**! I CAN'T SEE A **THING**!
IF YOU'RE IN SOME SORT OF TROUBLE, MAYBE WE SHOULD--

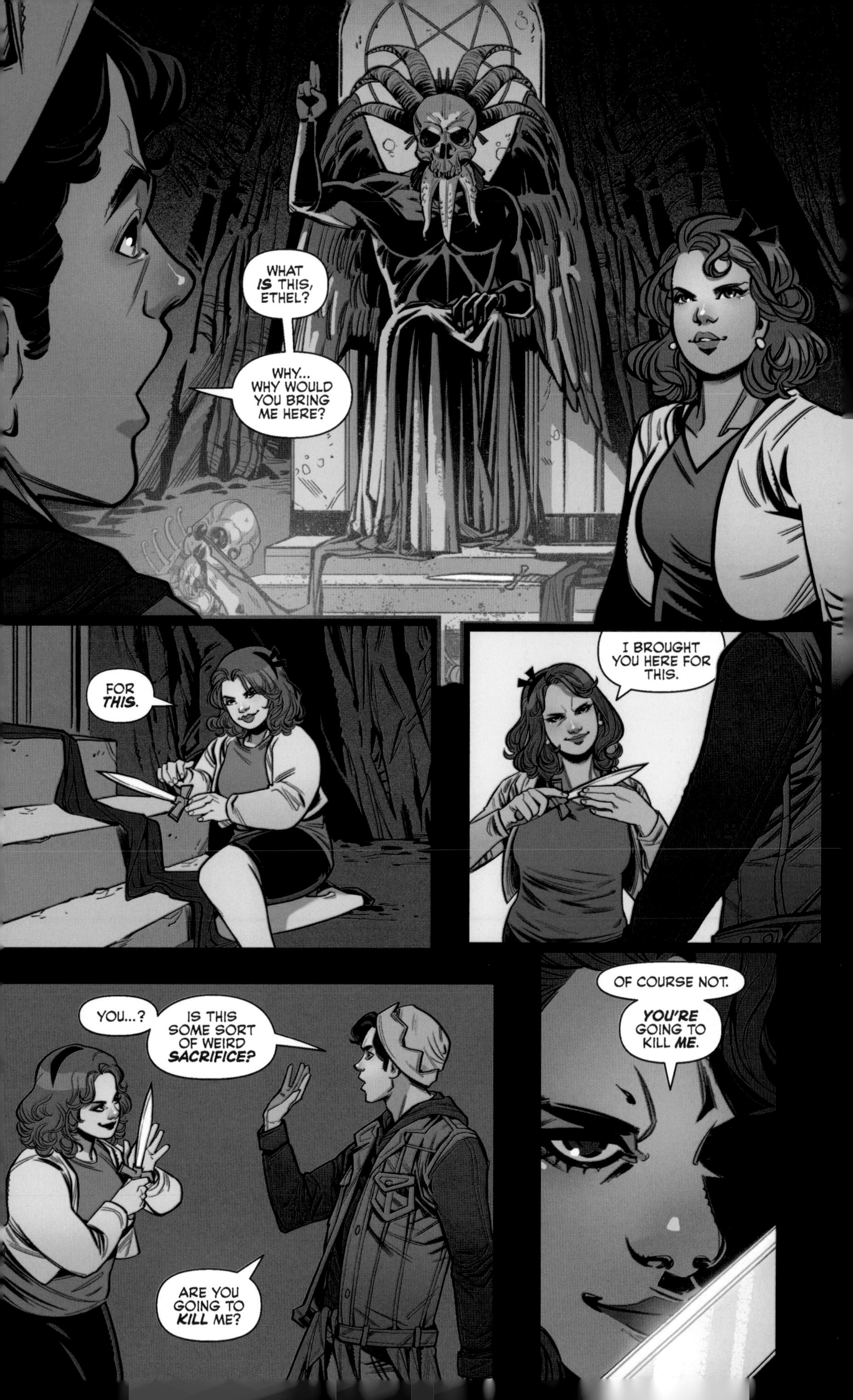
WHAT *IS* THIS, ETHEL?
WHY... WHY WOULD YOU BRING ME HERE?
FOR *THIS*.
I BROUGHT YOU HERE FOR THIS.
YOU...?
IS THIS SOME SORT OF WEIRD *SACRIFICE?*
ARE YOU GOING TO *KILL* ME?
OF COURSE NOT.
YOU'RE GOING TO KILL *ME*.

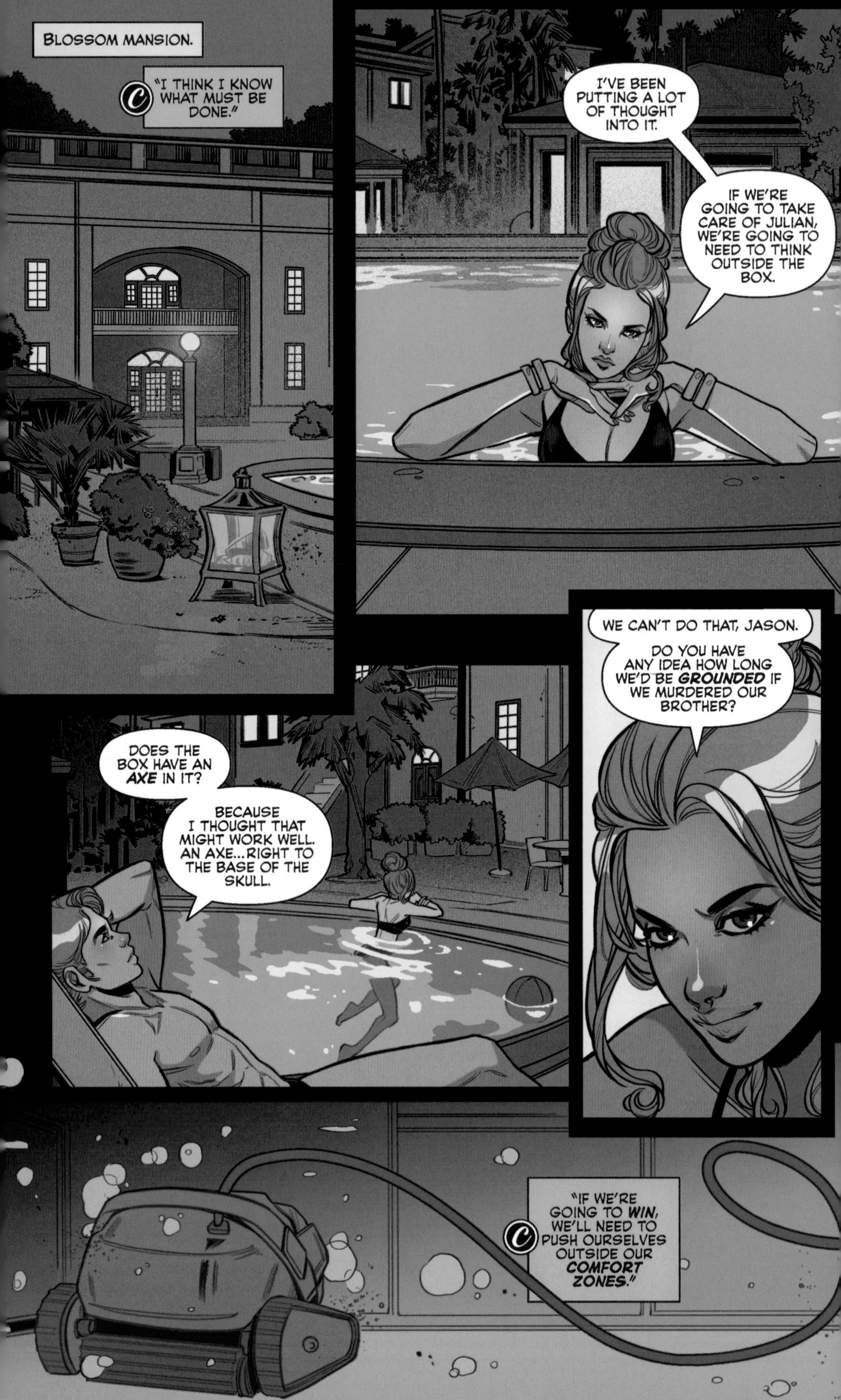
BLOSSOM MANSION.
"I THINK I KNOW WHAT MUST BE DONE."
I'VE BEEN PUTTING A LOT OF THOUGHT INTO IT.
IF WE'RE GOING TO TAKE CARE OF JULIAN, WE'RE GOING TO NEED TO THINK OUTSIDE THE BOX.
DOES THE BOX HAVE AN ***AXE*** IN IT?
BECAUSE I THOUGHT THAT MIGHT WORK WELL. AN AXE...RIGHT TO THE BASE OF THE SKULL.
WE CAN'T DO THAT, JASON.
DO YOU HAVE ANY IDEA HOW LONG WE'D BE ***GROUNDED*** IF WE MURDERED OUR BROTHER?
"IF WE'RE GOING TO ***WIN***, WE'LL NEED TO PUSH OURSELVES OUTSIDE OUR ***COMFORT ZONES***."

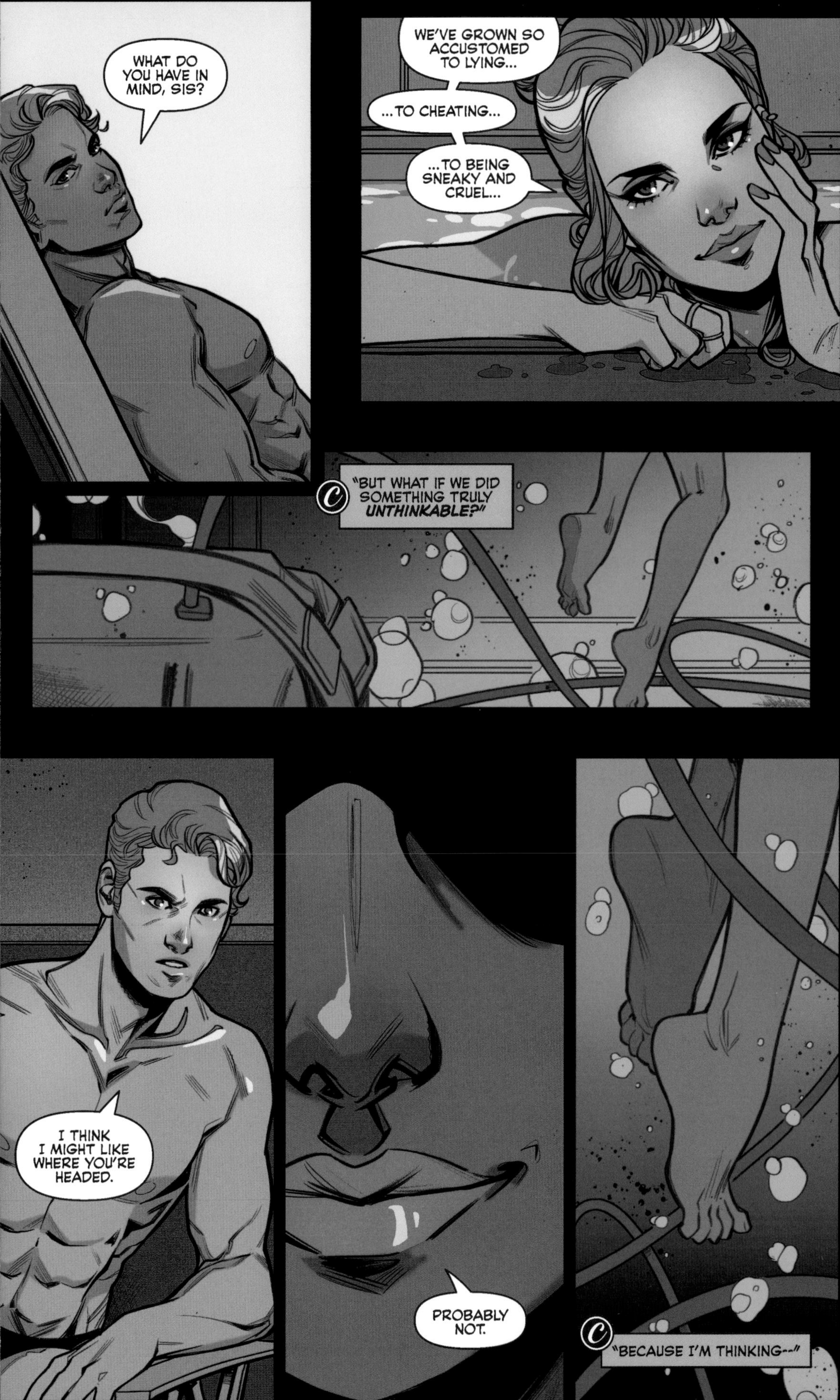

WHAT DO YOU HAVE IN MIND, SIS?
WE'VE GROWN SO ACCUSTOMED TO LYING...
...TO CHEATING...
...TO BEING SNEAKY AND CRUEL...
"BUT WHAT IF WE DID SOMETHING TRULY *UNTHINKABLE?*"
I THINK I MIGHT LIKE WHERE YOU'RE HEADED.
PROBABLY NOT.
"BECAUSE I'M THINKING--"

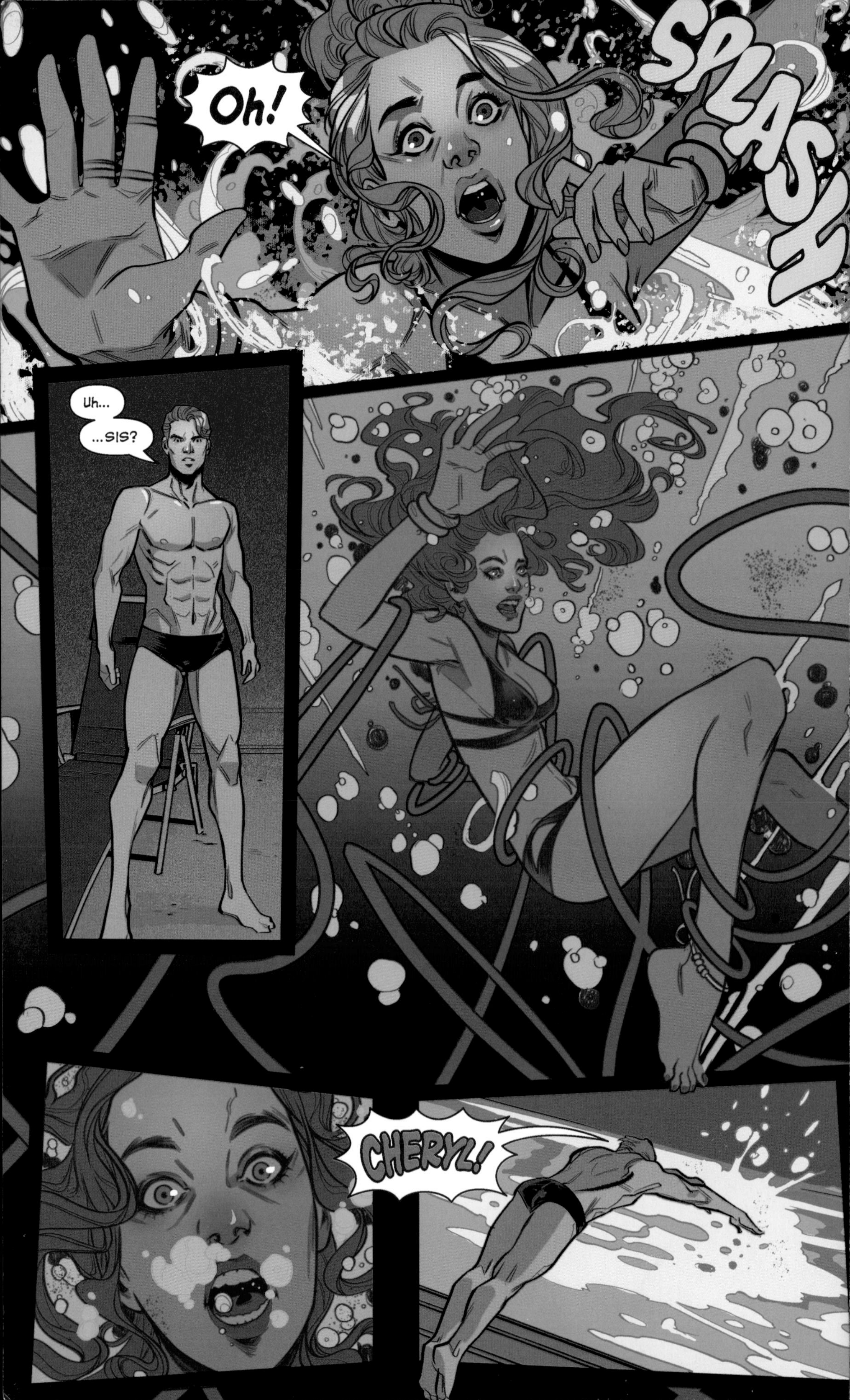
Oh!
SPLASH
Uh...
...SIS?
CHERYL!

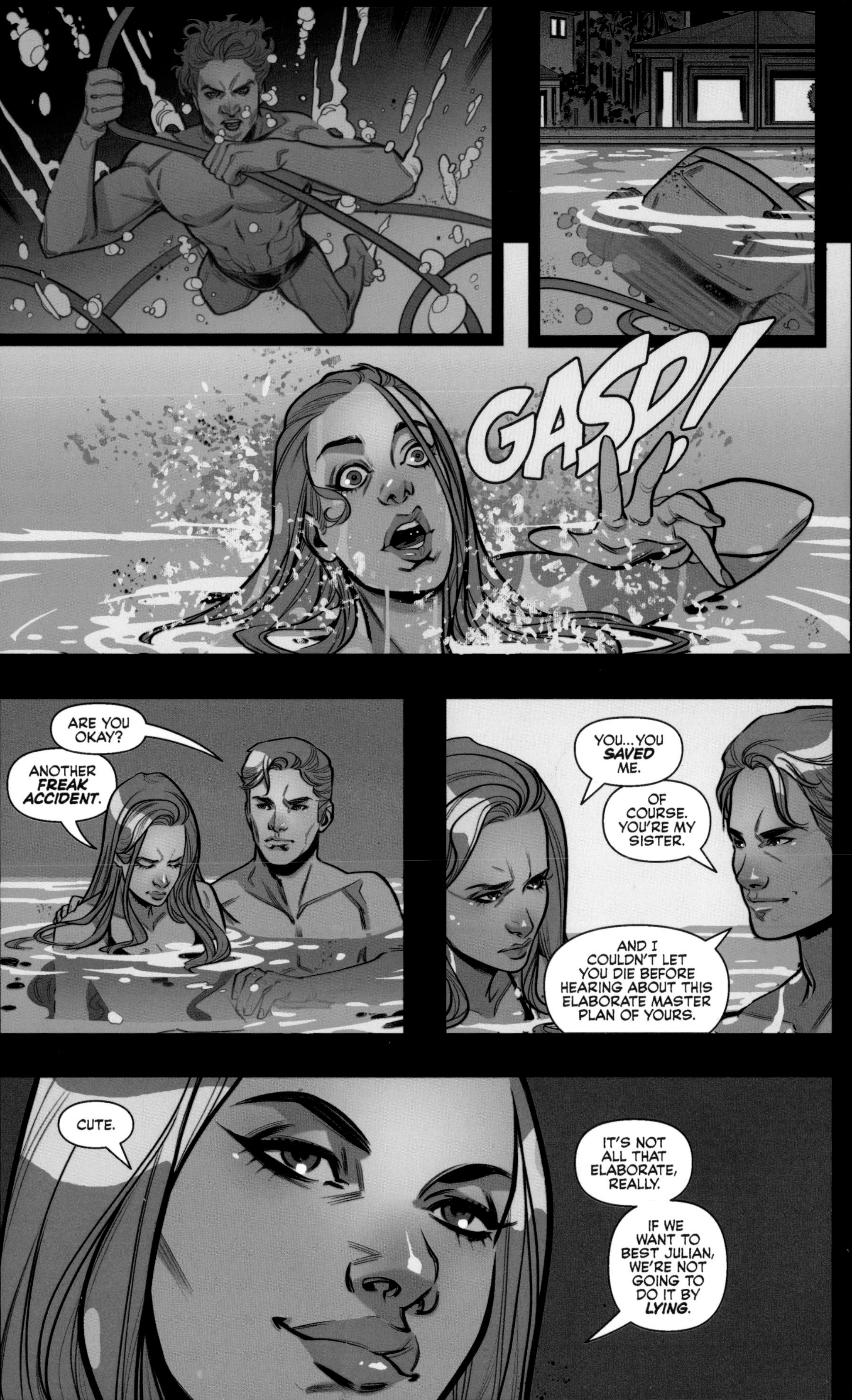
GASP!
ARE YOU OKAY?
ANOTHER FREAK ACCIDENT.
YOU... YOU SAVED ME.
OF COURSE. YOU'RE MY SISTER.
AND I COULDN'T LET YOU DIE BEFORE HEARING ABOUT THIS ELABORATE MASTER PLAN OF YOURS.
CUTE.
IT'S NOT ALL THAT ELABORATE, REALLY.
IF WE WANT TO BEST JULIAN, WE'RE NOT GOING TO DO IT BY LYING.

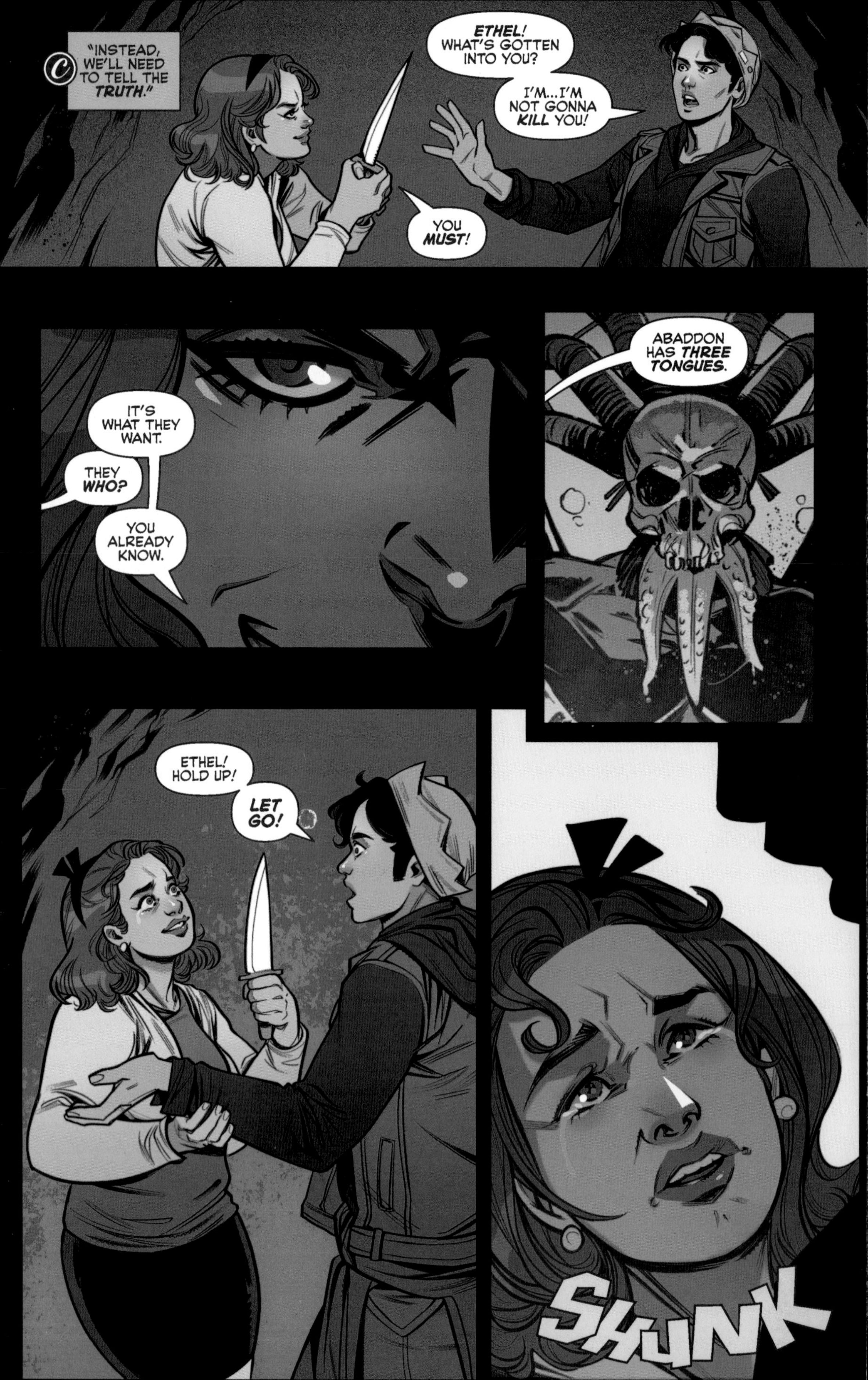
"INSTEAD, WE'LL NEED TO TELL THE TRUTH."
ETHEL! WHAT'S GOTTEN INTO YOU?
I'M...I'M NOT GONNA KILL YOU!
YOU MUST!
IT'S WHAT THEY WANT.
THEY WHO?
YOU ALREADY KNOW.
ABADDON HAS THREE TONGUES.
ETHEL! HOLD UP!
LET GO!
SHUNK

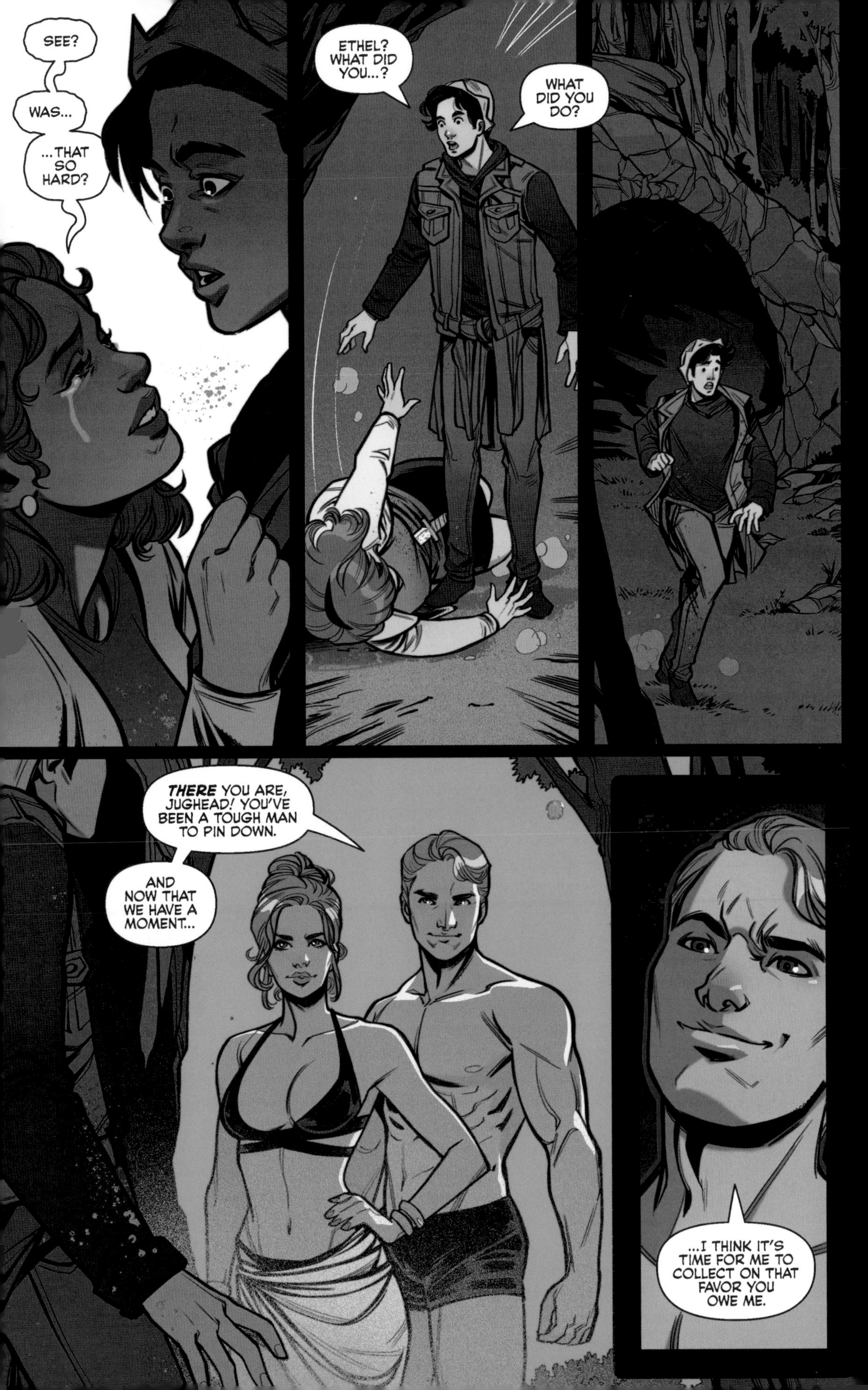
SEE?
WAS...
...THAT SO HARD?
ETHEL? WHAT DID YOU...?
WHAT DID YOU DO?
THERE YOU ARE, JUGHEAD! YOU'VE BEEN A TOUGH MAN TO PIN DOWN.
AND NOW THAT WE HAVE A MOMENT...
...I THINK IT'S TIME FOR ME TO COLLECT ON THAT FAVOR YOU OWE ME.

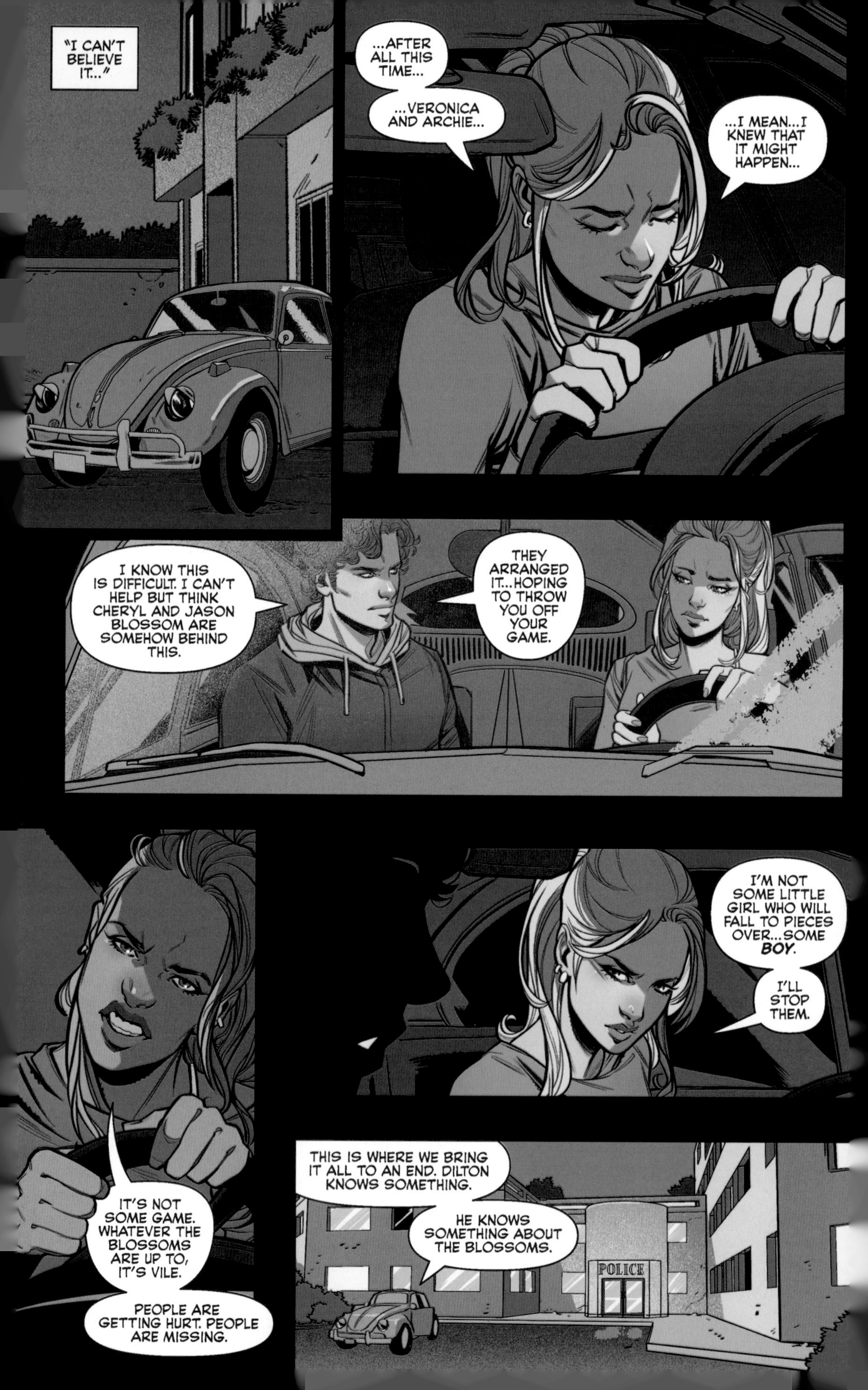
"I CAN'T BELIEVE IT..."
...AFTER ALL THIS TIME...
...VERONICA AND ARCHIE...
...I MEAN...I KNEW THAT IT MIGHT HAPPEN...
I KNOW THIS IS DIFFICULT. I CAN'T HELP BUT THINK CHERYL AND JASON BLOSSOM ARE SOMEHOW BEHIND THIS.
THEY ARRANGED IT...HOPING TO THROW YOU OFF YOUR GAME.
I'M NOT SOME LITTLE GIRL WHO WILL FALL TO PIECES OVER...SOME ***BOY***.
I'LL STOP THEM.
IT'S NOT SOME GAME. WHATEVER THE BLOSSOMS ARE UP TO, IT'S VILE.
PEOPLE ARE GETTING HURT. PEOPLE ARE MISSING.
THIS IS WHERE WE BRING IT ALL TO AN END. DILTON KNOWS SOMETHING.
HE KNOWS SOMETHING ABOUT THE BLOSSOMS.
POLICE

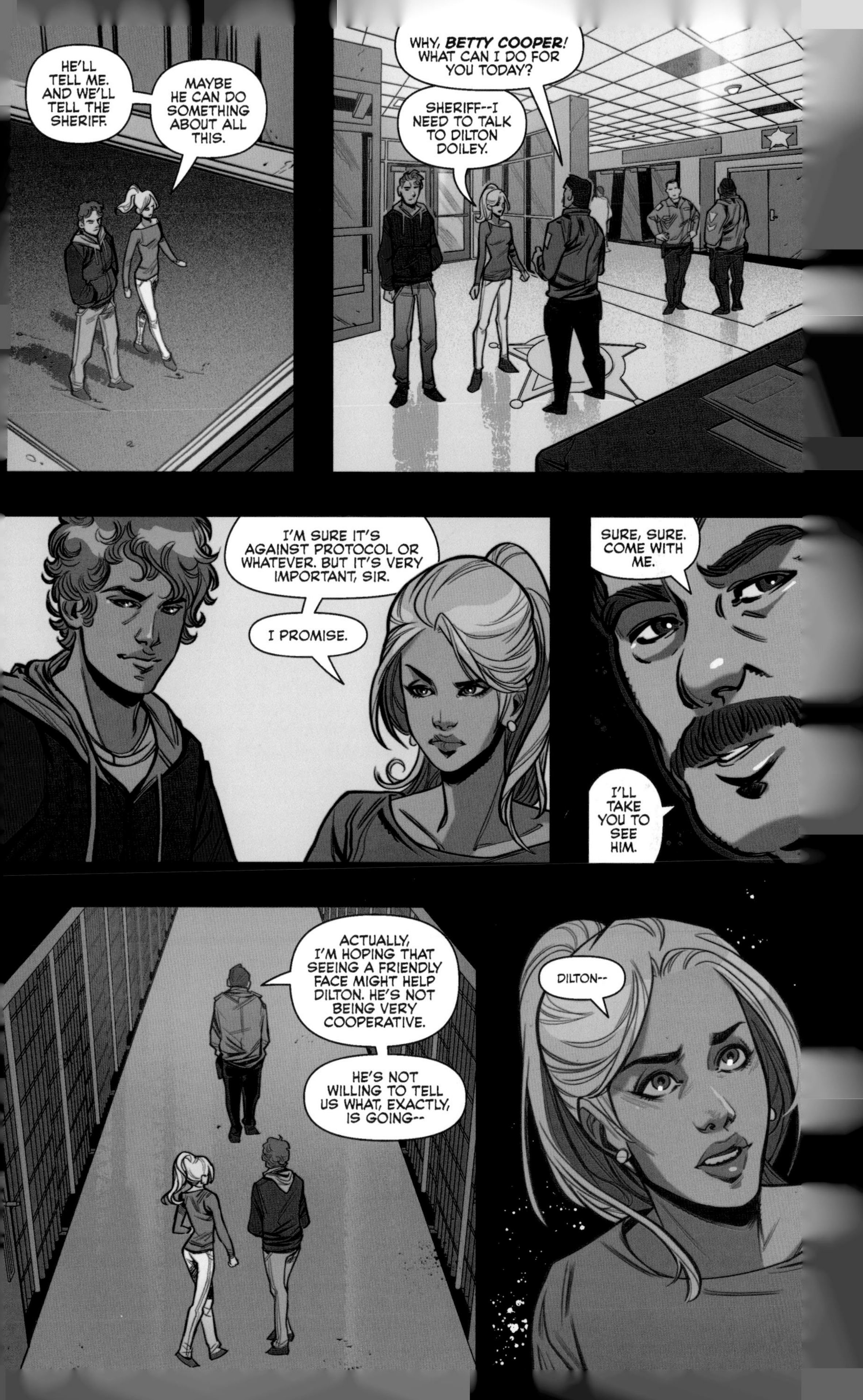
HE'LL TELL ME. AND WE'LL TELL THE SHERIFF.
MAYBE HE CAN DO SOMETHING ABOUT ALL THIS.
WHY, BETTY COOPER! WHAT CAN I DO FOR YOU TODAY?
SHERIFF--I NEED TO TALK TO DILTON DOILEY.
I'M SURE IT'S AGAINST PROTOCOL OR WHATEVER. BUT IT'S VERY IMPORTANT, SIR.
I PROMISE.
SURE, SURE. COME WITH ME.
I'LL TAKE YOU TO SEE HIM.
ACTUALLY, I'M HOPING THAT SEEING A FRIENDLY FACE MIGHT HELP DILTON. HE'S NOT BEING VERY COOPERATIVE.
HE'S NOT WILLING TO TELL US WHAT, EXACTLY, IS GOING--
DILTON--

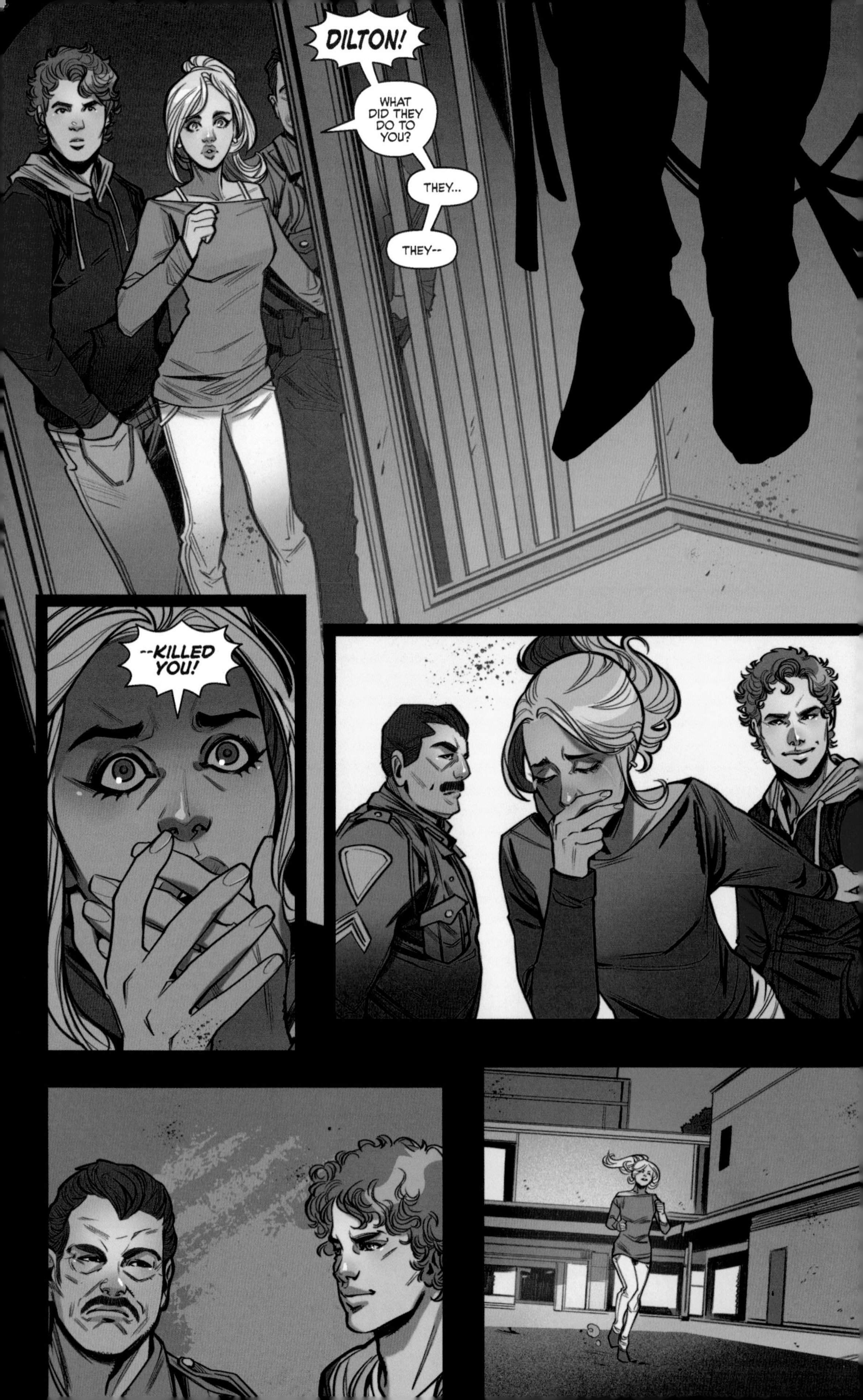
DILTON!
WHAT DID THEY DO TO YOU?
THEY...
THEY--
--KILLED YOU!

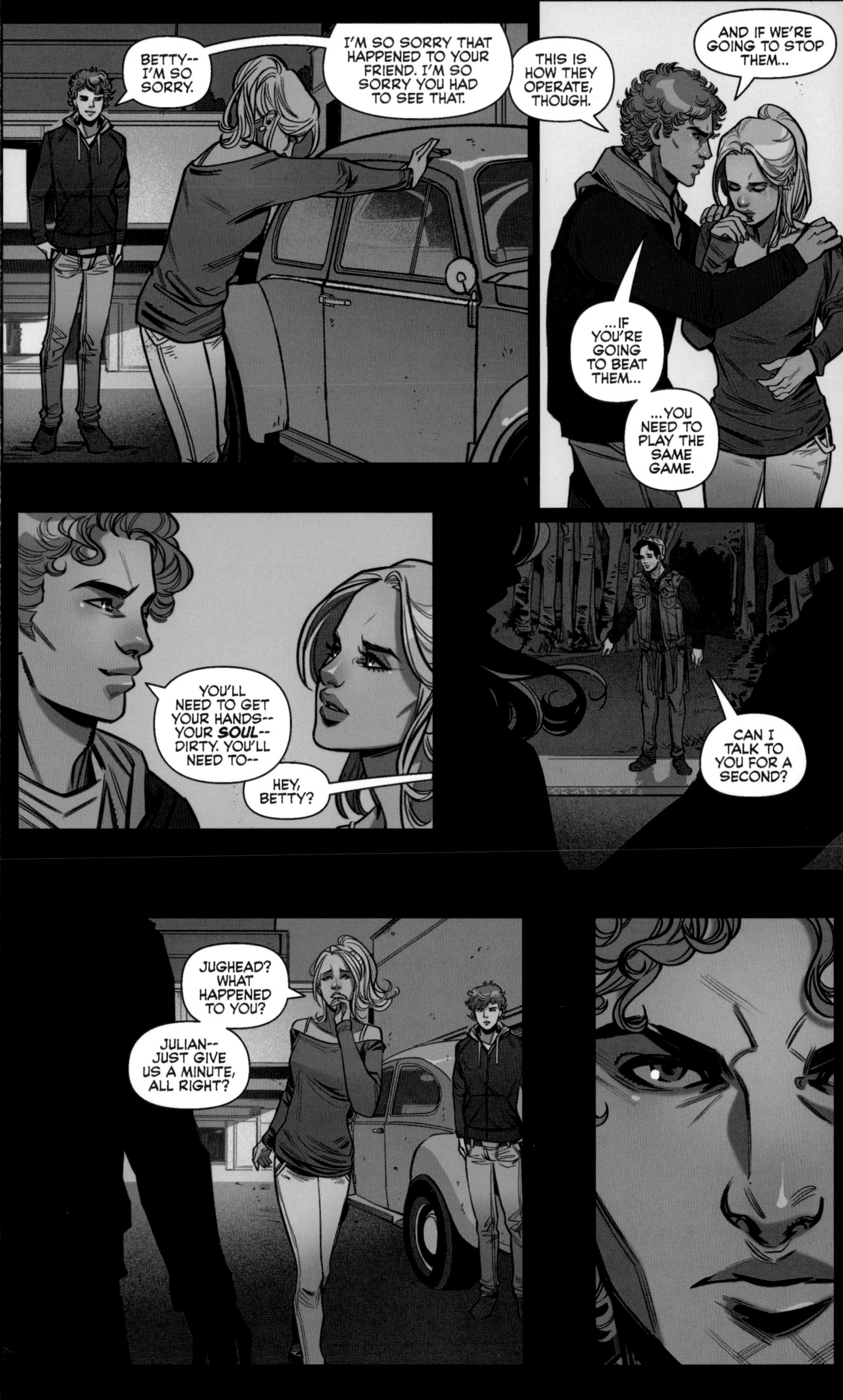
BETTY-- I'M SO SORRY.
I'M SO SORRY THAT HAPPENED TO YOUR FRIEND. I'M SO SORRY YOU HAD TO SEE THAT.
THIS IS HOW THEY OPERATE, THOUGH.
AND IF WE'RE GOING TO STOP THEM...
...IF YOU'RE GOING TO BEAT THEM...
...YOU NEED TO PLAY THE SAME GAME.
YOU'LL NEED TO GET YOUR HANDS-- YOUR SOUL-- DIRTY. YOU'LL NEED TO--
HEY, BETTY?
CAN I TALK TO YOU FOR A SECOND?
JUGHEAD? WHAT HAPPENED TO YOU?
JULIAN-- JUST GIVE US A MINUTE, ALL RIGHT?

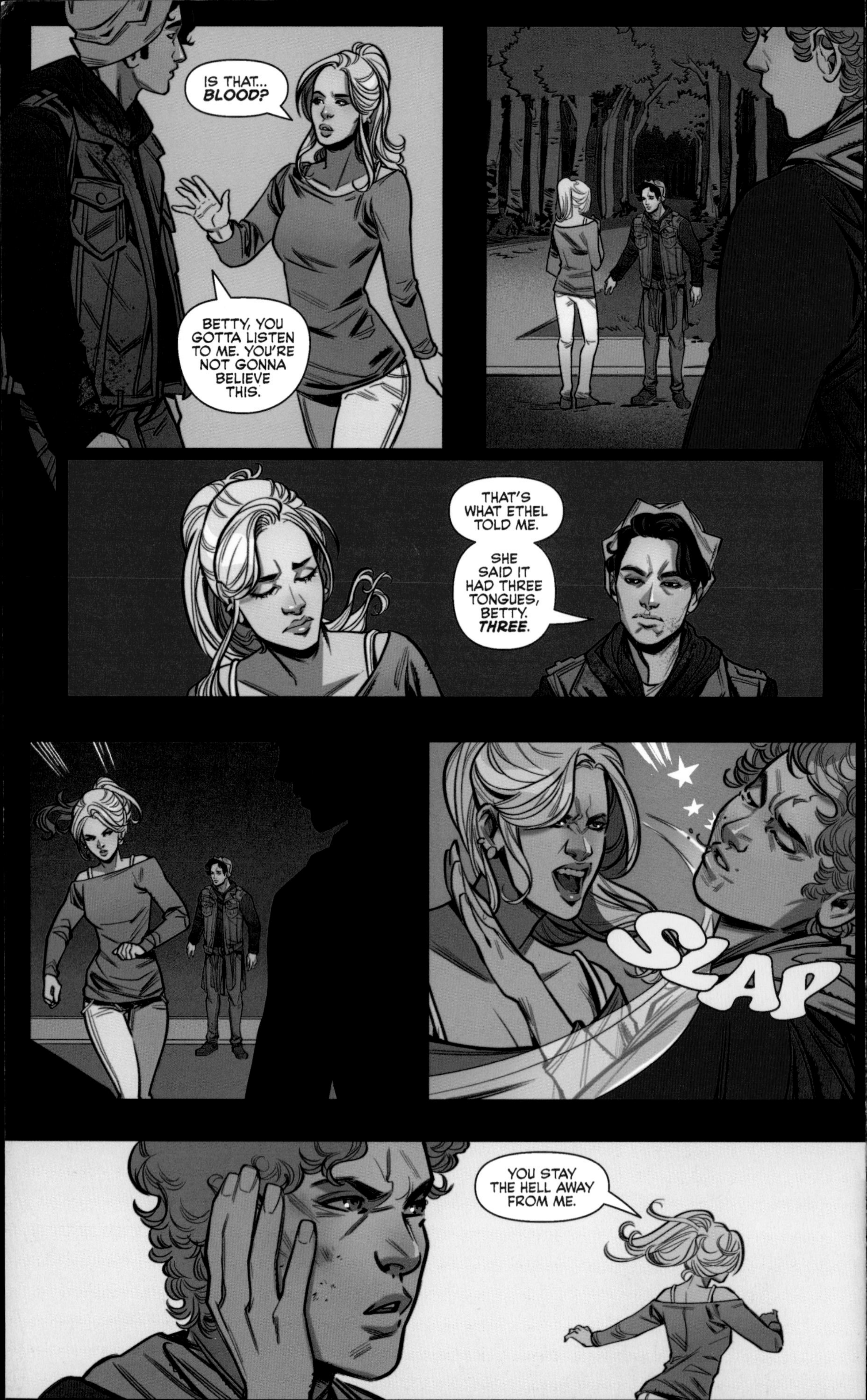
IS THAT... BLOOD?
BETTY, YOU GOTTA LISTEN TO ME. YOU'RE NOT GONNA BELIEVE THIS.
THAT'S WHAT ETHEL TOLD ME.
SHE SAID IT HAD THREE TONGUES, BETTY. THREE.
SLAP
YOU STAY THE HELL AWAY FROM ME.

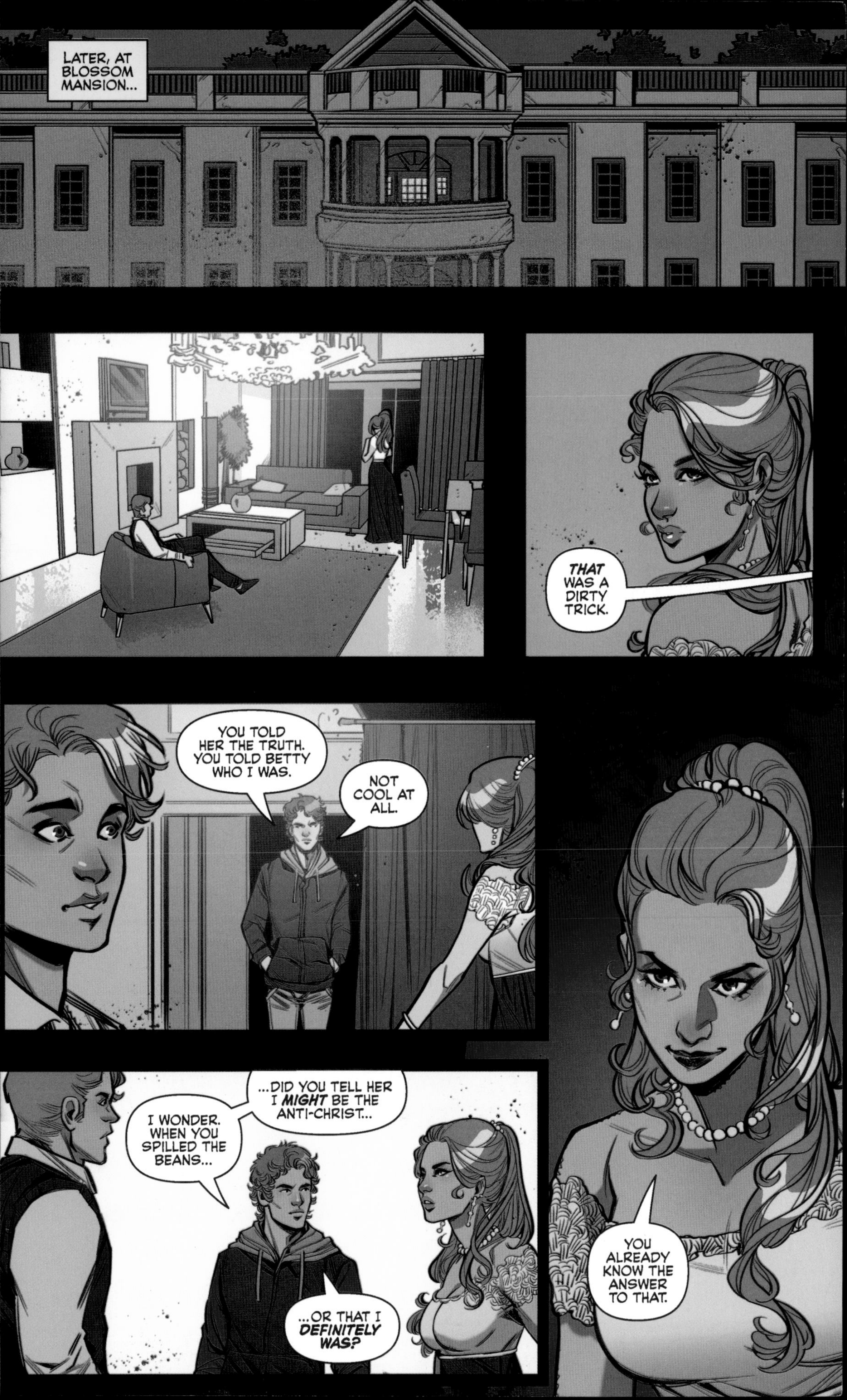
LATER, AT BLOSSOM MANSION...
THAT WAS A DIRTY TRICK.
YOU TOLD HER THE TRUTH. YOU TOLD BETTY WHO I WAS.
NOT COOL AT ALL.
I WONDER. WHEN YOU SPILLED THE BEANS...
...DID YOU TELL HER I MIGHT BE THE ANTI-CHRIST...
...OR THAT I DEFINITELY WAS?
YOU ALREADY KNOW THE ANSWER TO THAT.

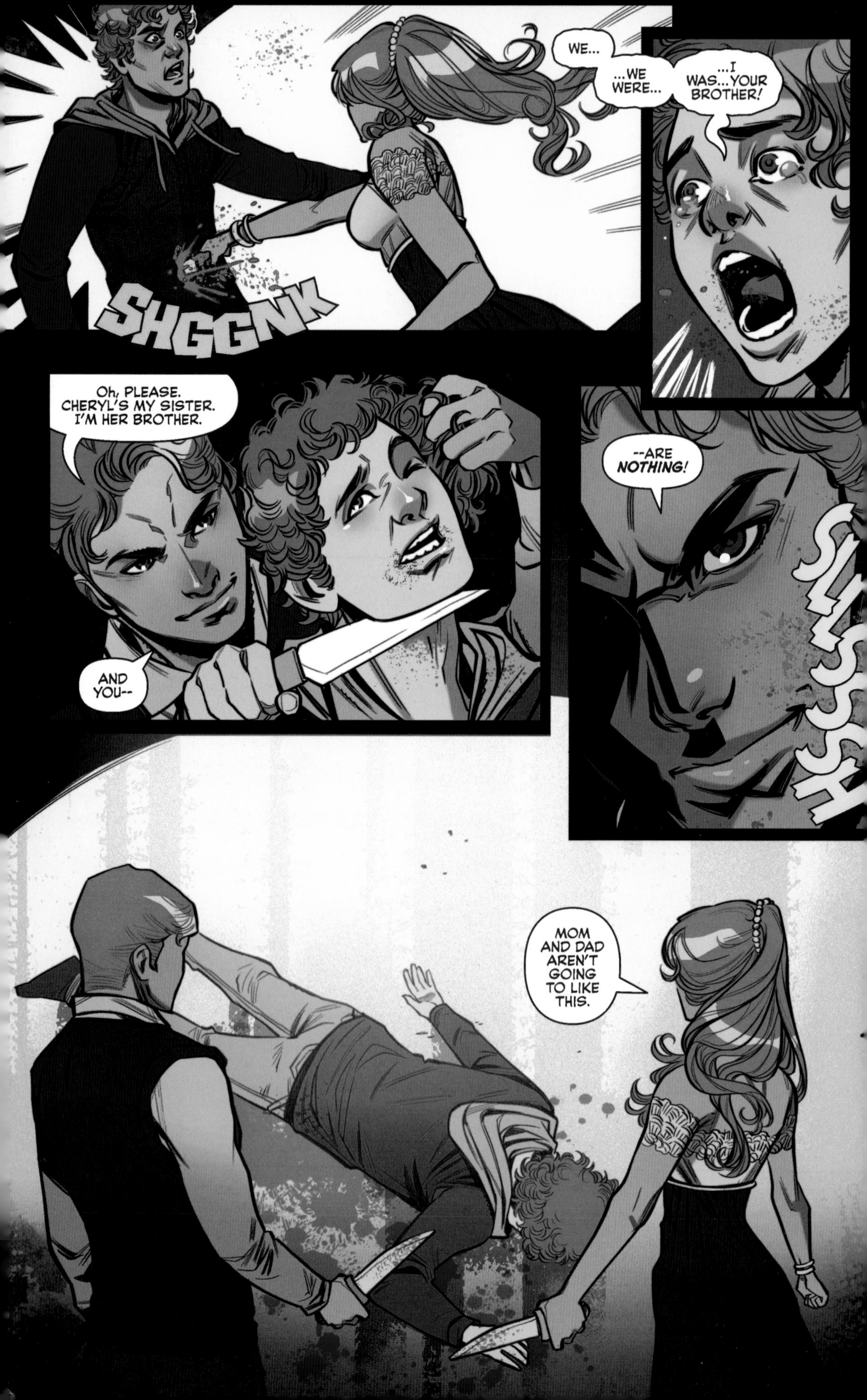
SHGGNK
WE...
...WE WERE...
...I WAS...YOUR BROTHER!
Oh, PLEASE. CHERYL'S MY SISTER. I'M HER BROTHER.
AND YOU--
--ARE NOTHING!
SLISSSH
MOM AND DAD AREN'T GOING TO LIKE THIS.

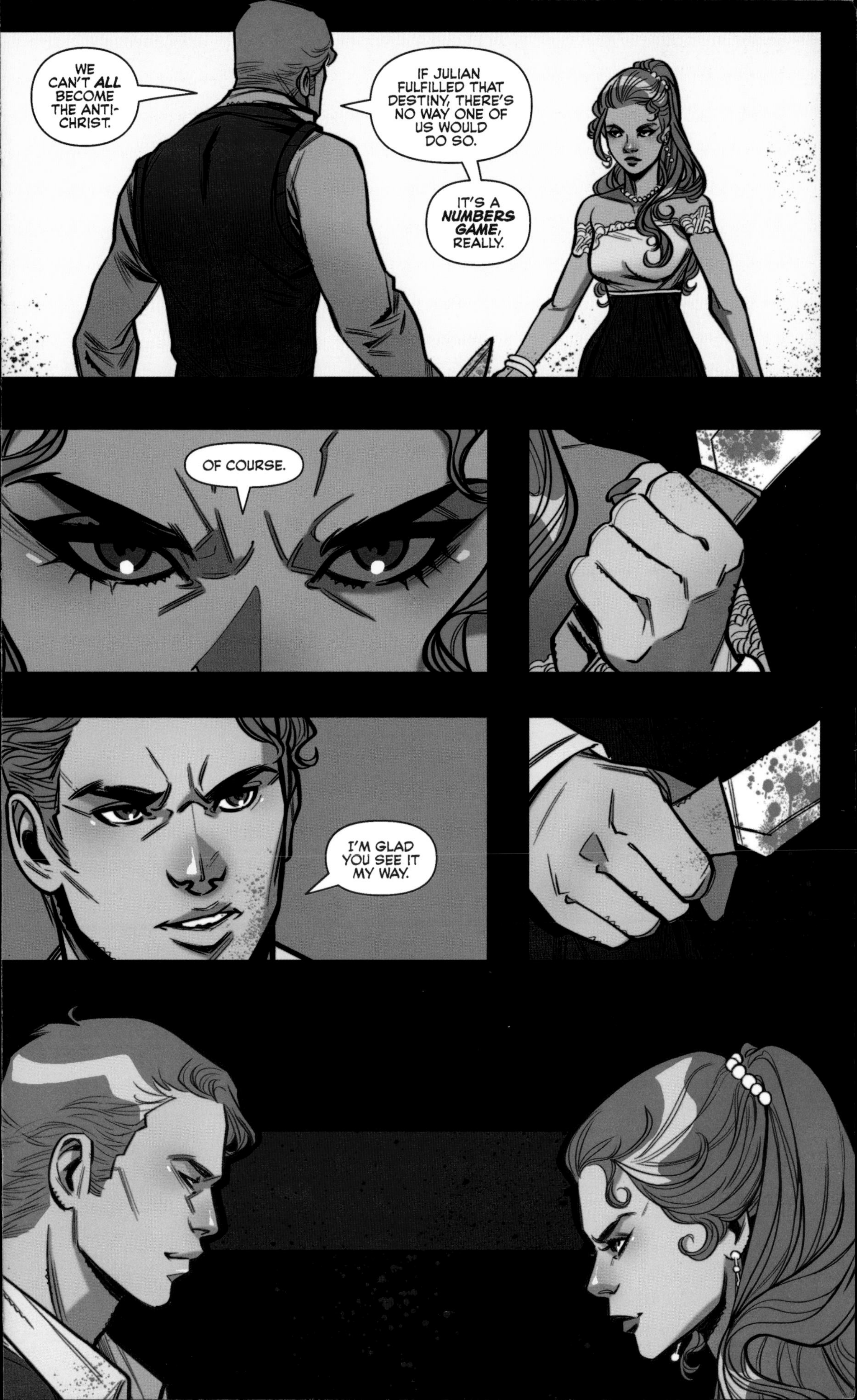
WE CAN'T ALL BECOME THE ANTI-CHRIST.
IF JULIAN FULFILLED THAT DESTINY, THERE'S NO WAY ONE OF US WOULD DO SO.
IT'S A NUMBERS GAME, REALLY.
OF COURSE.
I'M GLAD YOU SEE IT MY WAY.

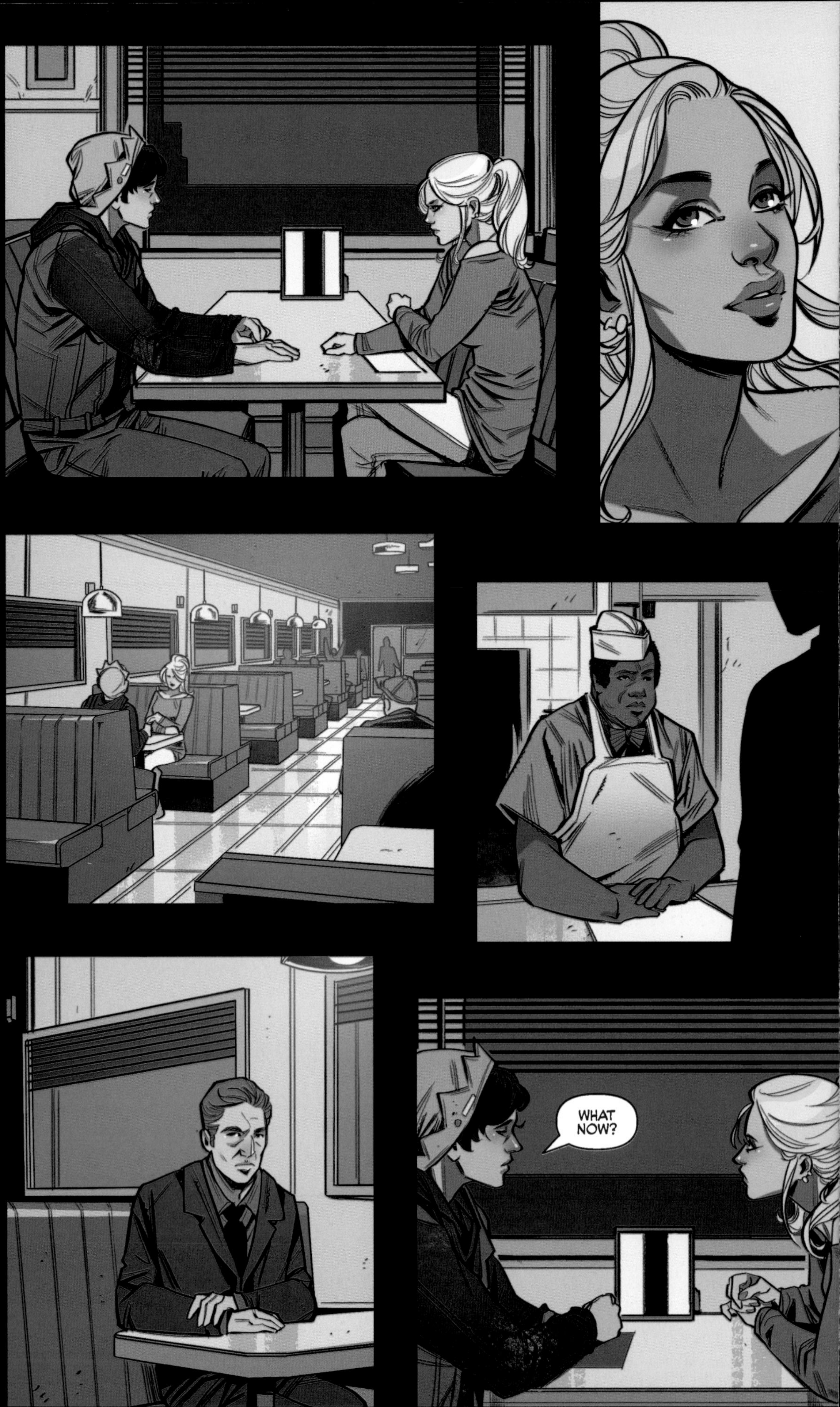
WHAT NOW?

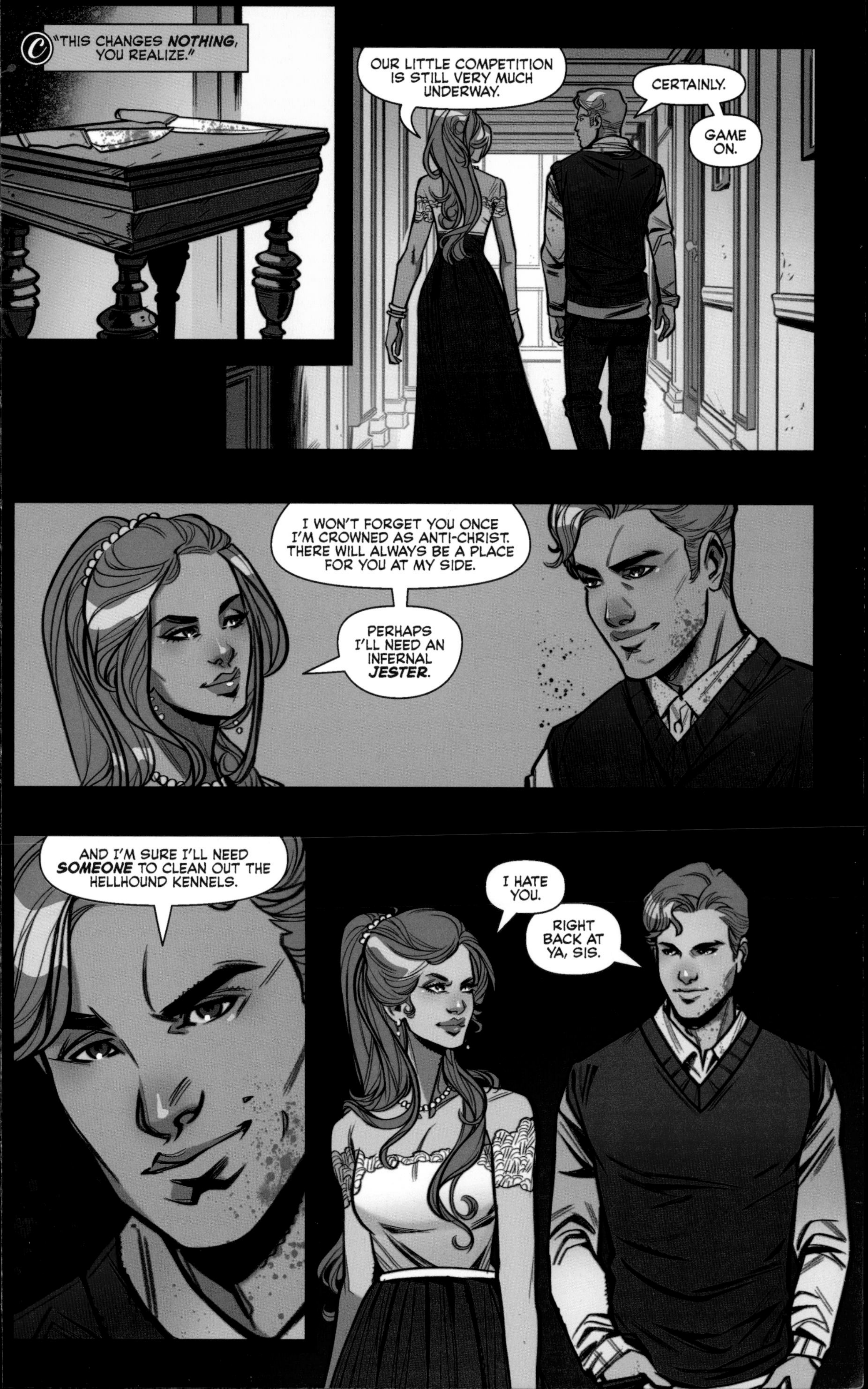
"THIS CHANGES NOTHING, YOU REALIZE."
OUR LITTLE COMPETITION IS STILL VERY MUCH UNDERWAY.
CERTAINLY.
GAME ON.
I WON'T FORGET YOU ONCE I'M CROWNED AS ANTI-CHRIST. THERE WILL ALWAYS BE A PLACE FOR YOU AT MY SIDE.
PERHAPS I'LL NEED AN INFERNAL JESTER.
AND I'M SURE I'LL NEED SOMEONE TO CLEAN OUT THE HELLHOUND KENNELS.
I HATE YOU.
RIGHT BACK AT YA, SIS.

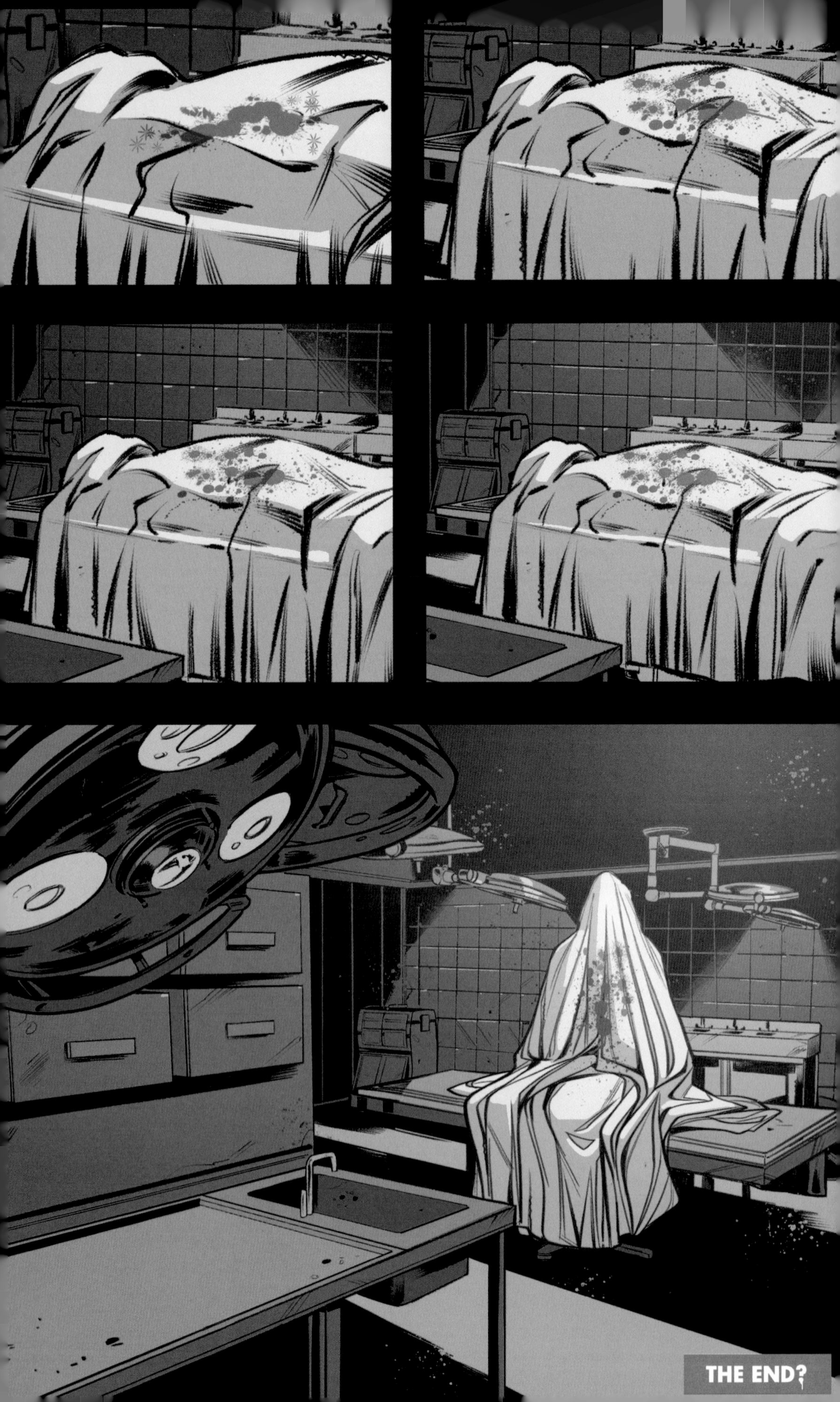
THE END?

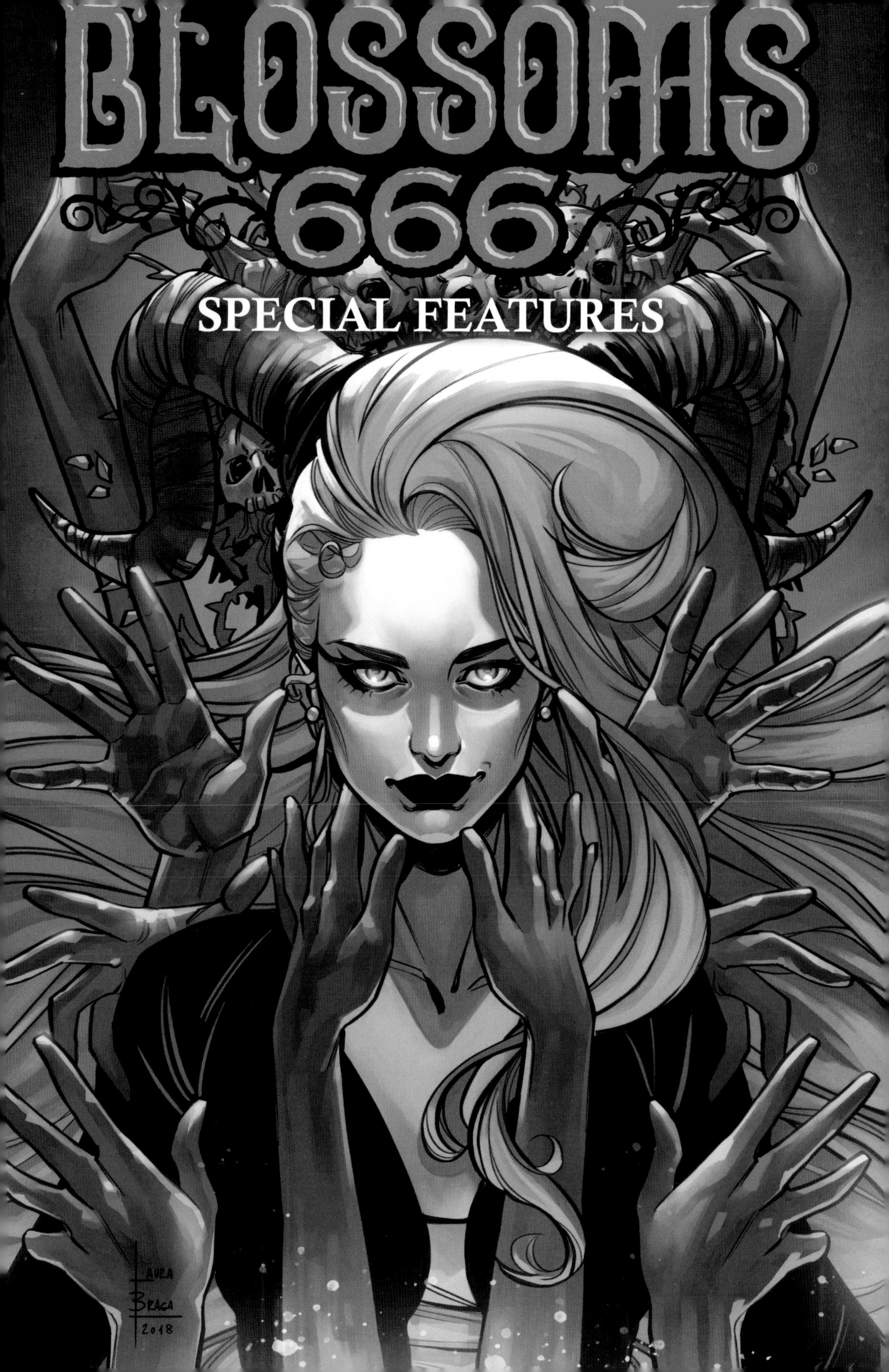
BLOSSOMS 666®
SPECIAL FEATURES
LAURA BRAGA 2018

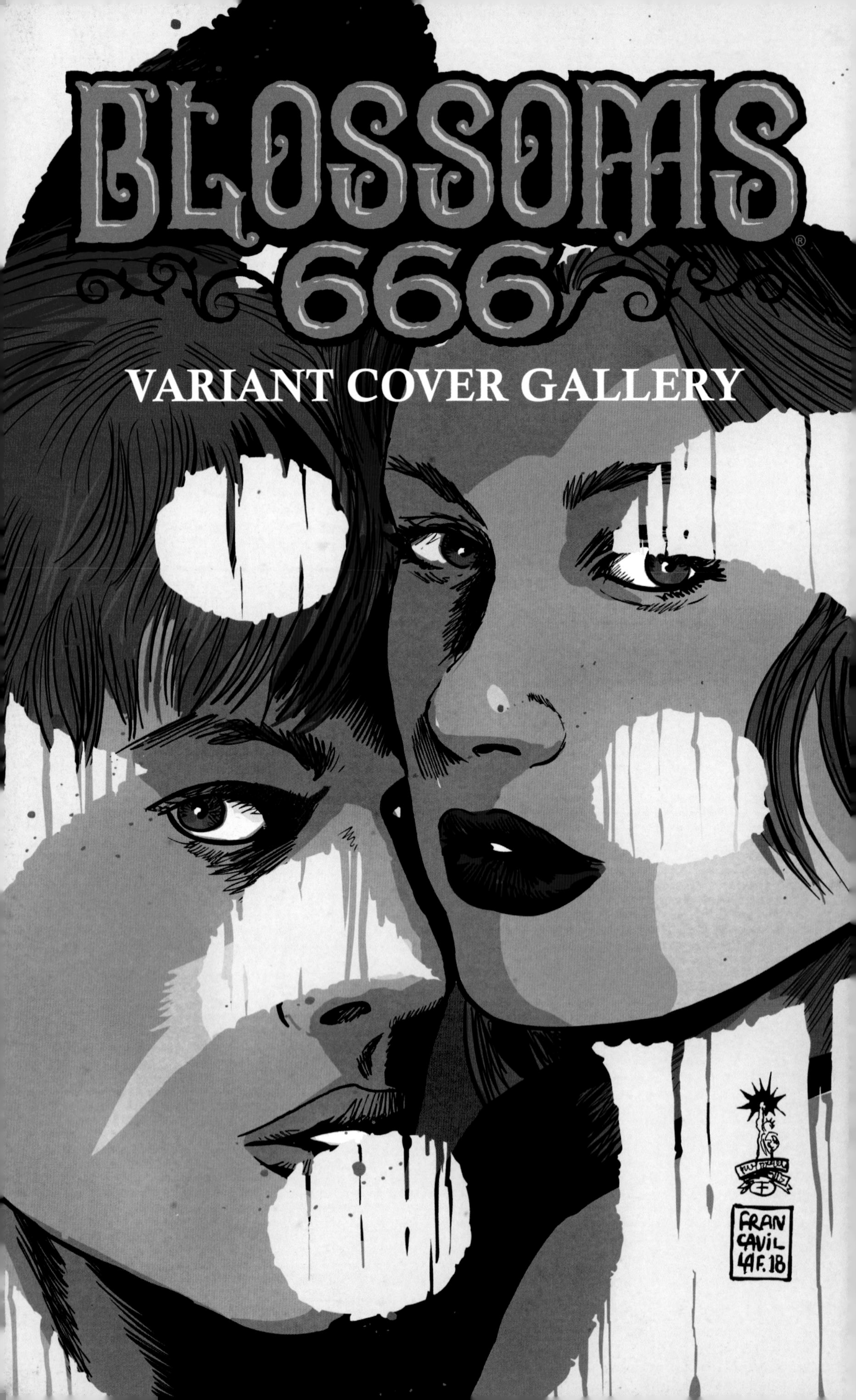
BLOSSOMS 666
VARIANT COVER GALLERY
FRAN CAVIL 14F.18

1.

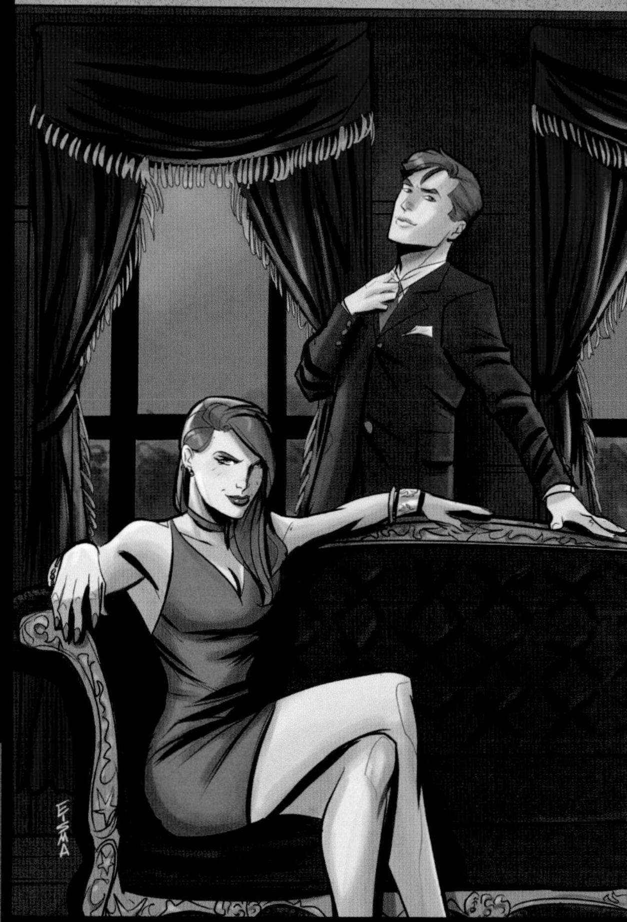
EISMA

2.

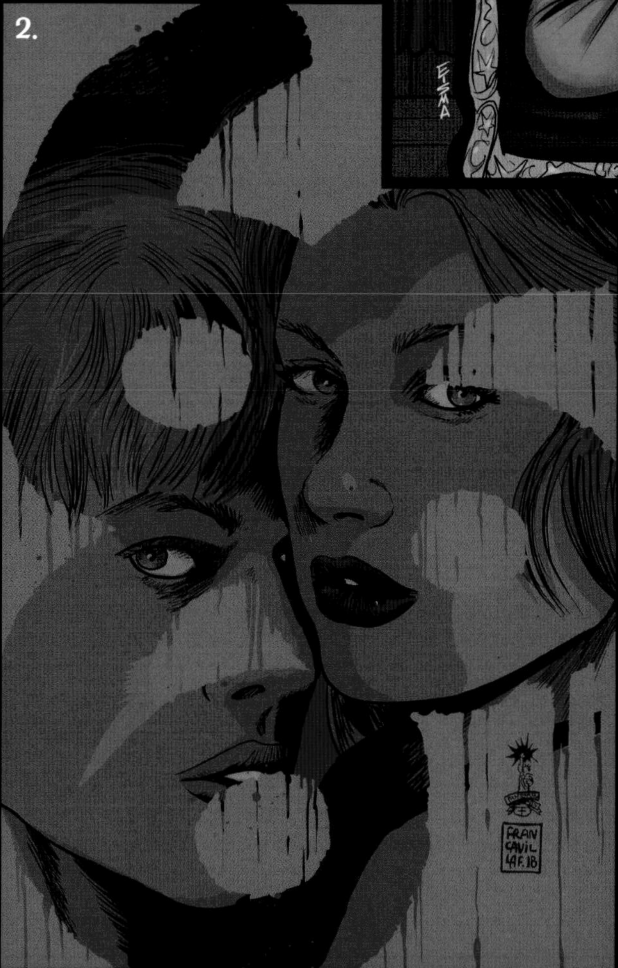

ISSUE ONE

1. JOE EISMA

2. FRANCESCO FRANCAVILLA

ISSUE ONE

3. ROBERT HACK

4. VIC MALHOTRA

3.

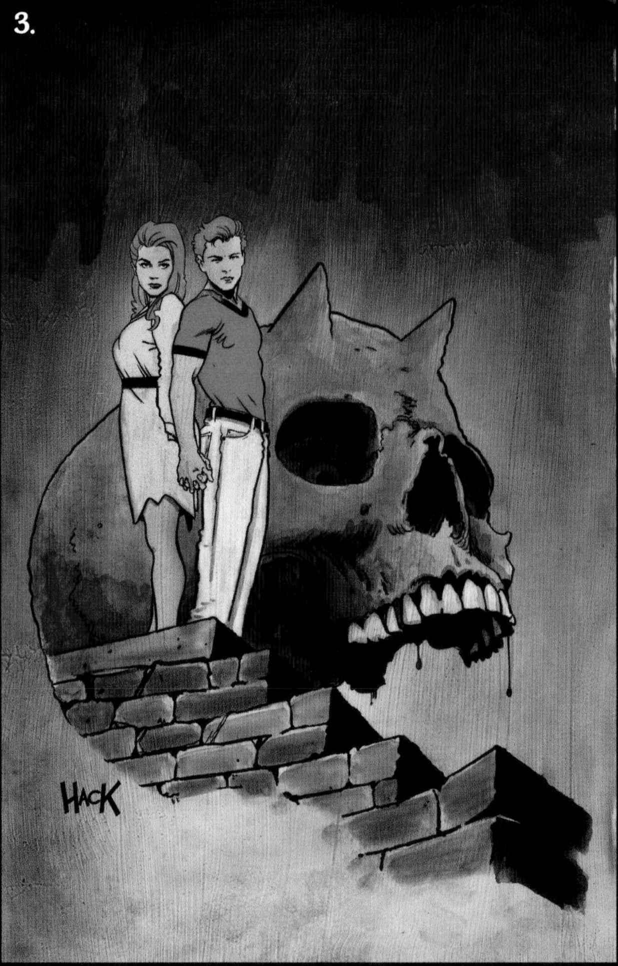
HACK

4.

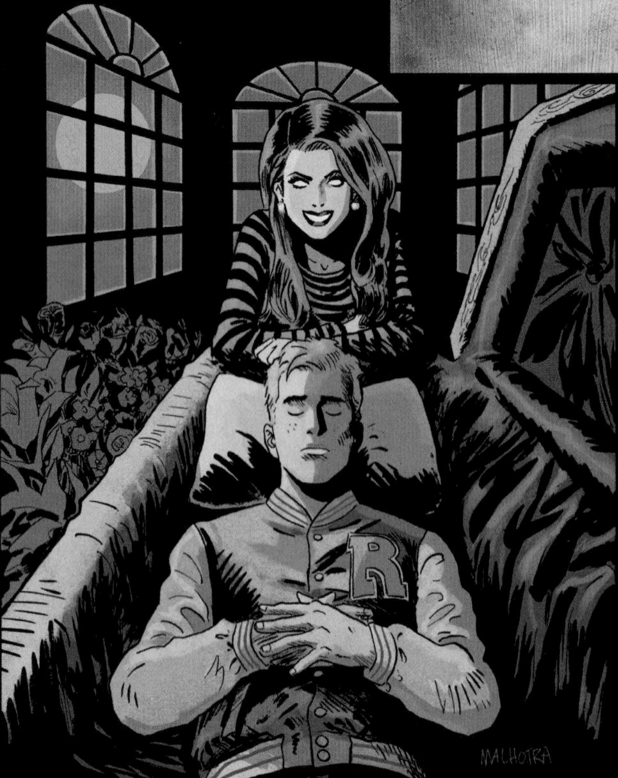
MALHOTRA

5.
BLOSSOMS 666
ARCHIE SERIES
ARCHIE HORROR GROUP
APPROVED BY THE STADIUM COMICS CODE AUTHORITY
NO.1
BLOSSOMS 666
Jason and Cheryl
FEATURING CHERYL, RIVERDALE'S CREEPIEST BOMBSHELL!
JASON & CHERYL: BLOSSOMS 666 #1
Betty
HACK

6.
FRAN CAVIL LA F. 18

ISSUE ONE

5. ROBERT HACK

(RETAILER VARIANT, STADIUM COMICS, BRAMPTON, ONTARIO CANADA)

6. FRANCESCO FRANCAVILLA

(SECOND PRINT)

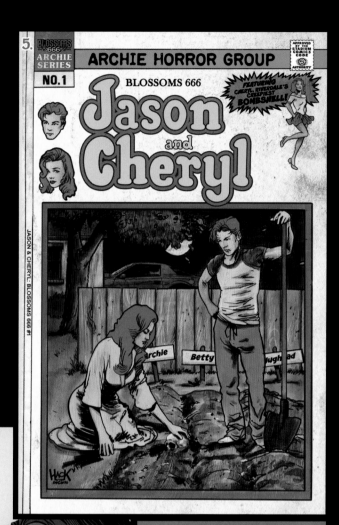

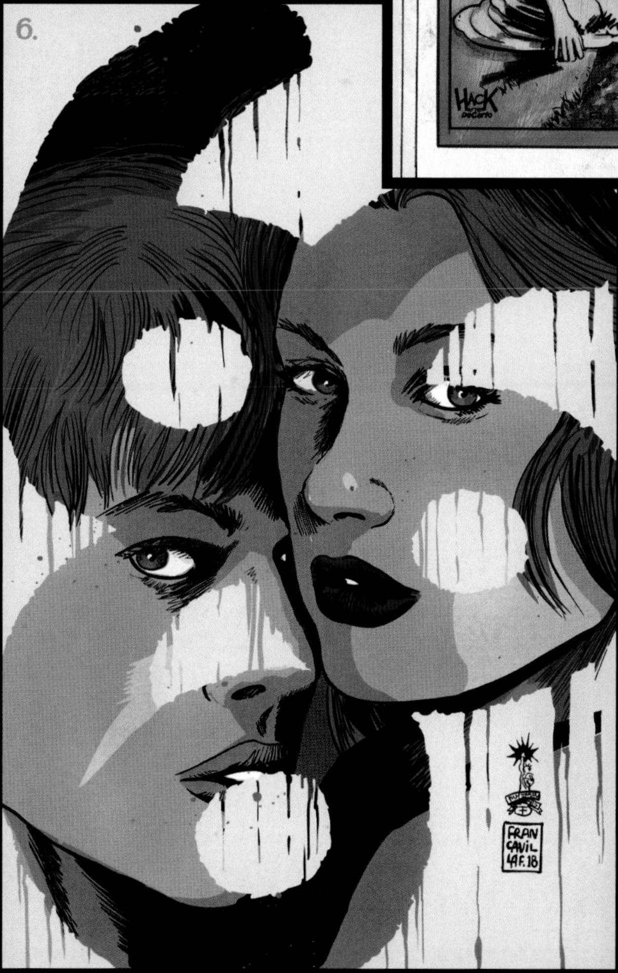

ISSUE TWO

1. AUDREY MOK

2. WILFREDO TORRES
   WITH KELLY FITZPATRICK

1.

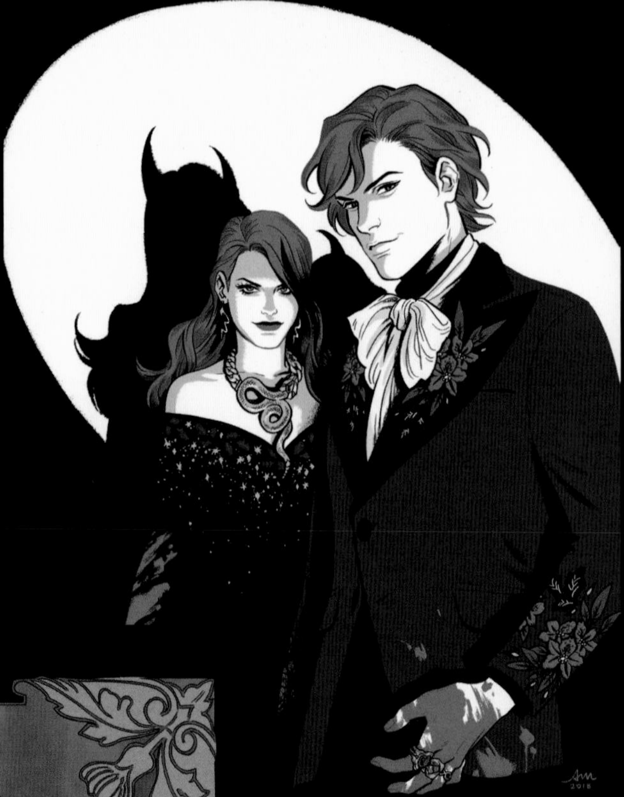

2.

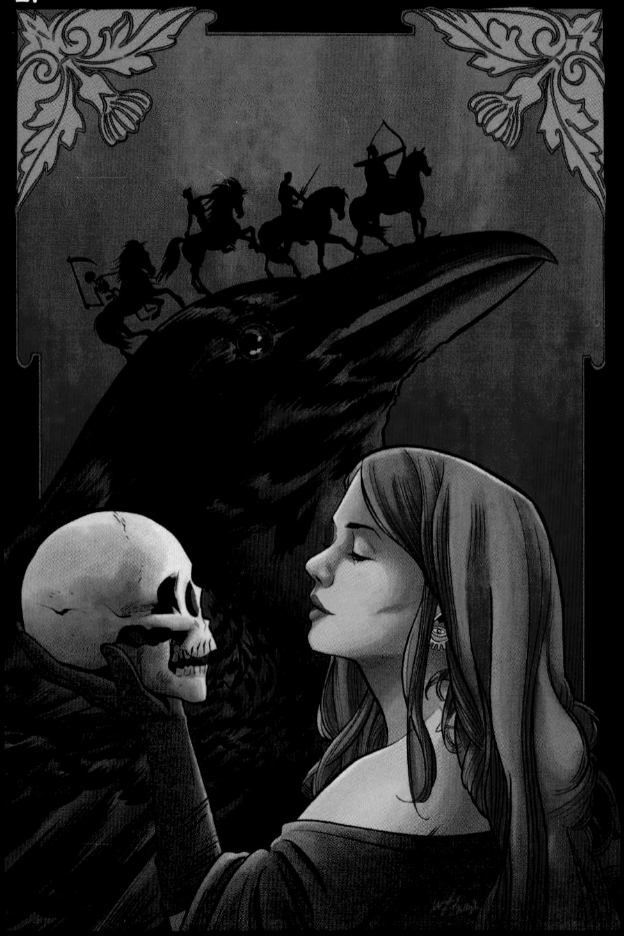

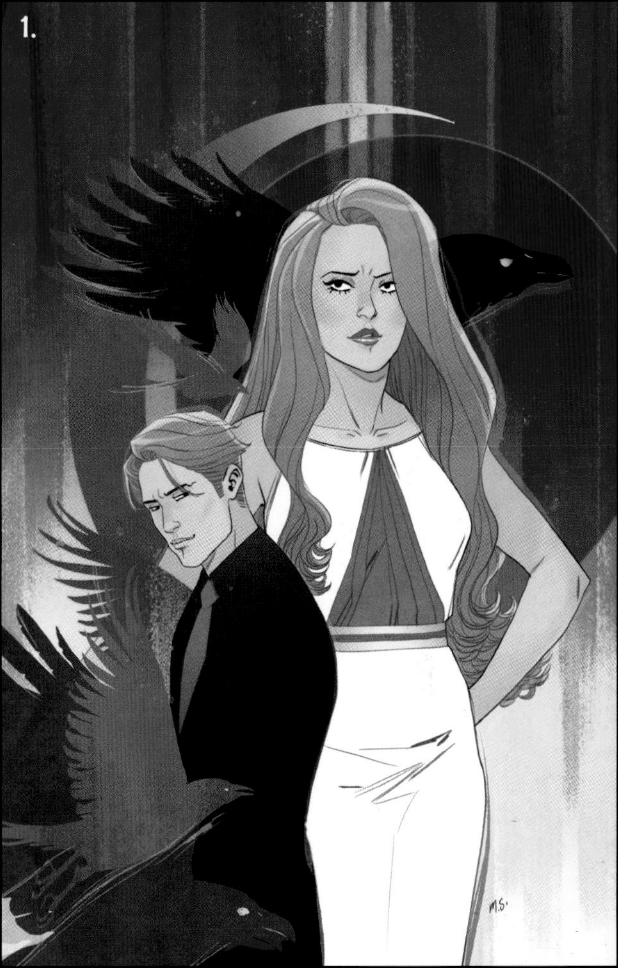
1.
M.S.

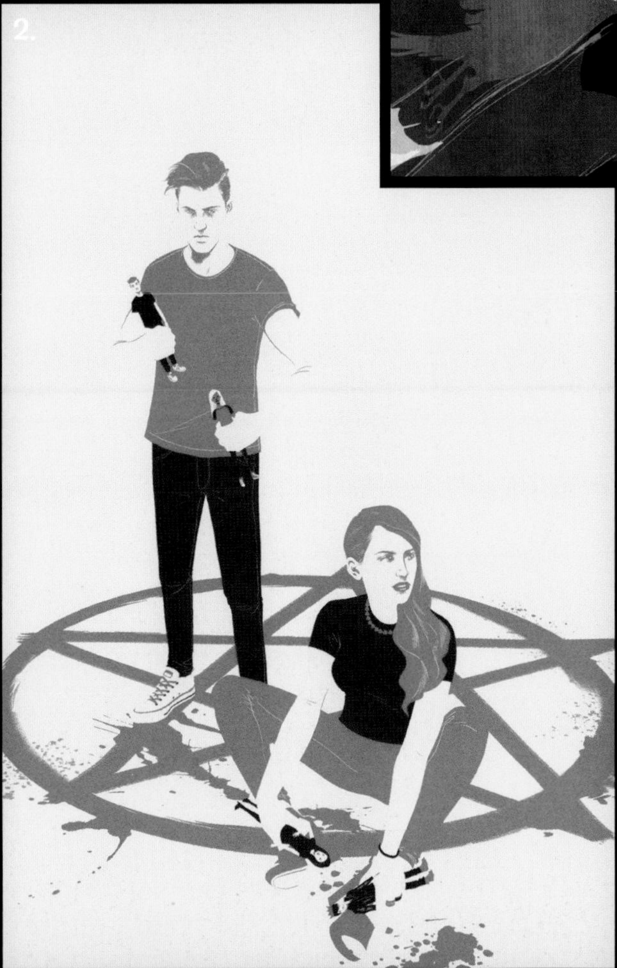
2.

ISSUE THREE

1. MARGUERITE SAUVAGE

2. MATTHEW TAYLOR

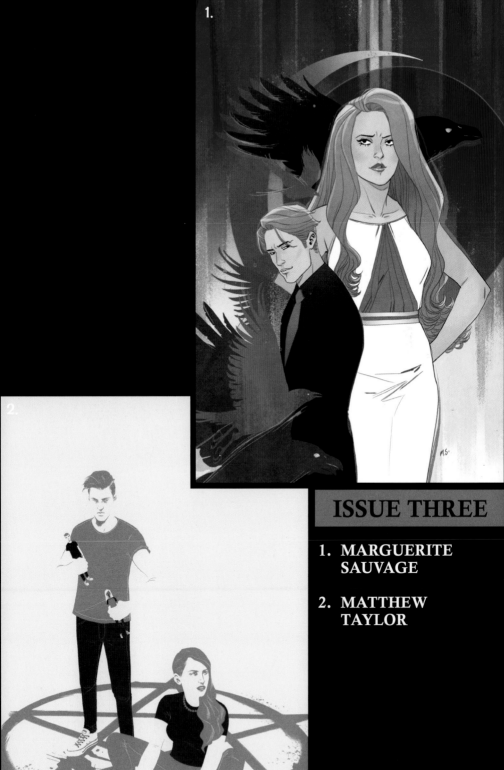

ISSUE FOUR

1. ELSA CHARRETIER
2. ERICA HENDERSON

1.

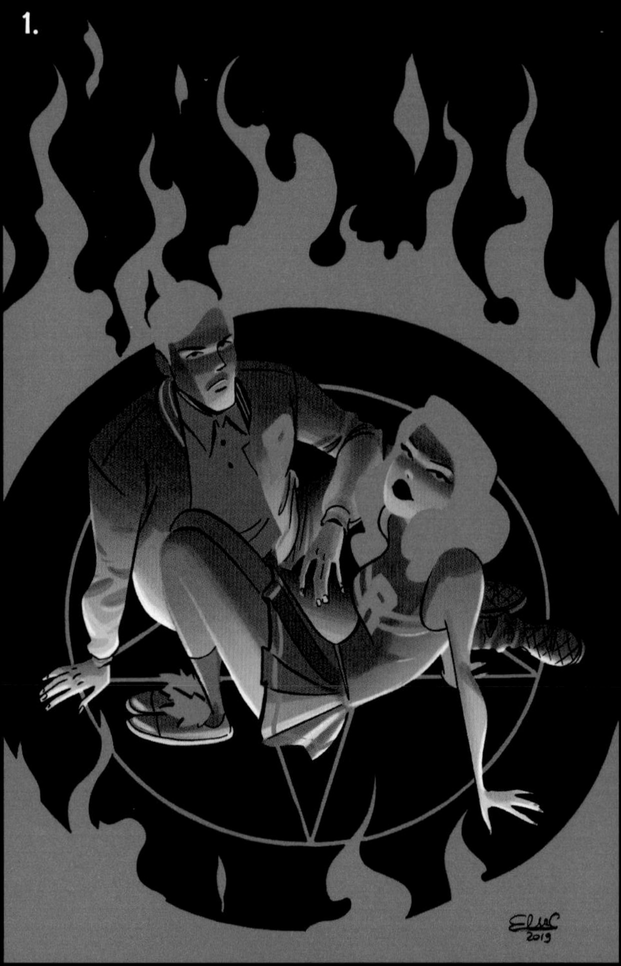

2.

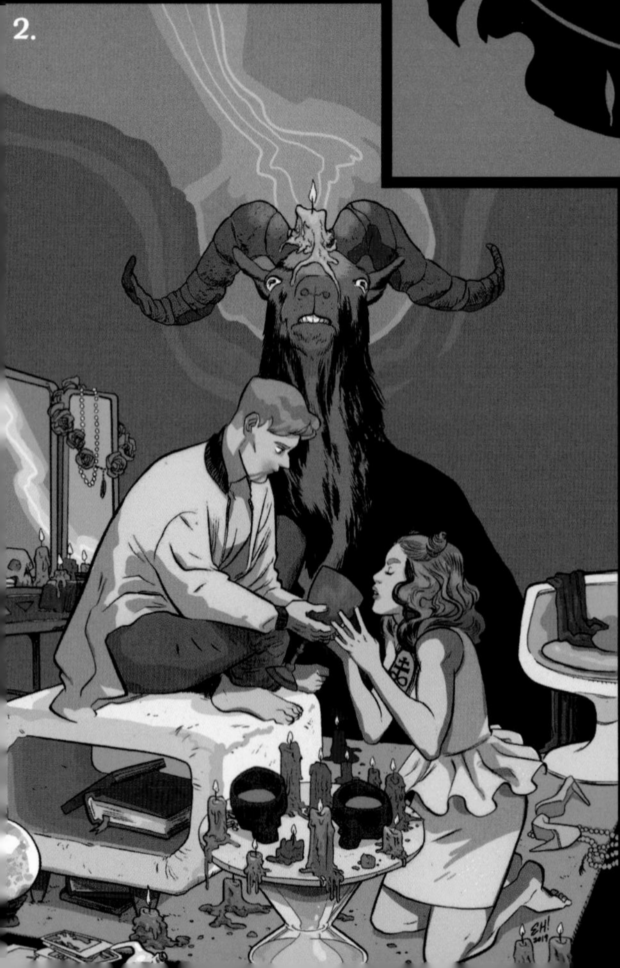

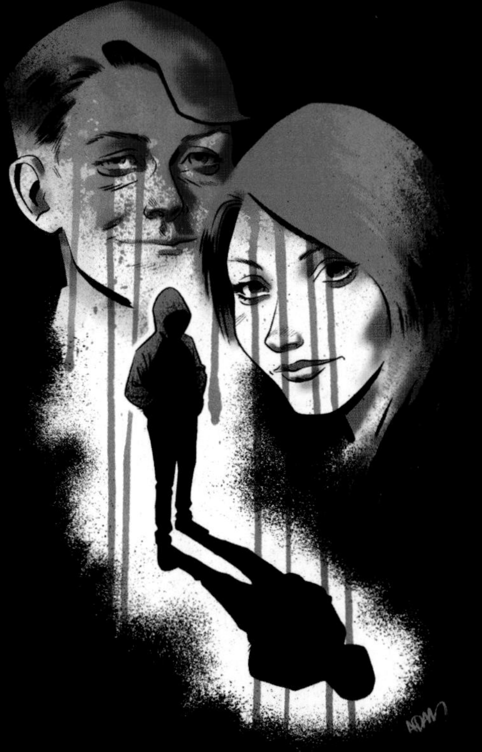

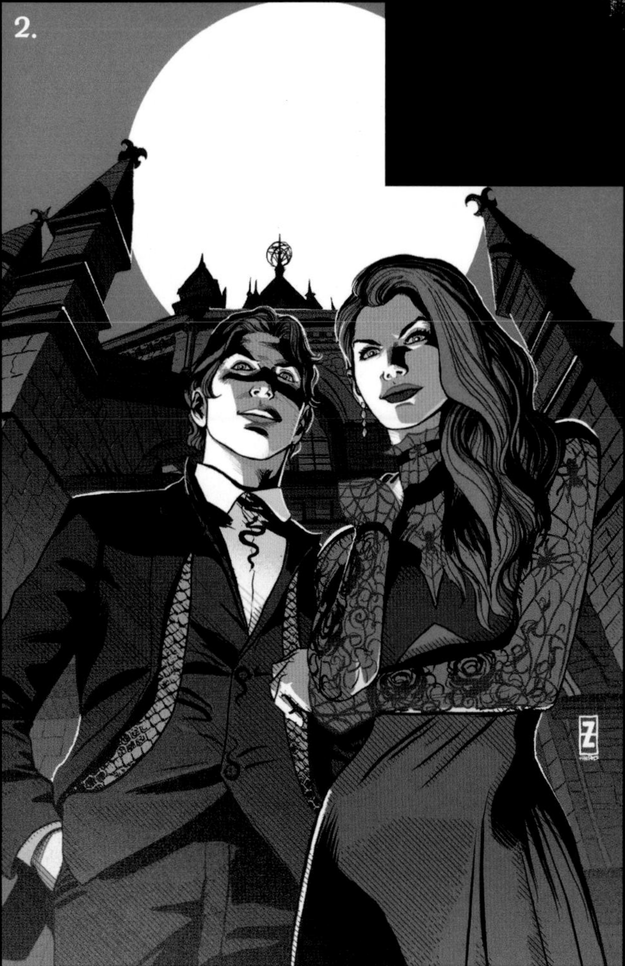
2.

ISSUE FIVE

1. ADAM GORHAM

2. PATRICK ZIRCHER
   WITH MATT HERMS

BLOSSOMS 666®

COVER SKETCHES

Before going ahead with the final cover, series artist Laura Braga submits cover sketches for the editorial team to review. Take a look at the sketches and final cover art for the first issue of *Blossoms 666*.

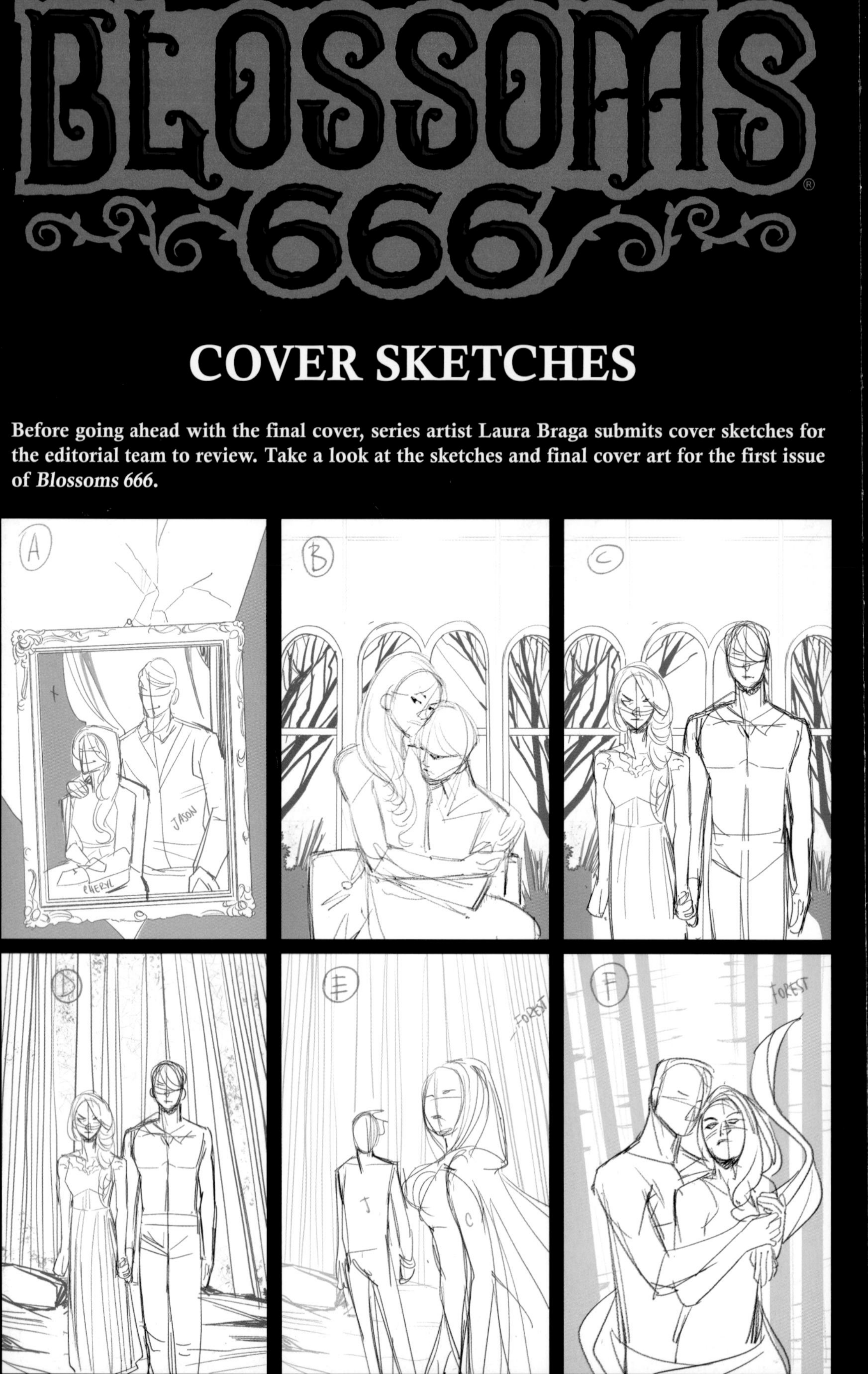

A
JASON
CHERYL
B
C
D
E
FOREST
J
C
F
FOREST

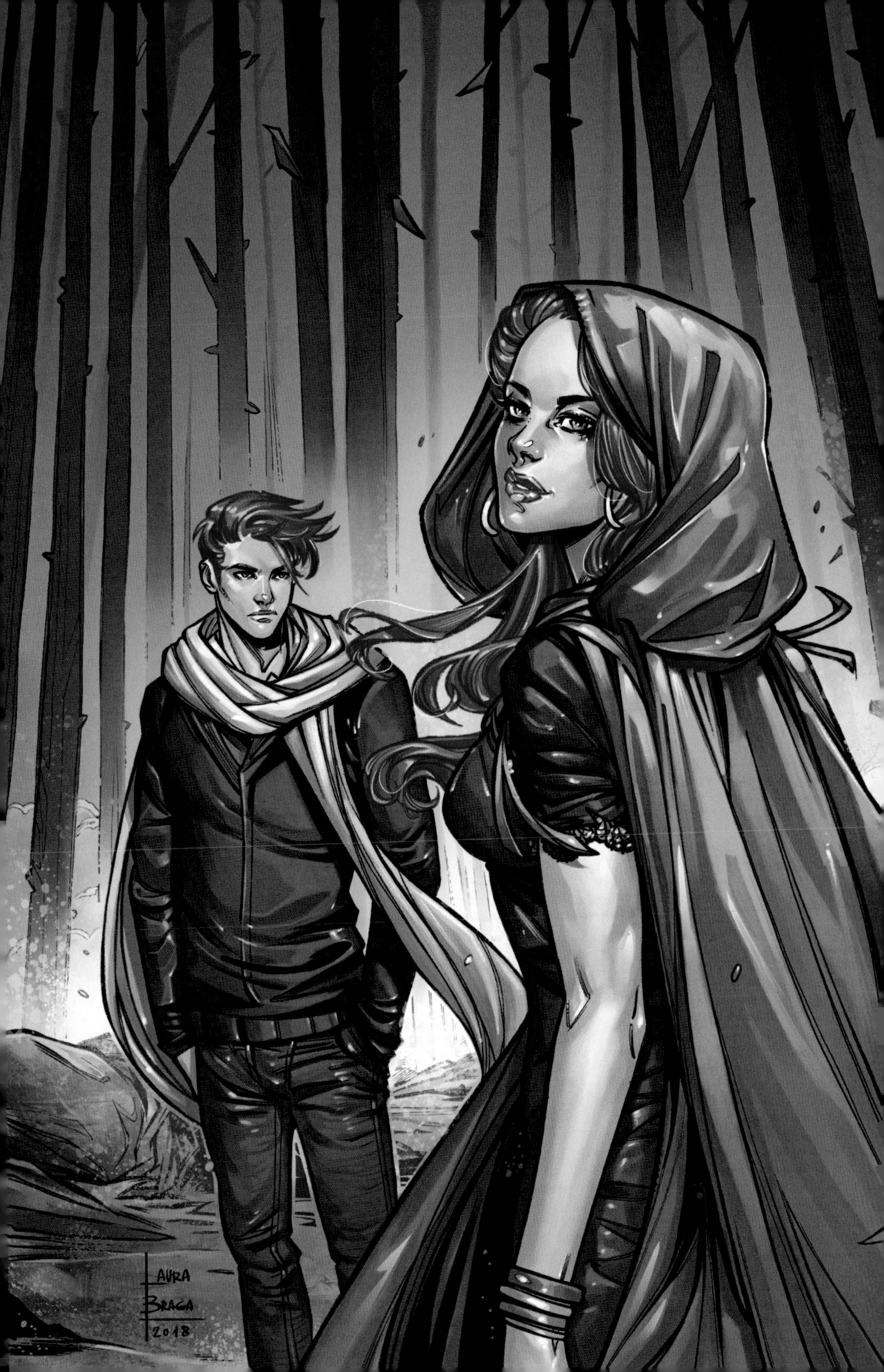
LAURA
BRAGA
2018

BONUS COMIC

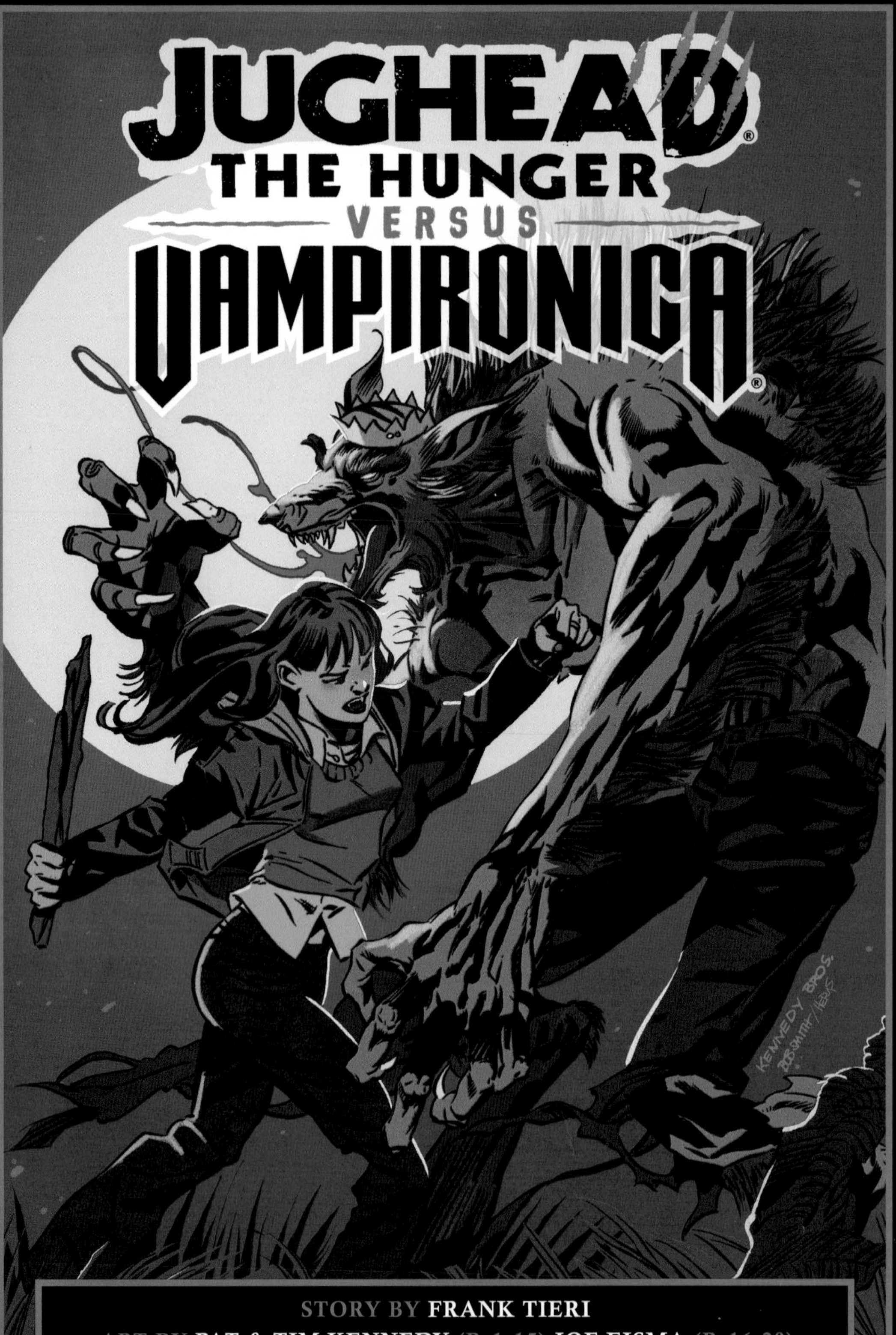
JUGHEAD®
THE HUNGER
VERSUS
VAMPIRONICA®
KENNEDY BROS.

STORY BY **FRANK TIERI**
ART BY **PAT & TIM KENNEDY** (P. 1-15) **JOE EISMA** (P. 16-20)
INKS BY **BOB SMITH** (P. 1-9,11,13-15) **RYAN JAMPOLE** (P. 10,12,14)
COLORING BY **MATT HERMS** LETTERING BY **JACK MORELLI**

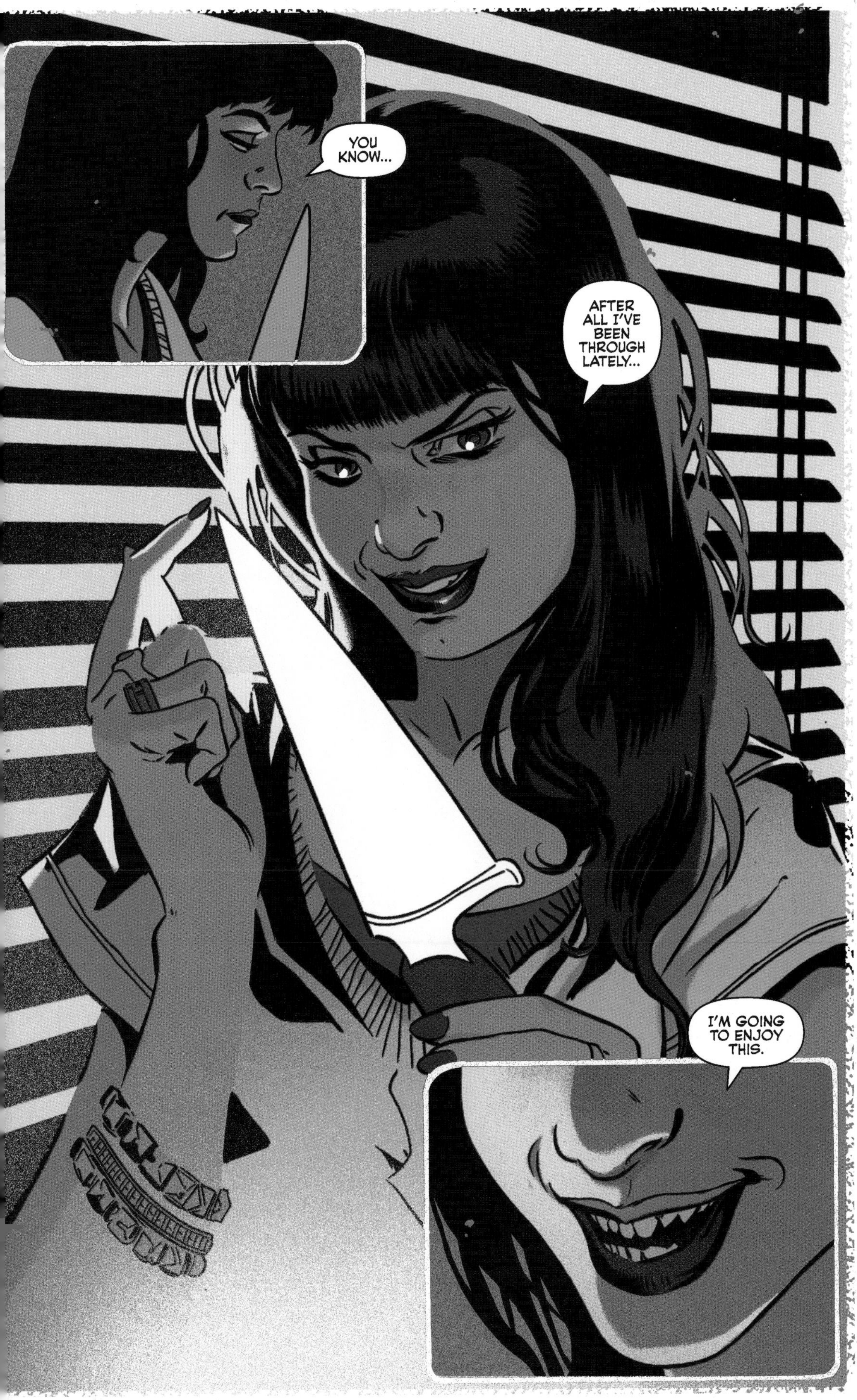
YOU KNOW...
AFTER ALL I'VE BEEN THROUGH LATELY...
I'M GOING TO ENJOY THIS.

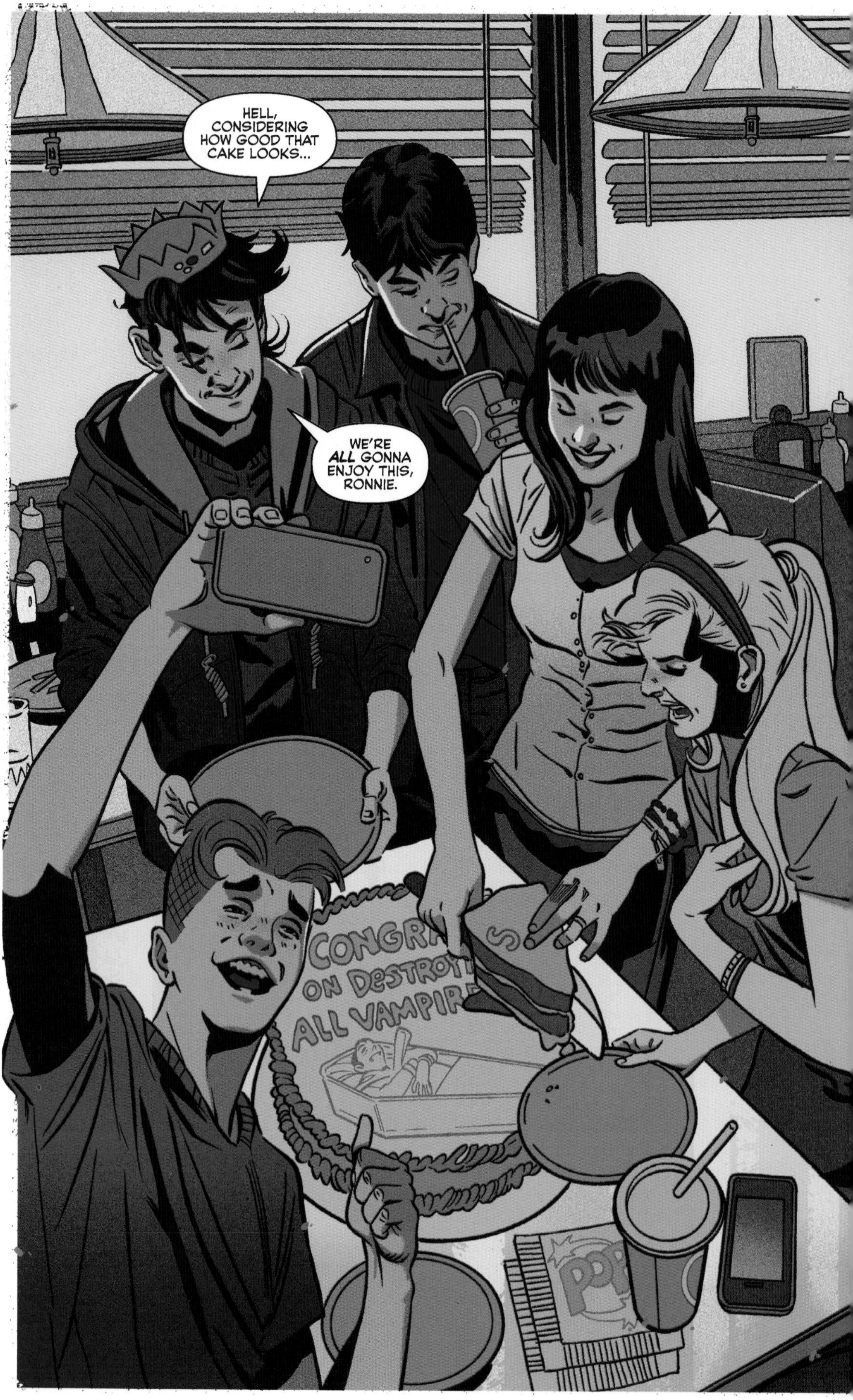
HELL, CONSIDERING HOW GOOD THAT CAKE LOOKS...
WE'RE ALL GONNA ENJOY THIS, RONNIE.

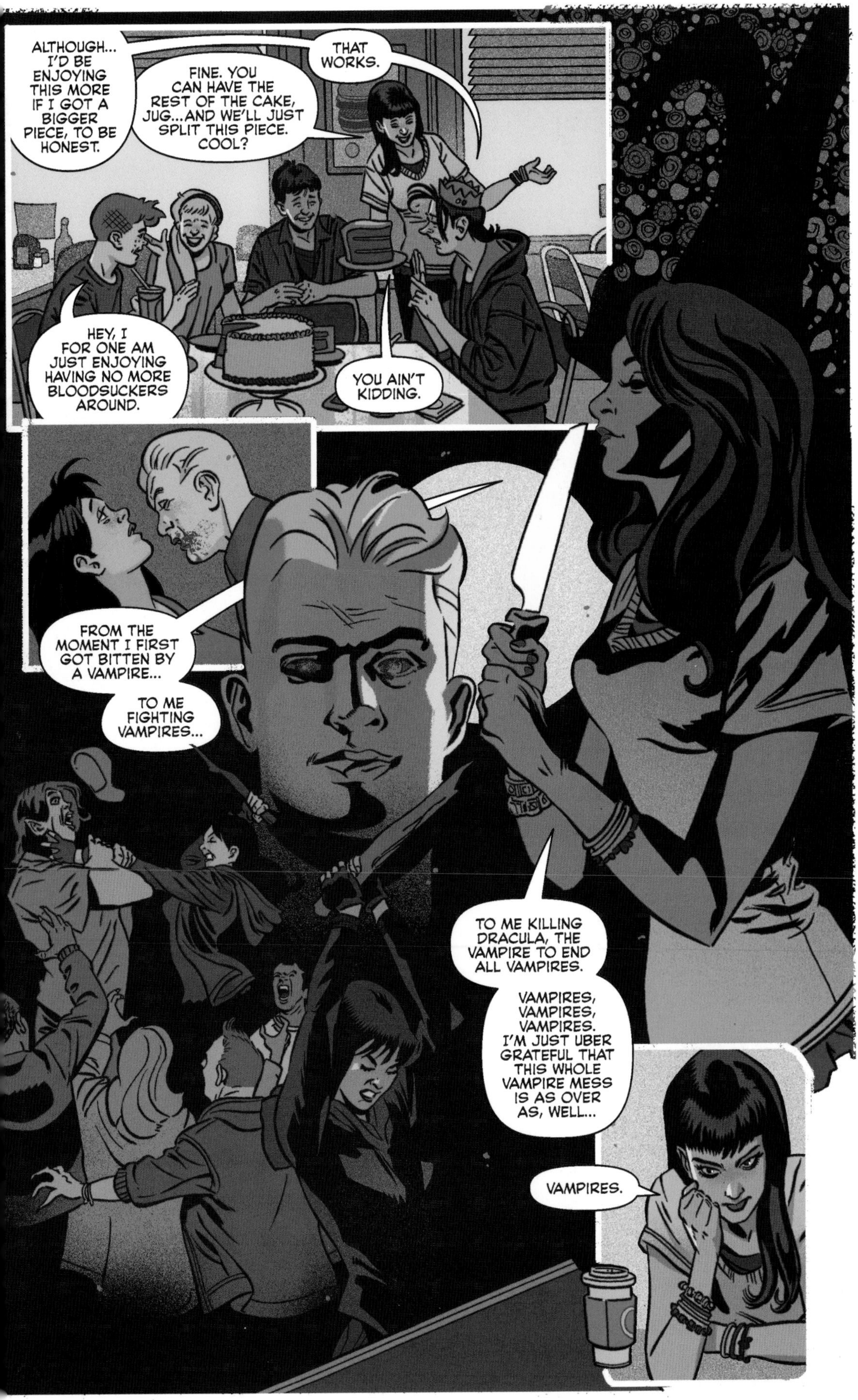
ALTHOUGH... I'D BE ENJOYING THIS MORE IF I GOT A BIGGER PIECE, TO BE HONEST.
FINE. YOU CAN HAVE THE REST OF THE CAKE, JUG...AND WE'LL JUST SPLIT THIS PIECE. COOL?
THAT WORKS.
HEY, I FOR ONE AM JUST ENJOYING HAVING NO MORE BLOODSUCKERS AROUND.
YOU AIN'T KIDDING.
FROM THE MOMENT I FIRST GOT BITTEN BY A VAMPIRE...
TO ME FIGHTING VAMPIRES...
TO ME KILLING DRACULA, THE VAMPIRE TO END ALL VAMPIRES.
VAMPIRES, VAMPIRES, VAMPIRES. I'M JUST UBER GRATEFUL THAT THIS WHOLE VAMPIRE MESS IS AS OVER AS, WELL...
VAMPIRES.

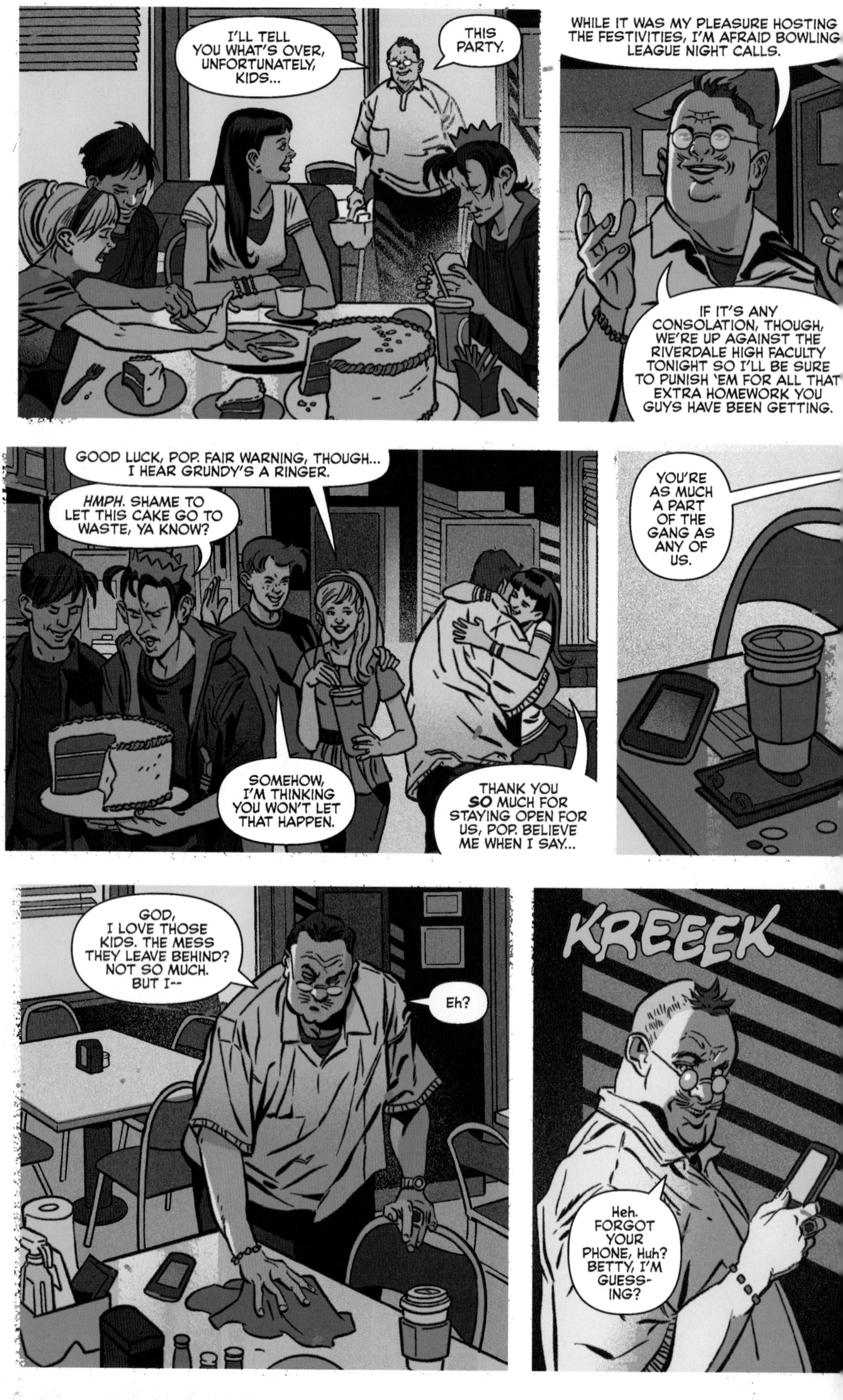
I'LL TELL YOU WHAT'S OVER, UNFORTUNATELY, KIDS...
THIS PARTY.
WHILE IT WAS MY PLEASURE HOSTING THE FESTIVITIES, I'M AFRAID BOWLING LEAGUE NIGHT CALLS.
IF IT'S ANY CONSOLATION, THOUGH, WE'RE UP AGAINST THE RIVERDALE HIGH FACULTY TONIGHT SO I'LL BE SURE TO PUNISH 'EM FOR ALL THAT EXTRA HOMEWORK YOU GUYS HAVE BEEN GETTING.
GOOD LUCK, POP. FAIR WARNING, THOUGH... I HEAR GRUNDY'S A RINGER.
HMPH. SHAME TO LET THIS CAKE GO TO WASTE, YA KNOW?
SOMEHOW, I'M THINKING YOU WON'T LET THAT HAPPEN.
THANK YOU **SO** MUCH FOR STAYING OPEN FOR US, POP. BELIEVE ME WHEN I SAY...
YOU'RE AS MUCH A PART OF THE GANG AS ANY OF US.
GOD, I LOVE THOSE KIDS. THE MESS THEY LEAVE BEHIND? NOT SO MUCH. BUT I--
Eh?
KREEEK
Heh. FORGOT YOUR PHONE, Huh? BETTY, I'M GUESS-ING?

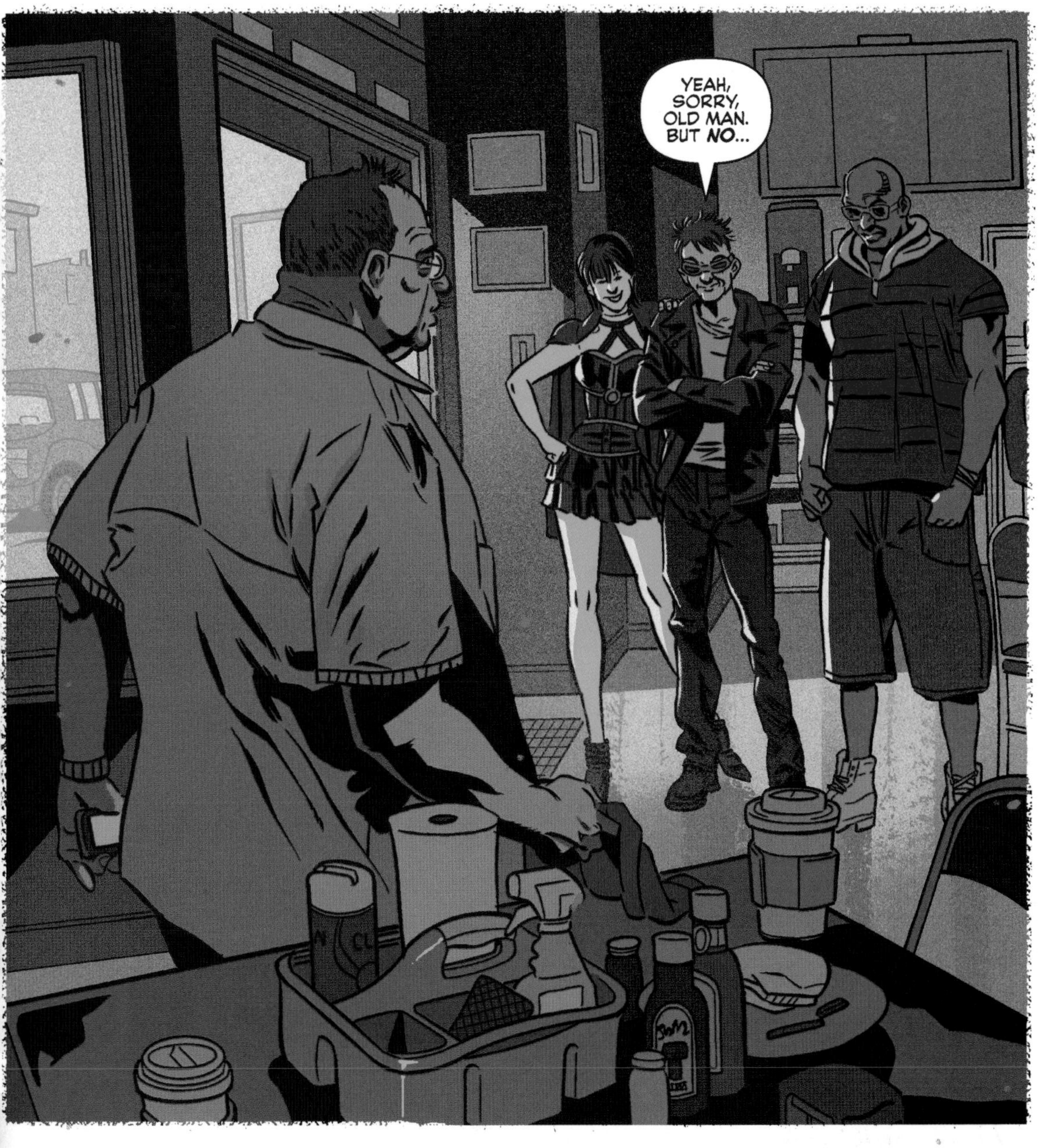
YEAH, SORRY, OLD MAN. BUT NO...

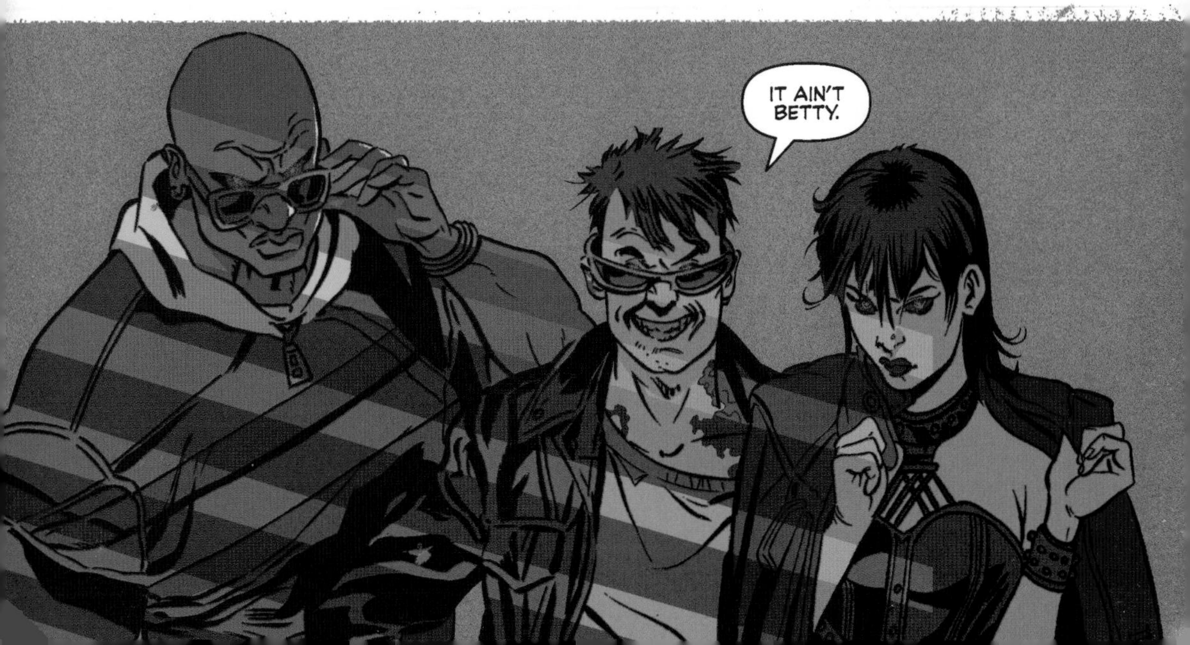
IT AIN'T BETTY.

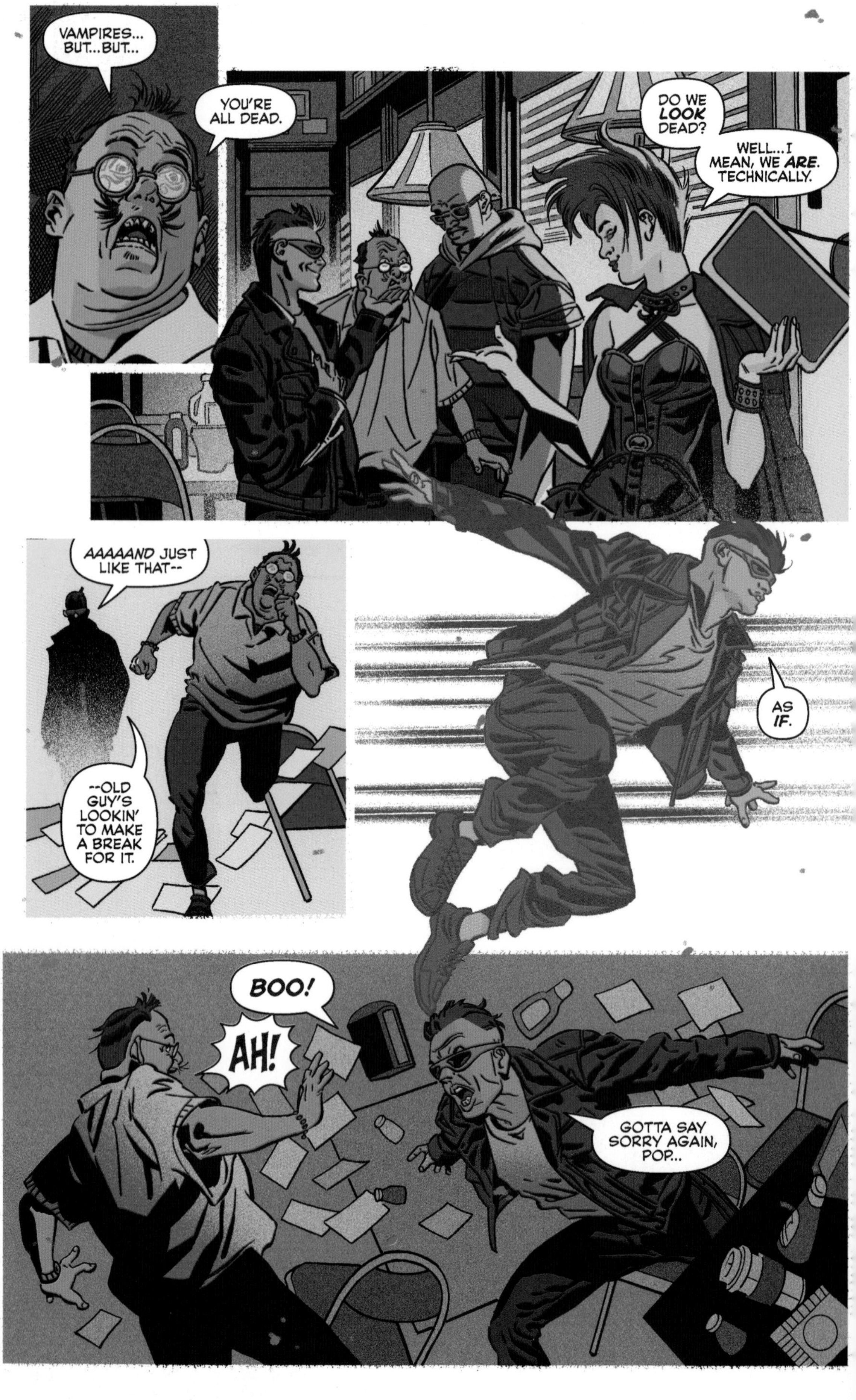
VAMPIRES... BUT...BUT...
YOU'RE ALL DEAD.
DO WE *LOOK* DEAD?
WELL...I MEAN, WE *ARE*. TECHNICALLY.
AAAAAND JUST LIKE THAT--
--OLD GUY'S LOOKIN' TO MAKE A BREAK FOR IT.
AS *IF*.
BOO!
AH!
GOTTA SAY SORRY AGAIN, POP...

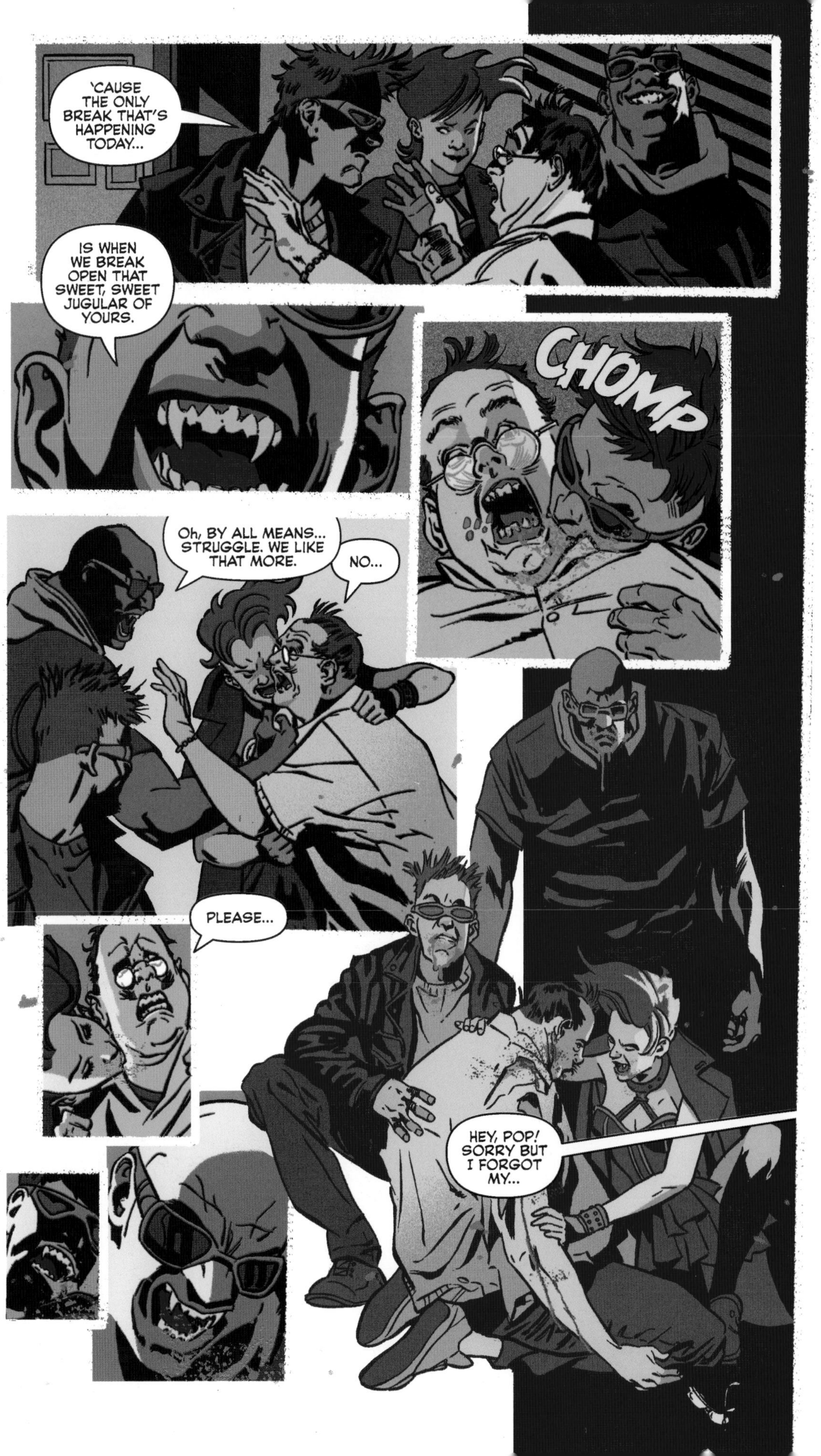
'CAUSE THE ONLY BREAK THAT'S HAPPENING TODAY...
IS WHEN WE BREAK OPEN THAT SWEET, SWEET JUGULAR OF YOURS.
CHOMP
Oh, BY ALL MEANS... STRUGGLE. WE LIKE THAT MORE.
NO...
PLEASE...
HEY, POP! SORRY BUT I FORGOT MY...

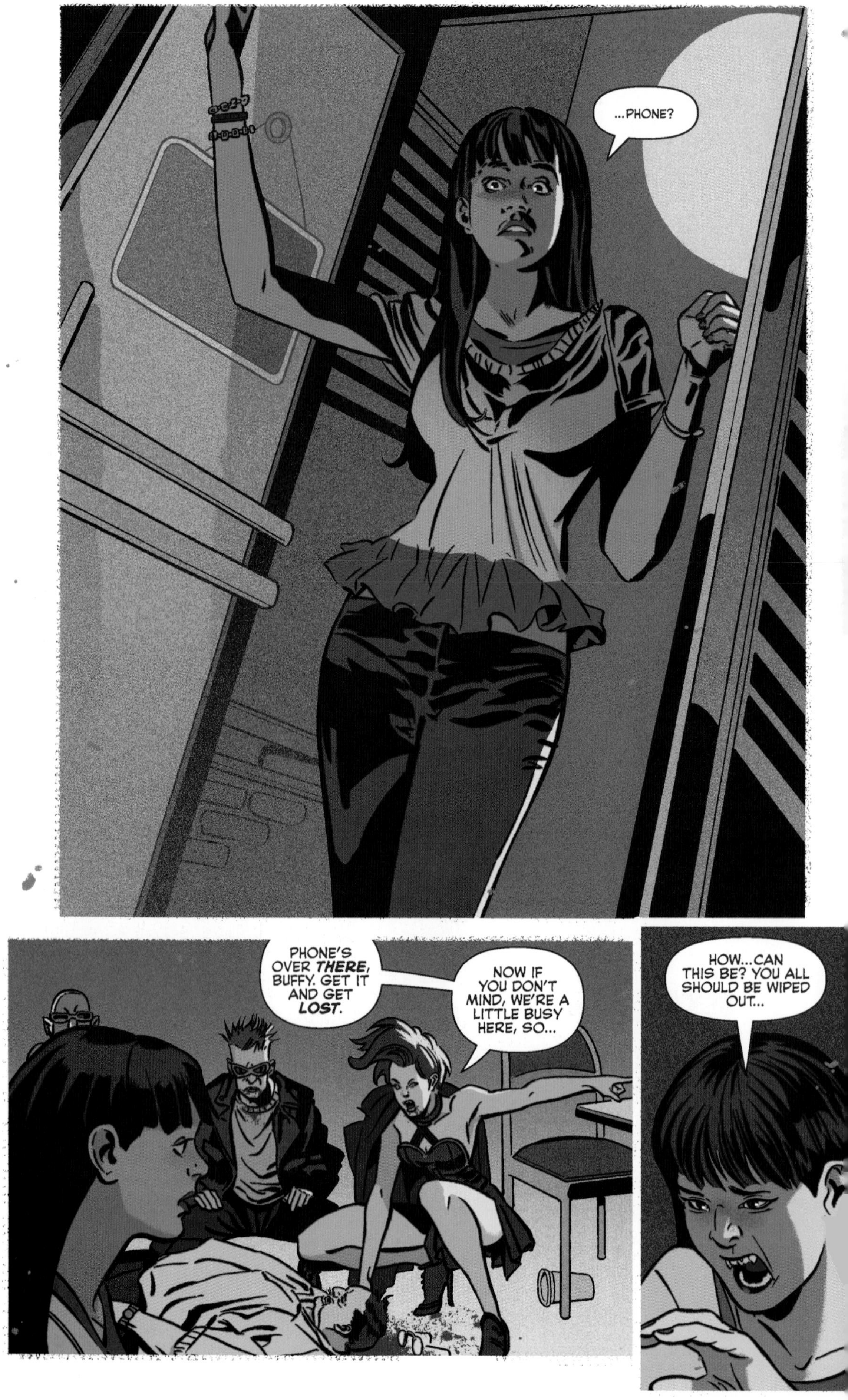
...PHONE?
PHONE'S OVER **THERE**, BUFFY. GET IT AND GET **LOST**.
NOW IF YOU DON'T MIND, WE'RE A LITTLE BUSY HERE, SO...
HOW...CAN THIS BE? YOU ALL SHOULD BE WIPED OUT...

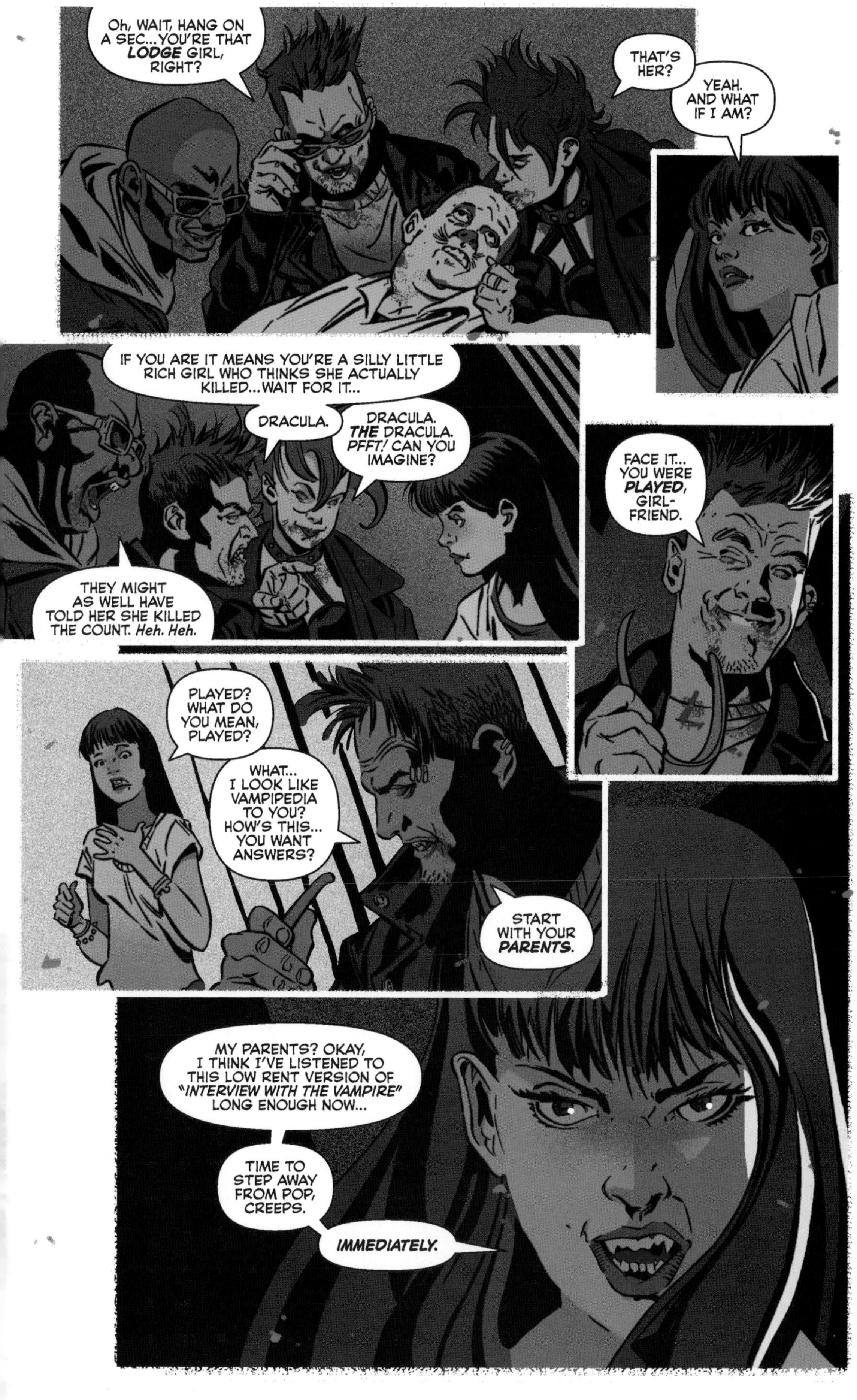
Oh, WAIT, HANG ON A SEC...YOU'RE THAT **LODGE** GIRL, RIGHT?
THAT'S HER?
YEAH. AND WHAT IF I AM?
IF YOU ARE IT MEANS YOU'RE A SILLY LITTLE RICH GIRL WHO THINKS SHE ACTUALLY KILLED...WAIT FOR IT...
DRACULA.
DRACULA. ***THE*** DRACULA. ***PFFT!*** CAN YOU IMAGINE?
THEY MIGHT AS WELL HAVE TOLD HER SHE KILLED THE COUNT. *Heh. Heh.*
FACE IT... YOU WERE ***PLAYED***, GIRL-FRIEND.
PLAYED? WHAT DO YOU MEAN, PLAYED?
WHAT... I LOOK LIKE VAMPIPEDIA TO YOU? HOW'S THIS... YOU WANT ANSWERS?
START WITH YOUR ***PARENTS***.
MY PARENTS? OKAY, I THINK I'VE LISTENED TO THIS LOW RENT VERSION OF "*INTERVIEW WITH THE VAMPIRE*" LONG ENOUGH NOW...
TIME TO STEP AWAY FROM POP, CREEPS.
IMMEDIATELY.

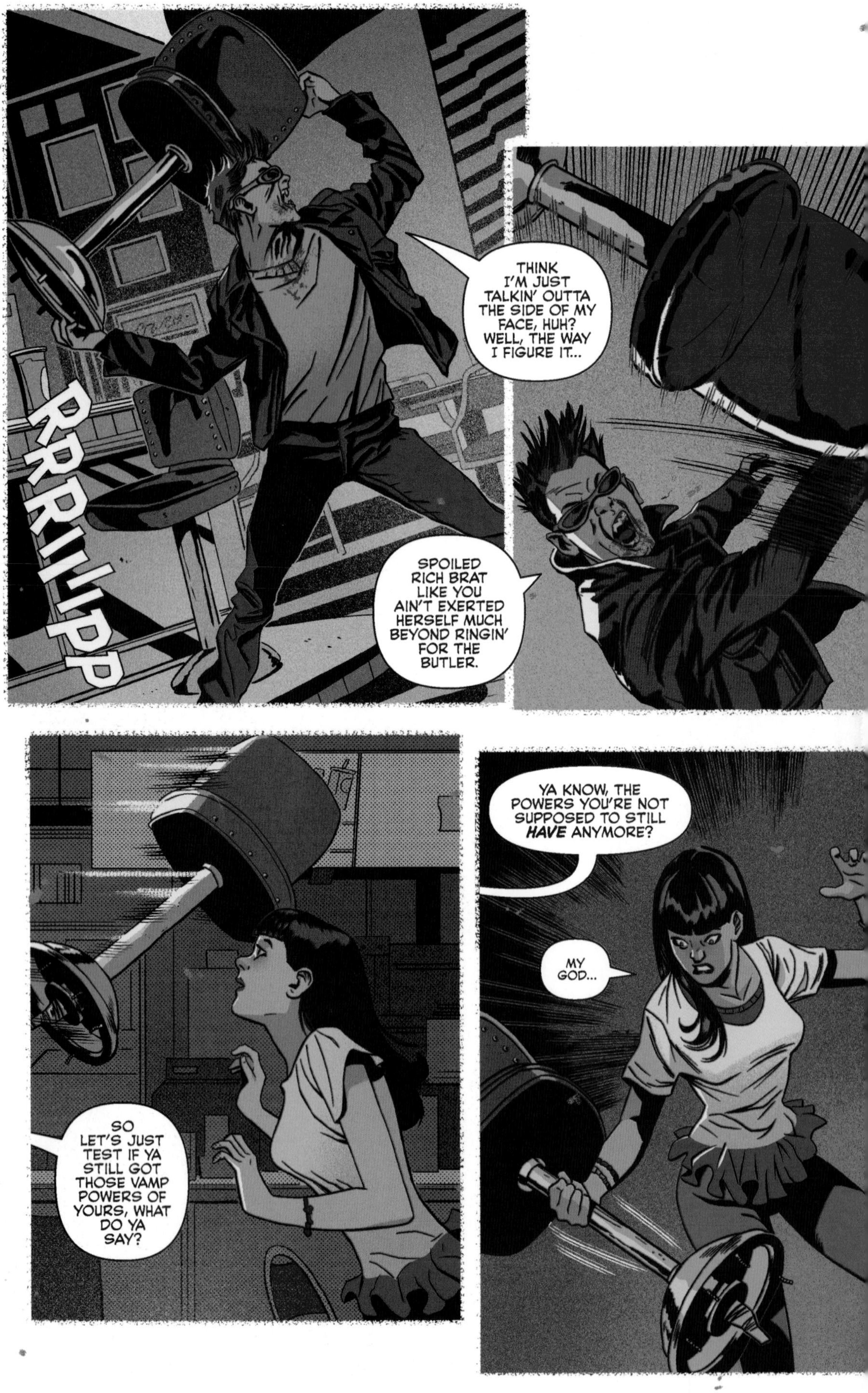
THINK I'M JUST TALKIN' OUTTA THE SIDE OF MY FACE, HUH? WELL, THE WAY I FIGURE IT...
SPOILED RICH BRAT LIKE YOU AIN'T EXERTED HERSELF MUCH BEYOND RINGIN' FOR THE BUTLER.
RRRIIIPP
SO LET'S JUST TEST IF YA STILL GOT THOSE VAMP POWERS OF YOURS, WHAT DO YA SAY?
YA KNOW, THE POWERS YOU'RE NOT SUPPOSED TO STILL *HAVE* ANYMORE?
MY GOD...

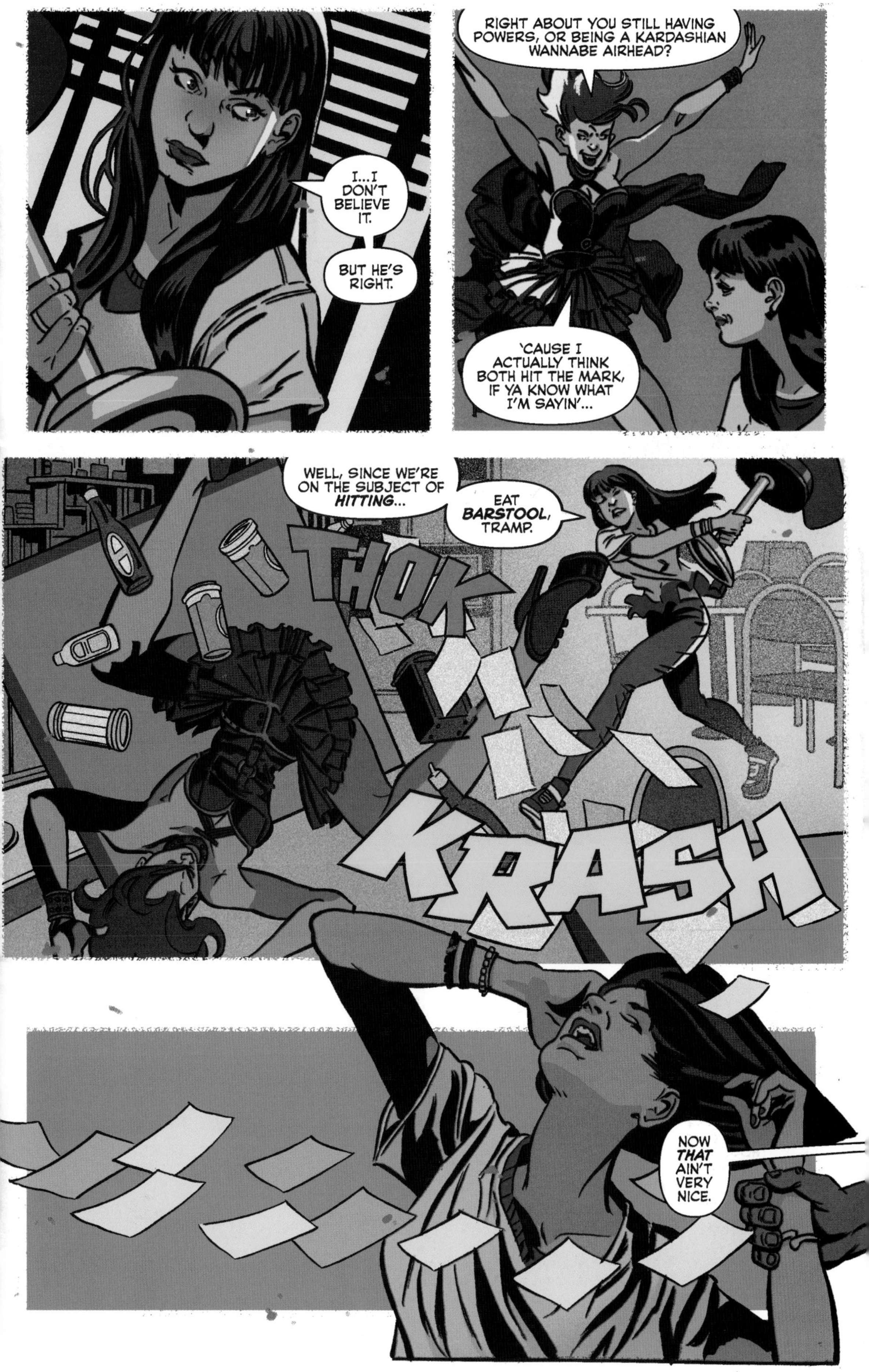
I...I DON'T BELIEVE IT.
BUT HE'S RIGHT.
RIGHT ABOUT YOU STILL HAVING POWERS, OR BEING A KARDASHIAN WANNABE AIRHEAD?
'CAUSE I ACTUALLY THINK BOTH HIT THE MARK, IF YA KNOW WHAT I'M SAYIN'...
WELL, SINCE WE'RE ON THE SUBJECT OF *HITTING*...
EAT *BARSTOOL*, TRAMP.
THOK
KRASH
NOW *THAT* AIN'T VERY NICE.

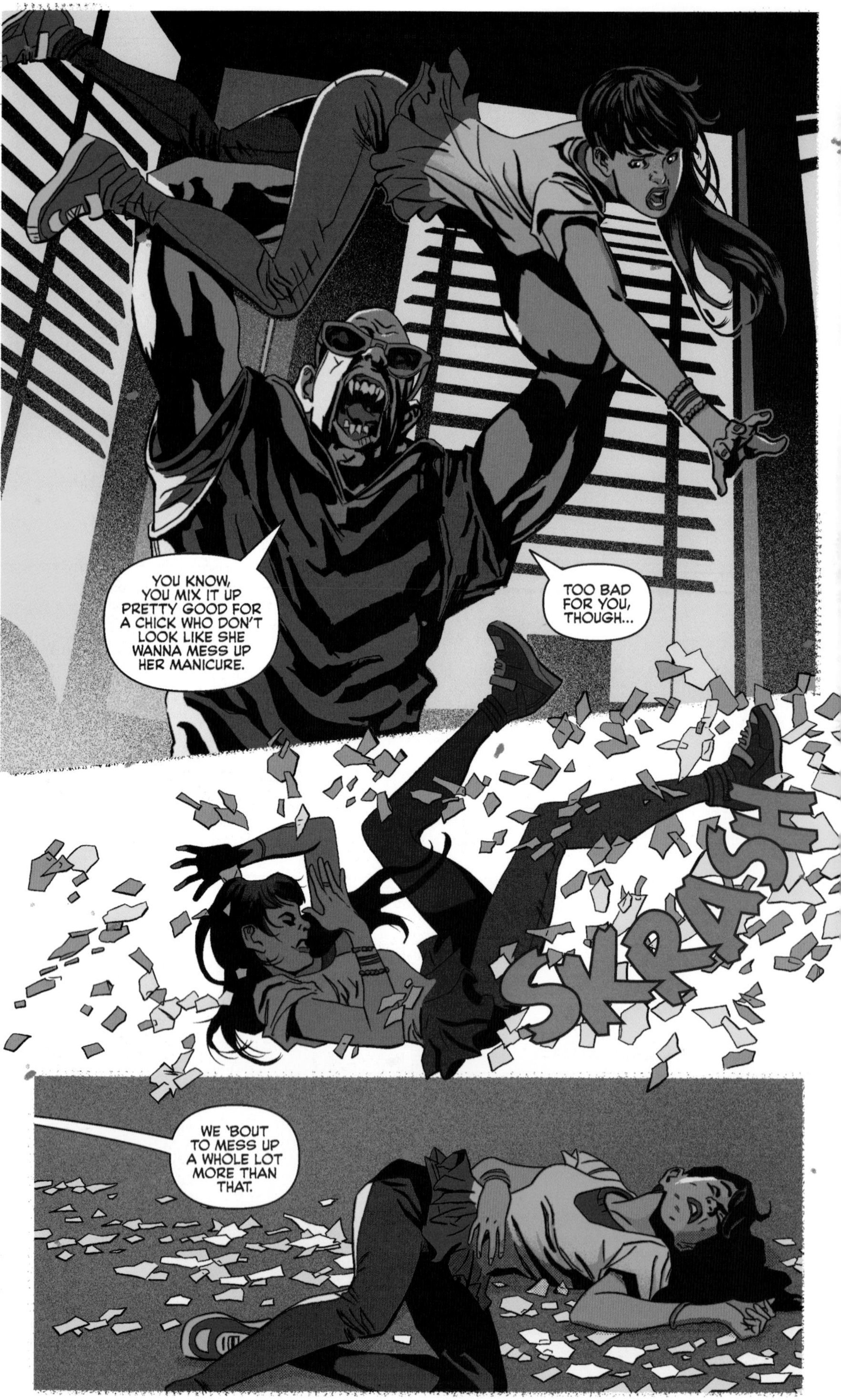
YOU KNOW, YOU MIX IT UP PRETTY GOOD FOR A CHICK WHO DON'T LOOK LIKE SHE WANNA MESS UP HER MANICURE.
TOO BAD FOR YOU, THOUGH...
SKRASH
WE 'BOUT TO MESS UP A WHOLE LOT MORE THAN THAT.

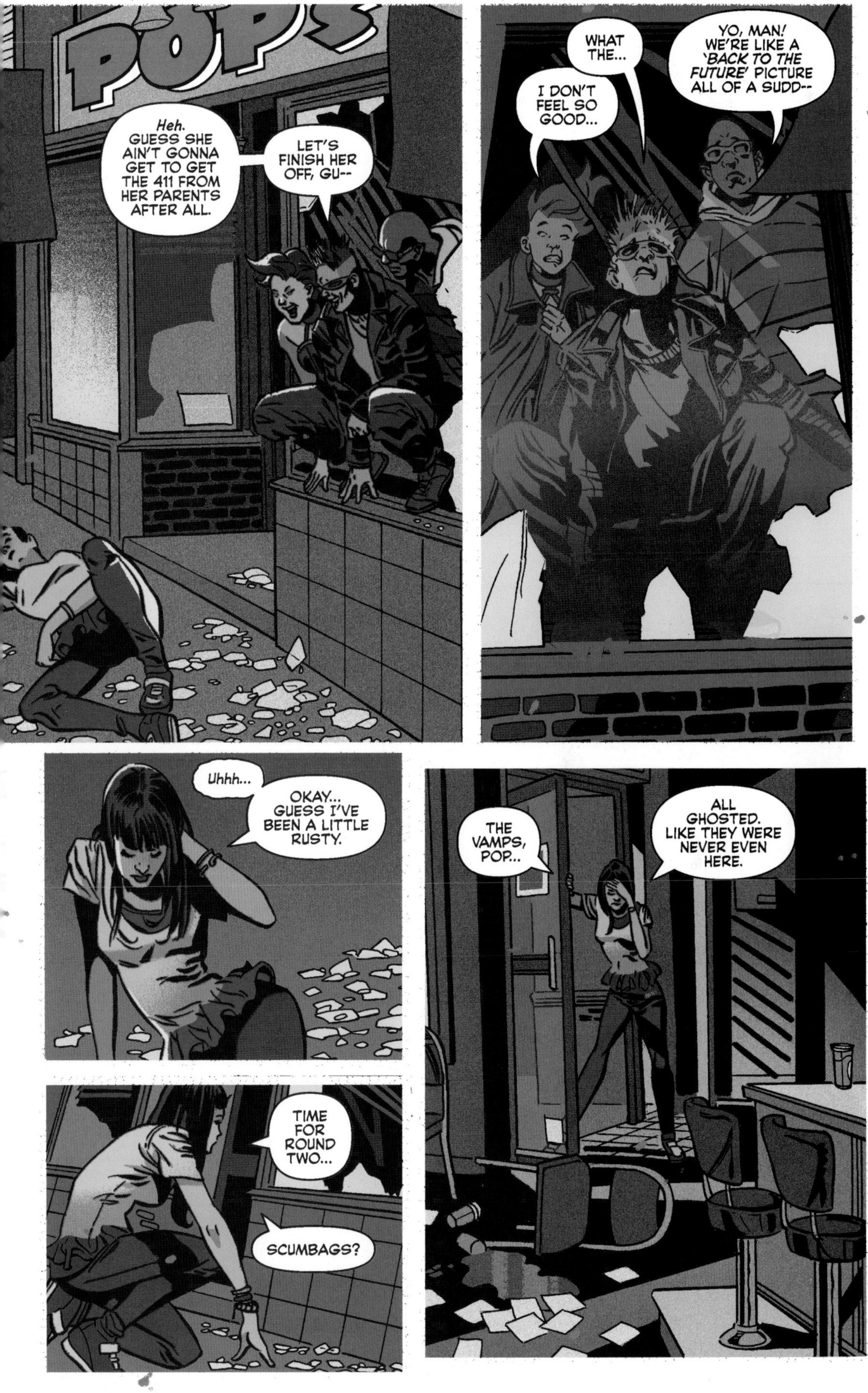
POPS
Heh. GUESS SHE AIN'T GONNA GET TO GET THE 411 FROM HER PARENTS AFTER ALL.
LET'S FINISH HER OFF, GU--
WHAT THE...
I DON'T FEEL SO GOOD...
YO, MAN! WE'RE LIKE A 'BACK TO THE FUTURE' PICTURE ALL OF A SUDD--
Uhhh...
OKAY... GUESS I'VE BEEN A LITTLE RUSTY.
TIME FOR ROUND TWO...
SCUMBAGS?
THE VAMPS, POP...
ALL GHOSTED. LIKE THEY WERE NEVER EVEN HERE.

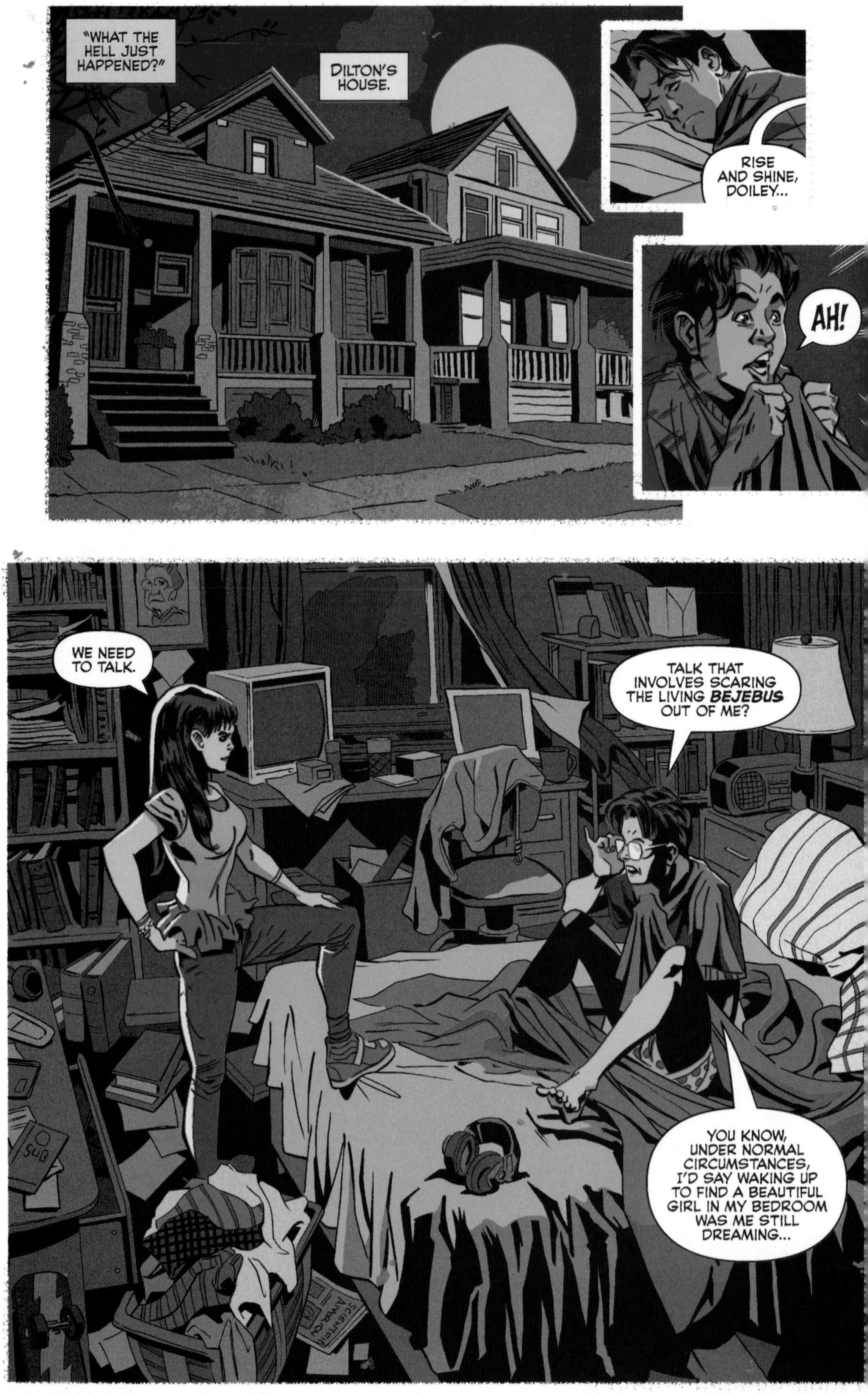
"WHAT THE HELL JUST HAPPENED?"
DILTON'S HOUSE.
RISE AND SHINE, DOILEY...
AH!
WE NEED TO TALK.
TALK THAT INVOLVES SCARING THE LIVING ***BEJEBUS*** OUT OF ME?
YOU KNOW, UNDER NORMAL CIRCUMSTANCES, I'D SAY WAKING UP TO FIND A BEAUTIFUL GIRL IN MY BEDROOM WAS ME STILL DREAMING...

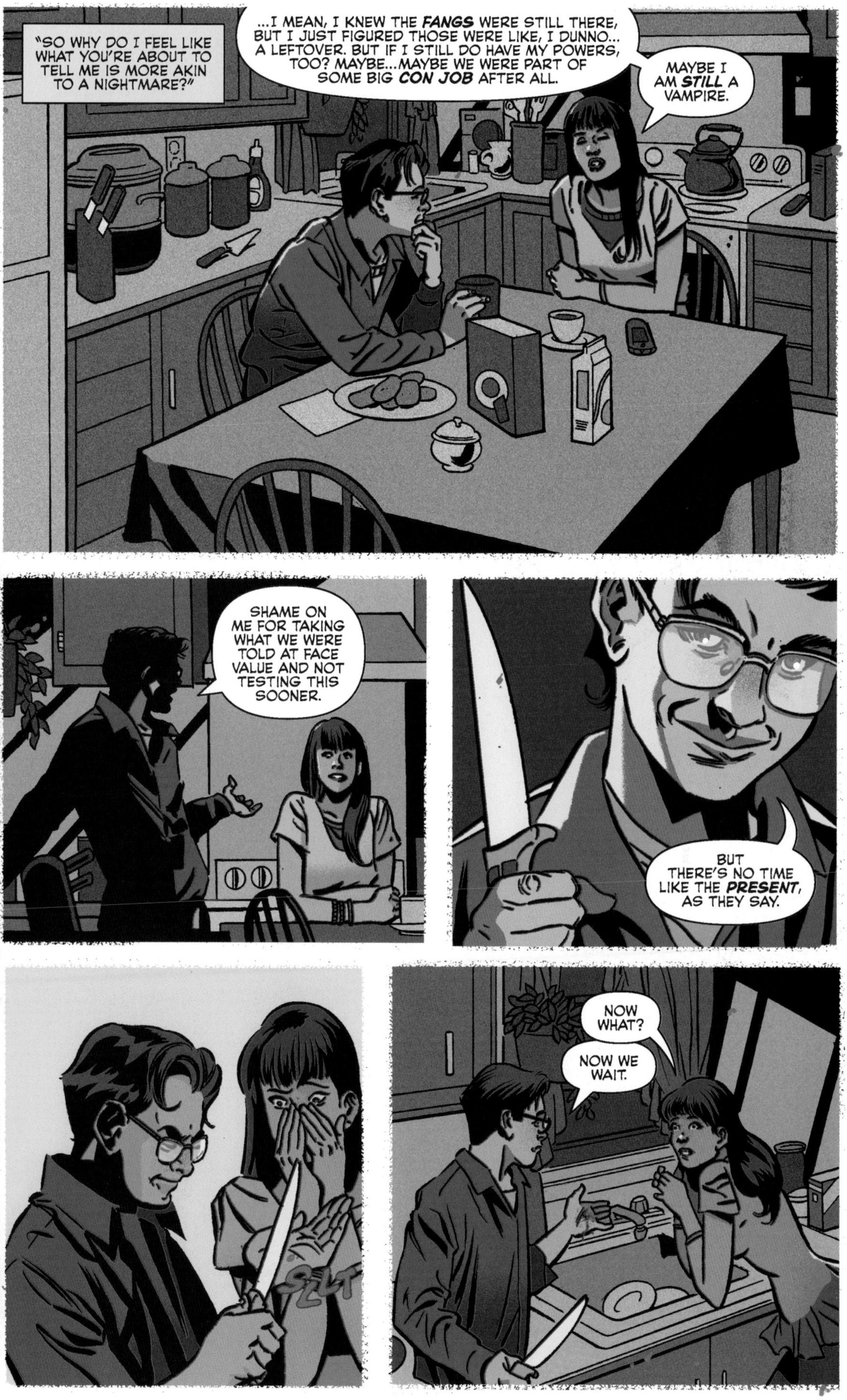
"SO WHY DO I FEEL LIKE WHAT YOU'RE ABOUT TO TELL ME IS MORE AKIN TO A NIGHTMARE?"
...I MEAN, I KNEW THE **FANGS** WERE STILL THERE, BUT I JUST FIGURED THOSE WERE LIKE, I DUNNO... A LEFTOVER. BUT IF I STILL DO HAVE MY POWERS, TOO? MAYBE...MAYBE WE WERE PART OF SOME BIG **CON JOB** AFTER ALL.
MAYBE I AM **STILL** A VAMPIRE.
SHAME ON ME FOR TAKING WHAT WE WERE TOLD AT FACE VALUE AND NOT TESTING THIS SOONER.
BUT THERE'S NO TIME LIKE THE **PRESENT**, AS THEY SAY.
NOW WHAT?
NOW WE WAIT.

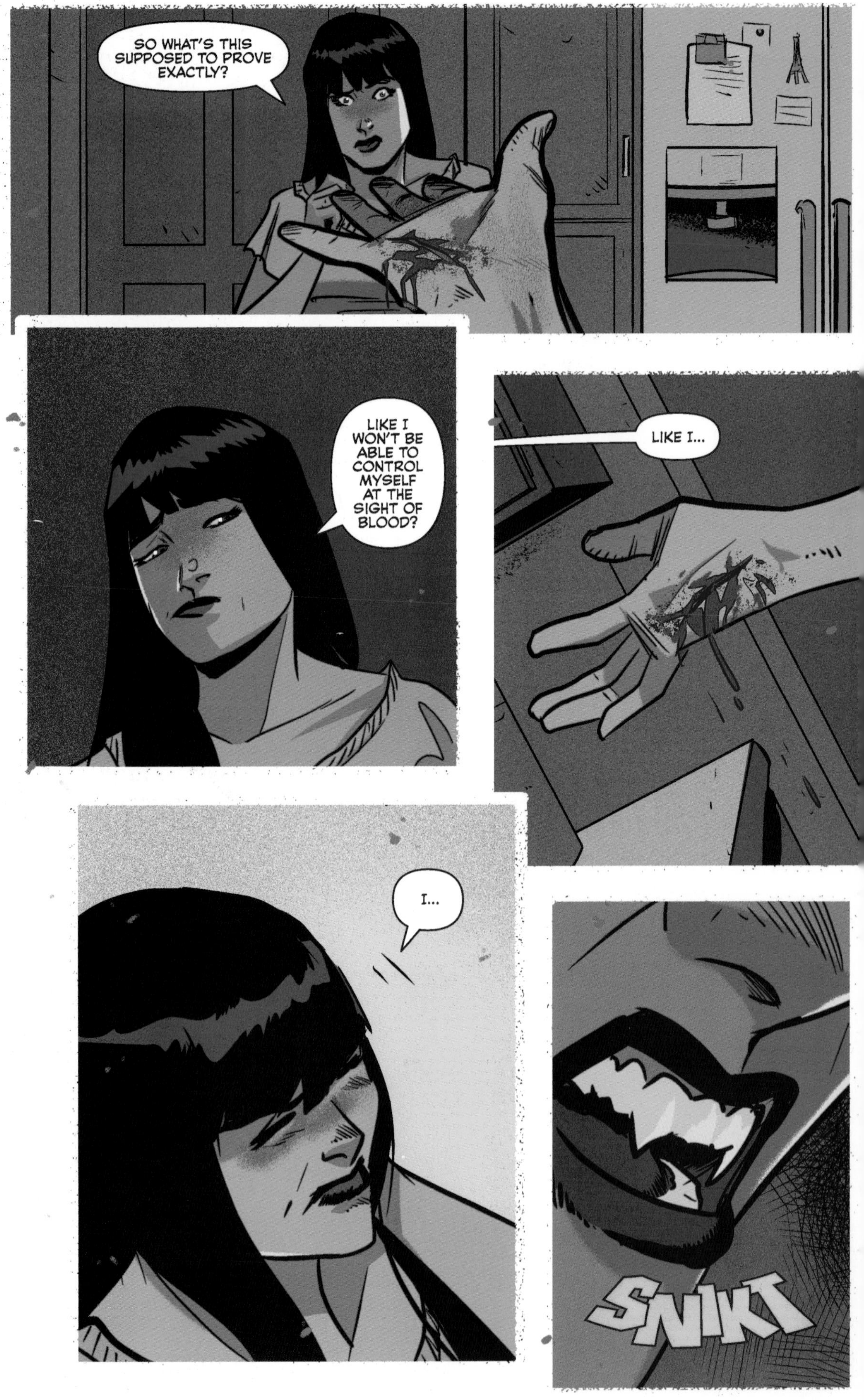
SO WHAT'S THIS SUPPOSED TO PROVE EXACTLY?
LIKE I WON'T BE ABLE TO CONTROL MYSELF AT THE SIGHT OF BLOOD?
LIKE I...
I...
SNIKT

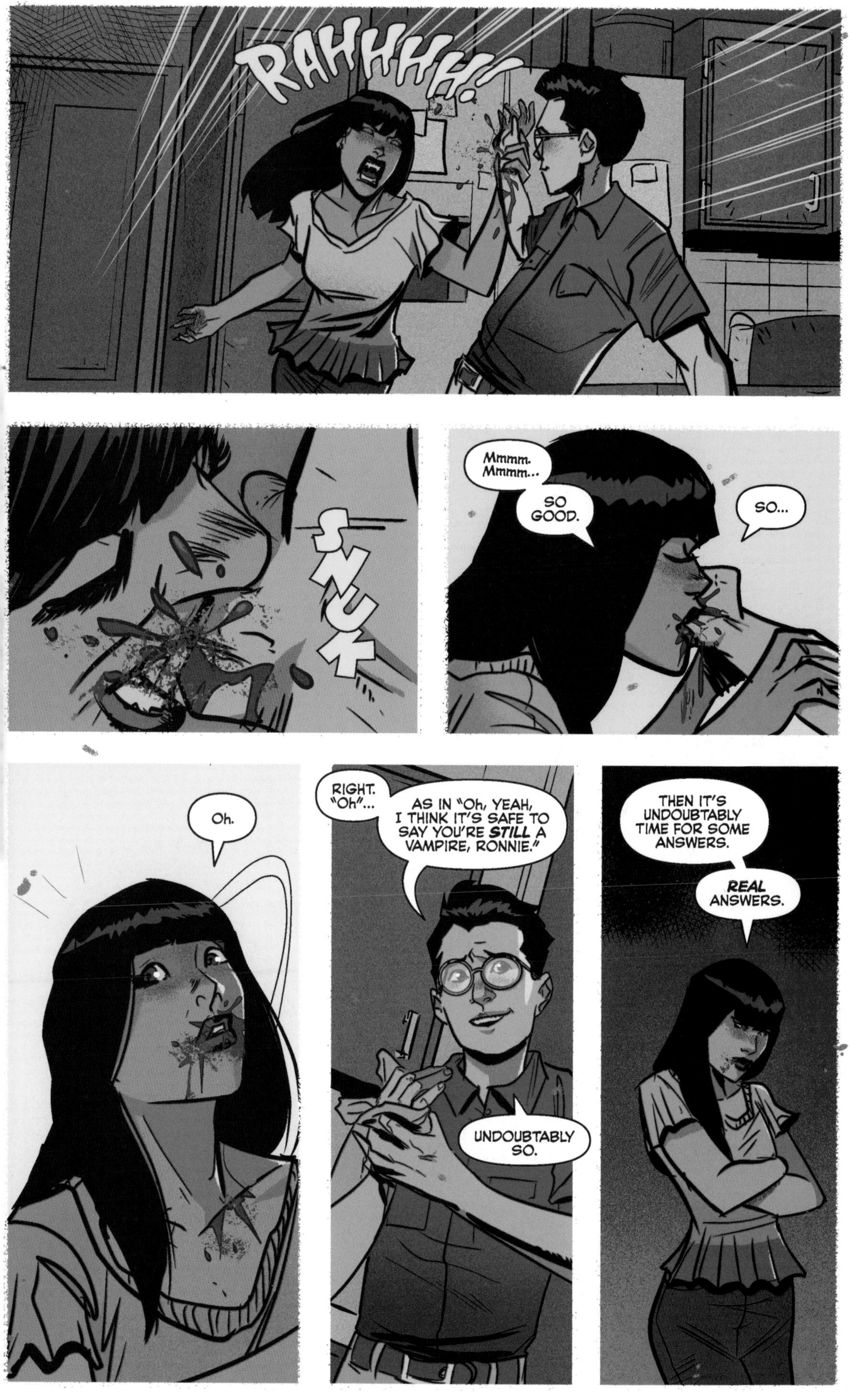
RAHHHH!!
SNUK
Mmmm. Mmmm...
SO GOOD.
SO...
Oh.
RIGHT. "Oh"...
AS IN "Oh, YEAH, I THINK IT'S SAFE TO SAY YOU'RE STILL A VAMPIRE, RONNIE."
UNDOUBTABLY SO.
THEN IT'S UNDOUBTABLY TIME FOR SOME ANSWERS.
REAL ANSWERS.

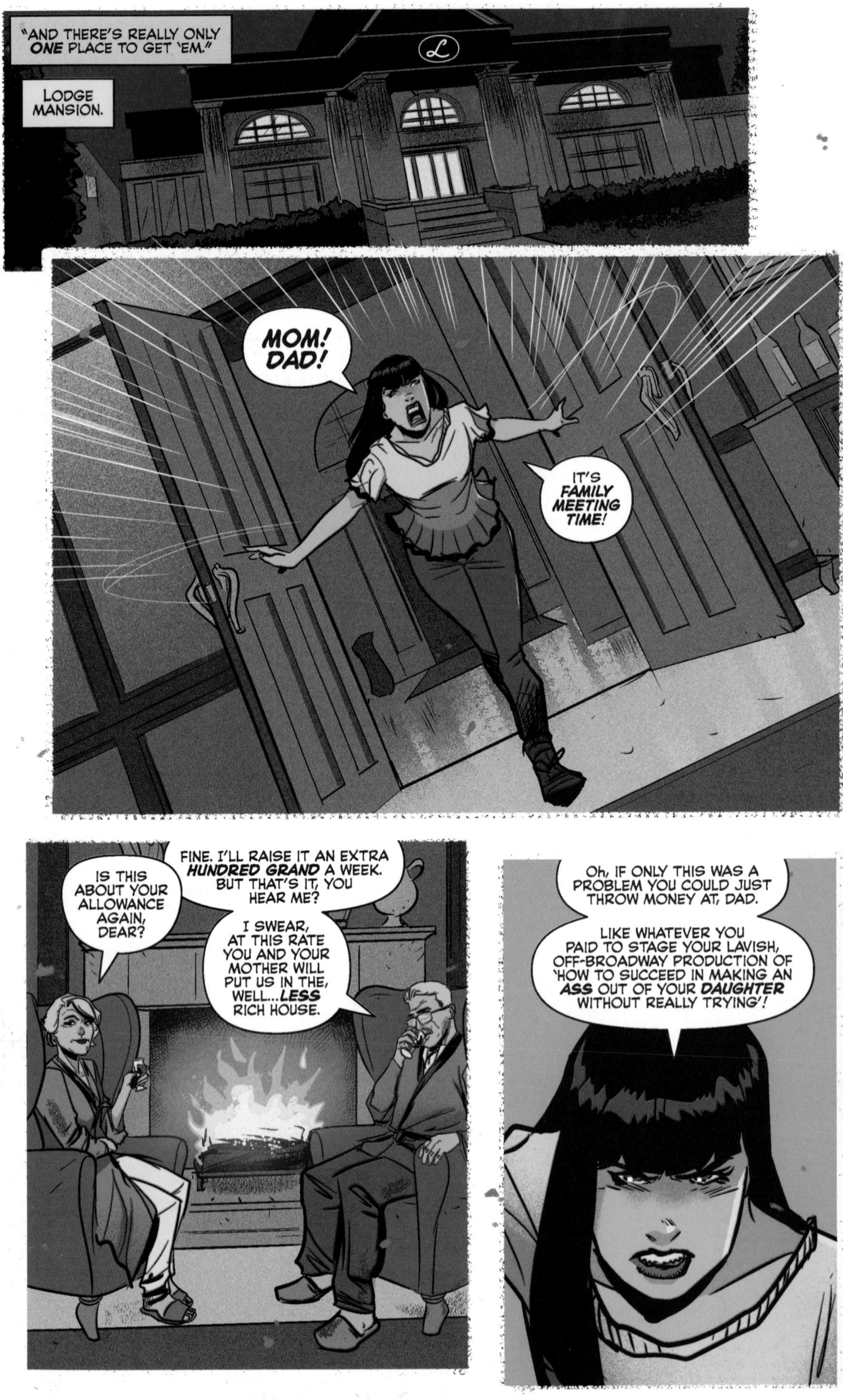
"AND THERE'S REALLY ONLY ONE PLACE TO GET 'EM."
LODGE MANSION.
MOM! DAD!
IT'S FAMILY MEETING TIME!
IS THIS ABOUT YOUR ALLOWANCE AGAIN, DEAR?
FINE. I'LL RAISE IT AN EXTRA HUNDRED GRAND A WEEK. BUT THAT'S IT, YOU HEAR ME?
I SWEAR, AT THIS RATE YOU AND YOUR MOTHER WILL PUT US IN THE, WELL...LESS RICH HOUSE.
Oh, IF ONLY THIS WAS A PROBLEM YOU COULD JUST THROW MONEY AT, DAD.
LIKE WHATEVER YOU PAID TO STAGE YOUR LAVISH, OFF-BROADWAY PRODUCTION OF 'HOW TO SUCCEED IN MAKING AN ASS OUT OF YOUR DAUGHTER WITHOUT REALLY TRYING'!

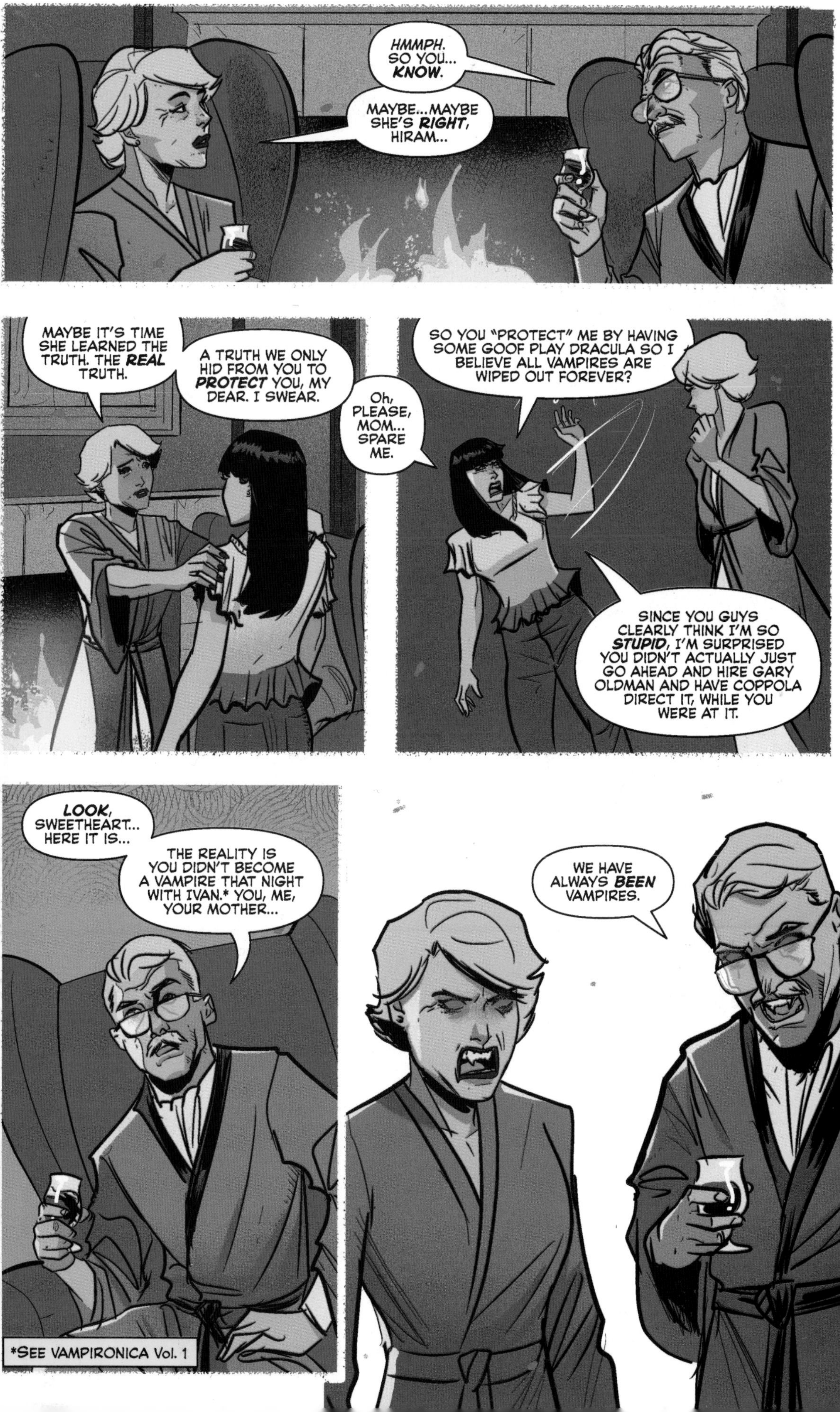
HMMPH. SO YOU... KNOW.
MAYBE...MAYBE SHE'S RIGHT, HIRAM...
MAYBE IT'S TIME SHE LEARNED THE TRUTH. THE REAL TRUTH.
A TRUTH WE ONLY HID FROM YOU TO PROTECT YOU, MY DEAR. I SWEAR.
Oh, PLEASE, MOM... SPARE ME.
SO YOU "PROTECT" ME BY HAVING SOME GOOF PLAY DRACULA SO I BELIEVE ALL VAMPIRES ARE WIPED OUT FOREVER?
SINCE YOU GUYS CLEARLY THINK I'M SO STUPID, I'M SURPRISED YOU DIDN'T ACTUALLY JUST GO AHEAD AND HIRE GARY OLDMAN AND HAVE COPPOLA DIRECT IT, WHILE YOU WERE AT IT.
LOOK, SWEETHEART... HERE IT IS...
THE REALITY IS YOU DIDN'T BECOME A VAMPIRE THAT NIGHT WITH IVAN.* YOU, ME, YOUR MOTHER...
*SEE VAMPIRONICA Vol. 1
WE HAVE ALWAYS BEEN VAMPIRES.

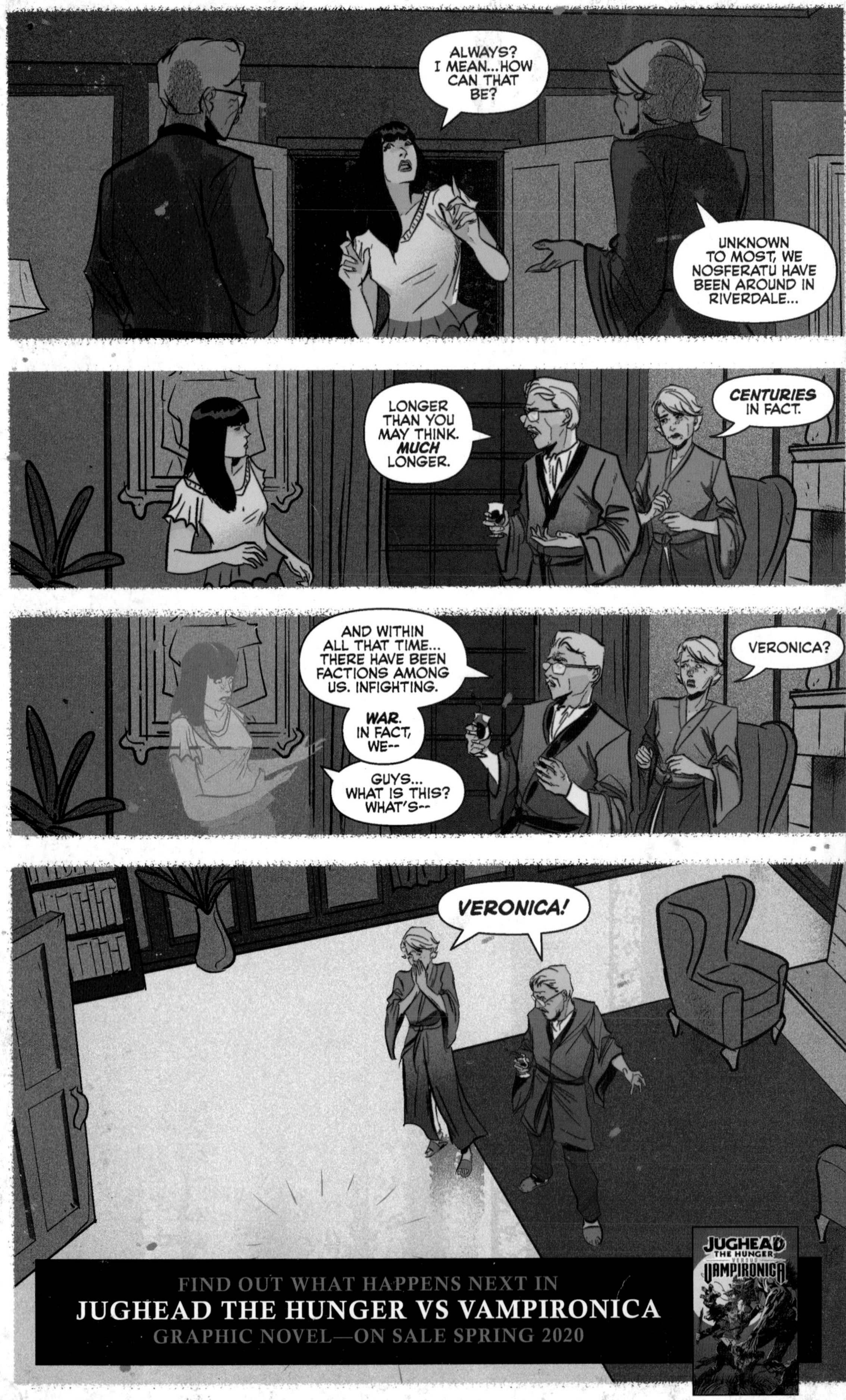
ALWAYS? I MEAN...HOW CAN THAT BE?
UNKNOWN TO MOST, WE NOSFERATU HAVE BEEN AROUND IN RIVERDALE...
LONGER THAN YOU MAY THINK. *MUCH* LONGER.
CENTURIES IN FACT.
AND WITHIN ALL THAT TIME... THERE HAVE BEEN FACTIONS AMONG US. INFIGHTING.
WAR. IN FACT, WE--
GUYS... WHAT IS THIS? WHAT'S--
VERONICA?
VERONICA!
FIND OUT WHAT HAPPENS NEXT IN
JUGHEAD THE HUNGER VS VAMPIRONICA
GRAPHIC NOVEL—ON SALE SPRING 2020
JUGHEAD THE HUNGER VERSUS VAMPIRONICA